C000094420

ROYAL HISTORICAL SOCIETY

STUDIES IN HISTORY

New Series

ROBERT SOUTHEY AND ROMANTIC APOSTASY

POLITICAL ARGUMENT IN BRITAIN, 1780–1840

Studies in History New Series

Editorial Board

Professor John Morrill (*Convenor*)
Dr Arthur Burns
Dr S. D. Church
Dr Neil Gregor
Dr Rachel Hammersley
Professor Colin Kidd
Dr J. M. Lawrence (*Literary Director*)
Professor M. Overton (*Economic History Society*)
Dr Jonathan Parry (*Honorary Treasurer*)
Professor Alexandra Walsham (*Past and Present Society*)

This series is supported by annual subventions from the
Economic History Society and from the Past and Present Society

'Robert Southey', by Edward Nash, from the frontispiece to *The doctor*,
ed. J. W. Warter, London 1848.

ROBERT SOUTHEY
AND ROMANTIC APOSTASY

POLITICAL ARGUMENT IN BRITAIN, 1780–1840

David M. Craig

THE ROYAL HISTORICAL SOCIETY
THE BOYDELL PRESS

© David M. Craig 2007

All Rights Reserved. Except as permitted under current legislation
no part of this work may be photocopied, stored in a retrieval system,
published, performed in public, adapted, broadcast,
transmitted, recorded or reproduced in any form or by any means,
without the prior permission of the copyright owner

The right of David M. Craig to be identified as
the author of this work has been asserted in accordance with
sections 77 and 78 of the Copyright, Designs and Patents Act 1988

First published 2007

A Royal Historical Society publication
Published by The Boydell Press
an imprint of Boydell & Brewer Ltd
PO Box 9, Woodbridge, Suffolk IP12 3DF, UK
and of Boydell & Brewer Inc.
668 Mt Hope Avenue, Rochester, NY 14620, USA
website: www.boydellandbrewer.com

ISBN 9–780–86193–291–7

ISSN 0269–2244

A CIP catalogue record for this book is available
from the British Library

This publication is printed on acid-free paper

Printed in Great Britain by
Antony Rowe Ltd, Chippenham, Wiltshire

FOR MUM AND DAD

Contents

Publication of this volume was aided by a generous grant
from the University of Durham.

Acknowledgements

This book has taken too long to write, so it is with some relief that I can finally say thank you to those who have helped along the way. It began life, or at least the first five chapters did, as a doctoral dissertation at the University of Cambridge, while the writing of the final four was greatly assisted by two terms of matching research leave from the University of Durham and the Arts and Humanities Research Board. At a time when academic publishers seem increasingly reluctant to publish academic work, I am particularly grateful to the editorial board of the Studies in History series, and to Colin Kidd and Christine Linehan for advice and encouragement in the final, and occasionally frantic, stages of preparing the manuscript.

I'm not much of a 'networker', so my debts are comparatively few (and the errors all my own). At the head of the list, though, are my parents, who have over the years supported me in many ways, not the least of which was financial, and often when they were facing hard times of their own. More specifically, various friends and colleagues have aided the gestation of this book. I would like to thank Geoff Baldwin, Philip Connell, David Eastwood, Boyd Hilton, Nigel Leask, Lynda Pratt, Michael Sonenscher, Miles Taylor and Philip Williamson. My greatest intellectual debt is to Gareth Stedman Jones, who in supervising my doctorate always encouraged me to see the wood for the trees. I hope this book remains true to that lesson.

Then there are those friends who make an evening in the pub particularly stimulating. With Elizabeth Emens, Max Jones, Joanna Lewis, Glyn Redworth, Amanda Rees, Richard Reid and, especially, Adrian Green and James Thompson, I have discussed all manner of matters. If only I could remember what they were ... Finally, Colin Davey has made all the difference. Not by his contribution to this book – which never much interested him – but by his invigorating love of laughter and sobering sense of perspective. Without ever saying so, he has taught me that historians should not take themselves too seriously.

David M. Craig
August 2006

Abbreviations

Works by Southey

BOTC   *The book of the Church*, London 1824
CPB   *Common-place book*, ed. J. W. Warter, London 1849–51
HB   *The history of Brazil*, London 1810–19
LC   *The life and correspondence of Robert Southey*, ed. C. C. Southey, London 1849–50
LE   *Letters from England: by Don Manuel Alvarez Espriella*, London 1807
LW   *The life of Wesley and the rise and progress of Methodism*, London 1820
NL   *New letters of Robert Southey*, ed. K. Curry, New York 1965
SL   *Selections from the letters of Robert Southey*, ed. J. W. Warter, London 1856
STM   *Sir Thomas More: colloquies on the progress and prospects of society*, London 1829

Works by Coleridge

CL   *Collected letters of Samuel Taylor Coleridge*, ed. E. L. Griggs, Oxford 1956–71
EOT   *Essays on his times in the* Morning Post *and the* Courier, ed. D. V. Erdman, London–Princeton 1978
LS   *Lay sermons*, ed. R. J. White, London–Princeton 1972
TF   *The Friend*, ed. B. E. Rooke, London–Princeton 1969

Works by Wordsworth

CC   *The Convention of Cintra*, London 1809, in *The prose works of William Wordsworth*, ed. W. J. B. Owen and J. W. Smyser, Oxford 1974, i

Other abbreviations

AR   *Annual Review*
EAR   *Edinburgh Annual Register*
EHR   *English Historical Review*

ER	*Edinburgh Review*
HHS	*History of the Human Sciences*
HJ	*Historical Journal*
JBS	*Journal of British Studies*
JEH	*Journal of Ecclesiastical History*
JRH	*Journal of Religious History*
PMLA	*Publications of the Modern Language Association of America*
PQ	*Philological Quarterly*
QR	*Quarterly Review*
RN	*Romanticism on the Net*
SP	*Studies in Philology*
WC	*The Wordsworth Circle*

Introduction

'I did not fall into the error of those who having been the friends of France when they imagined that the cause of liberty was implicated in her success, transferred their attachment from the Republic to the Military Tyranny in which it ended, and regarded with complacency the progress of oppression, because France was the Oppressor. "They had turned their faces towards the east in the morning to worship the rising sun, and in the evening they were looking Eastward still, obstinately affirming that still the sun was there".[1] I, on the contrary, altered my position as the world went round': Robert Southey, *A letter to William Smith, Esq. MP*, London 1817, 27–8.

'It is not always that a simile runs on all-fours; but this does. The sun indeed passes from the East to the West, but it rises in the East again: yet Mr. Southey is still looking in the West – for his pension. The world has gone round a second time, but he has not altered his position – at the Treasury door': William Hazlitt, 'A letter to William Smith, Esq. MP, from Robert Southey', *The Examiner*, 18 May 1817, 316.

Imagine Robert Southey's surprise when, on 14 February 1817, he read in the *Morning Chronicle* that his long-forgotten dramatic poem *Wat Tyler* was to be published by Sherwood, Neeley and Jones. Written hastily in the autumn of 1794, it was a sympathetic dramatisation of the Peasants' Revolt, which was also intended to express the social and political truths of the French Revolution. The manuscript was given to the printer James Ridgeway for publication but it never appeared, and Southey soon forgot about it. By 1817 he was poet laureate, and a staunch conservative who recommended restricting the liberty of the press and transporting the purveyors of sedition. The flooding of the marketplace with cheap editions of this poem was greeted with glee by those eager to embarrass an ideological enemy. During the debate on the Seditious Meetings Bill, the noted reformer William Smith read excerpts from both *Wat Tyler* and Southey's recent essay against 'Parliamentary reform' in the *Quarterly Review*, and argued that the author of the latter would recommend prosecuting the author of the former. At this point Southey began to write a pamphlet in his defence: the *Letter to William Smith* was announced by John Murray on 26 April, and four editions had been published by the end of the year. But for radicals and Whigs it merely furnished further evidence of the poet laureate's apostasy.[2]

---

[1] Southey was quoting himself: 'The history of Europe, 1808', *EAR* i (1810), i. 23.
[2] See F. T. Hoadley, 'The controversy over Southey's *Wat Tyler*', *SP* xxxviii (1941), 81–96, and R. A. Manogue, 'Southey and William Winterbotham: new light on an old quarrel', *Charles Lamb Bulletin* n.s. xxxviii (1982), 105–14.

The debate about Southey's political position was extensive and bilious, and he himself observed that his name had become 'the very shuttlecock of discussion'.[3] No radical was more dogged than William Hazlitt, whose essays exhaustively detailed the full extent of Southey's tergiversation by comparing his 'Jacobin' works of the 1790s with his recent efforts in defence of 'Toryism'.[4] It is worth quoting Hazlitt at length to appreciate how strongly he drew this contrast: 'The author of *Wat Tyler* was an Ultra-jacobin; the author of Parliamentary Reform is an Ultra-royalist; the one was a frantic demagogue, the other is a servile court-tool.' The former was so appalled by abuses of power that he 'vilified kings, priests and nobles' in support of anarchy, while the latter could only perceive the horror of resistance by the people and so he endorsed despotism. '[T]he one was for universal suffrage and perfect equality; the other is for seat-selling and the increasing influence of the Crown: the one admired the preaching of John Ball; the other recommends the Suspension of the Habeas Corpus, and the putting down of the *Examiner* by the sword, the dagger, or the thumb-screw.'[5] Hazlitt was doing his very best to show that Southey had utterly changed his views. The only similarity between his earlier and later positions was their extremism: no moderate person would countenance them and yet all who disagreed were damned as fools. 'What is right in him, is wrong in them', Hazlitt argued, 'Whatever he does, is proper: whatever he thinks, is true and profound.'[6] The other main accusation was that Southey had sold out to line his own pockets. Having realised that supporting the cause of liberty in France undermined the pursuit of riches in Britain, he abandoned the former for the latter. In throwing his principles to the wind he embraced servility and sycophancy. 'He has no feeling left, but of "tickling commodity"; no ears but for court whispers: no understanding but of his interest; no passion but his vanity.' Hazlitt was convinced that 'if Mr. Southey is not an apostate, we should like to know who ever was?'[7]

Coleridge was quick to leap to the defence in *The Courier*. Hazlitt had recently lambasted his style, politics and metaphysics in a number of articles, and had reminded the public that the Trinitarian who in 1816 eulogised the fusion of Church and State had in 1798 been a Unitarian preaching their separation.[8] In defending Southey, Coleridge was also defending himself: he downplayed early radicalism, contrasted supposedly boyish views with manly opinions and insisted that Southey had changed long before he had become poet laureate.[9] He repeated this tactic in his *Biographia literaria*, which appeared in July 1817 and subsequently became infamous for its denial that

---

3 R. Southey, *A letter to William Smith, Esq. MP*, London 1817, 12.
4 Collected as W. Hazlitt, *Political essays, with sketches of public characters*, London 1819, reprinted in *The selected writings of William Hazlitt*, ed. D. Wu, London 1998, iv.
5 Ibid. iv. 158.
6 Ibid. iv. 175. See also p. 158.
7 Ibid. iv. 173, 168.
8 Ibid. iv. 107–21.
9 EOT ii. 449–60, 466–78.

he had more than a passing acquaintance with the radicalism of the 1790s. This work, however, also made a more positive case for Southey. Coleridge wanted to defend him from the charge that he was an unprincipled hireling who would sing any tune as long as he was paid well enough. He might be presented as 'Mr Feathernest' in Peacock's *Melincourt*, but Coleridge was keen to deny this and to praise his friend's talents. Southey was unequalled as an historian and an essayist and few could convey 'so much truth and knowledge with so much life and fancy'. 'As a writer, he has uniformly made his talents subservient to the best interests of humanity, of public virtue and domestic piety; his cause has ever been the cause of pure religion and of liberty, of national independence and of national illumination.'[10] Even more than his poetry, Coleridge claimed, his histories and essays would be approved by posterity. So, in 1817, Coleridge was trying both to play down the accusation of apostasy by softening the poets' earlier politics, and to rescue Southey from charges of financial opportunism by insisting that he must be recognised as a serious and principled writer.

In his *Letter to William Smith*, Southey agreed that his politics had evolved but rejected the charge of outright apostasy. Unlike Coleridge he made no attempt to whitewash his formative years. Although he admitted that *Wat Tyler* was full of errors, he claimed that if he were to write it again there would be much to add but little to alter.[11] The opinions he had held in the 1790s were 'right in themselves, and wrong only in their direction' and he now wrote in the 1810s with 'the same heart and the same desires, but with a ripened understanding and competent stores of knowledge'.[12] The word 'ripened' highlights the way he saw his mature politics as a development of his youthful ideals. He no longer thought that old monarchical countries were capable of republican government, and had ceased to think that revolution was desirable even in countries that needed reform.

> But he has not ceased to love liberty with all his heart, and with all his soul, and with all his strength; he has not ceased to detest tyranny wherever it exists, and in whatever form. He has not ceased to abhor the wickedness of ambition, and to sympathise with those who were engaged in the defence of their country and in a righteous cause.[13]

Southey claimed that the 'whole tenour of my writings, whether in prose, or verse' was directed towards encouraging the improvement of mankind, and in the final part of the pamphlet he listed some of the schemes he had proposed to that end.[14] He was annoyed that Smith and Hazlitt appeared successful in presenting him as an ally of reactionary despotism when he thought himself a

---

[10] S. T. Coleridge, *Biographia literaria*, ed. J. Engell and W. J. Bate, London–Princeton 1983, i. 63–4, 66–7.
[11] Southey, *William Smith*, 6, 15.
[12] Ibid. 8, 15.
[13] Ibid. 24–5.
[14] Ibid. 27.

friend to freedom and progress. The image of the sun quoted in the epigraph above was important to him because it conveyed his belief that although his politics had changed on the ground, his eyes remained fixed on enlightenment in the heavens.

The politics of 'romanticism'

It seems virtually impossible to assess the politics of the lake poets without recourse to the concept of romanticism. This term, however, is notoriously difficult. The original German founders of the movement used the word 'romantic' to refer to 'modern' as opposed to 'classical' literature, and while their writings spawned an extensive debate in Europe about aesthetics, its impact in Britain was relatively limited. No early nineteenth-century writer would have described themselves as 'romantic', and indeed it was only towards the end of the century that the word became fashionable. In the meantime, however, the ideas of the lake poets grew in influence. Coleridge was presumed to have articulated a counter-tradition to the spiritually impoverished reductionism of utilitarianism,[15] while, by the end of the century, Southey was thought to have foreseen the problems of industrial society. In the *Dictionary of national biography* Richard Garnett passed judgement on Macaulay's critical review of *Sir Thomas More: or colloquies on the progress and prospects of society*. The 'view of social evils to which Southey there gave expression, often in anticipation of Mr. Ruskin, was in many respects deeper and truer than that of his optimistic critic'.[16] A little later A. V. Dicey, in his last published and least known work, dealt with the *Statesmanship of Wordsworth* in which he argued that this poet anticipated the doctrine of nationalism by forty years.[17] In other words, by the turn of the twentieth century there was interest in the social and political ideas of the lake poets, but the concept of romanticism was not yet required in order to explicate them.

This was the very period when scholarship on 'romanticism' grew rapidly. These studies were literary in focus, and were generally more preoccupied with how revolution shaped poetry than with the ideas of the lake poets as such. Studies of German 'romanticism', however, did approach it as a movement of social and political thought. These romantics, it was argued, abandoned their early support for the French Revolution, with its mechanistic and rationalistic understandings of society, in favour of organic and historical approaches. For this reason they increasingly saw religion and medievalism as antidotes to modern individualism. It appeared that they were 'radicals' who had become 'conservatives', albeit idiosyncratic ones. This paradigm was

---

15 See P. Connell, *Romanticism, economics and the question of 'culture'*, Oxford 2001, 274–96.

16 [R. Garnett], 'Robert Southey', in *The dictionary of national biography*, ed. L. Stephen and S. Lee, London 1885–1900, liii. 288.

17 A. V. Dicey, *The statesmanship of Wordsworth: an essay*, Oxford 1917.

understandably applied to the lake poets. Alfred Cobban's *Edmund Burke and the revolt against the eighteenth century* of 1929 was perhaps the most influential work which depicted the lake poets as critics of the Enlightenment.[18] It argued that the 'fundamental ideas' of the eighteenth century were sensationalist psychology and natural law, and that these formed the foundations of utilitarian ethics, classical economics and conceptions of individual rights. In Burke and the lake poets, Cobban argued, were the outlines of an alternative tradition which taught that 'individuals must always be taken as they exist in society, on the one hand, and on the other, that political society is simply a feeling of relationship in the minds of individuals'.[19] Burke developed a new theory of nationality, which was subsequently deepened by Wordsworth, while Coleridge supplied a coruscating critique of eighteenth-century philosophy and politics. Southey, finally, showed the harmful effects of commerce and manufacturing. Taken together, the lake poets provided a vision of community which formed a contrast to stale Victorian individualism. While Cobban did not dwell on the concept of romanticism, Crane Brinton's *Political ideas of the English romanticists* of 1926 had laboured it, and thereby impressed the notion of romantic social and political thought into British intellectual history.[20]

While this approach to 'romantic' thought has been enormously influential, it is also problematic. The links between German and English romanticism have been intensively studied, but the evidence for an extensive exchange of ideas remains inconclusive. In any case, the concept of romantic social and political thought is misleading. It, and with it Isaiah Berlin's later work on the 'counter-Enlightenment', creates the impression that there was a relatively unified Enlightenment which was superseded by a relatively unified romanticism.[21] This has helped instantiate a fault-line in intellectual history between the eighteenth and nineteenth centuries, but it has long been clear that such a sharp conceptual break between two rudimentary typologies is unhelpful. Indeed, Cobban hinted as much in the second edition of his pioneering work when he suggested that perhaps Burke and the lake poets owed more to the ideas of the eighteenth century than he had formerly claimed: 'not so much a denial as an enlargement and liberalisation of its ideas'.[22] All this suggests that the points first raised by A. O. Lovejoy in 1924 remain valid. He had noted that in a couple of decades romanticism had come to be defined in a

---

[18] A. Cobban, *Edmund Burke and the revolt against the eighteenth century: a study of the political and social thinking of Burke, Wordsworth, Coleridge and Southey*, 2nd edn, London 1960.

[19] Ibid. 271–2.

[20] C. Brinton, *The political ideas of the English romanticists*, Oxford 1926.

[21] I. Berlin, 'The counter-Enlightenment', in P. P. Wiener (ed.), *The dictionary of the history of ideas: studies of selected pivotal ideas*, New York 1973, ii. 100–12; R. Wokler, 'Isaiah Berlin's Enlightenment and counter-Enlightenment', in R. Wokler and J. Mali (eds), *Isaiah Berlin's counter-Enlightenment*, Philadelphia 2003, 13–31.

[22] Cobban, *Burke*, p. xiv.

multiplicity of ways. 'The result is a confusion of words and ideas. ... The word "romantic" has come to mean so many things that, by itself, it means nothing.' The 'really radical solution' was one that he knew would not be adopted, 'that we should all cease talking about Romanticism'.[23] At the very least he suggested that the plural – romanticisms – should be used as a looser way of indicating the range of changes occurring in the late eighteenth and early nineteenth centuries. His concerns were met halfway by René Wellek, who counselled that the term be used more carefully. In the last couple of decades, however, various literary scholars have either started to unpick the 'romantic ideology' or have set it aside as a diversion from reading writers in their actual historical context.[24]

Since the 1970s new paradigms have emerged out of the growing interest in eighteenth-century intellectual life and political ideology in Britain. The most influential has undoubtedly been J. G. A. Pocock's work on 'civic humanism', which he presented as a competing tradition to natural jurisprudence, and so was able to argue that the evolution of 'liberalism' – political and economic individualism – was by no means simple or unchallenged.[25] The civic tradition developed in eighteenth-century Britain as a critique of the supposed corruption being engineered by court Whiggery. These enlightened 'moderns' embraced 'politeness': they argued in favour of the social progress wrought by the financial revolution and commercial society and insisted that freedom was a recent invention that had little to do with the past. The country party, by contrast, believed that these changes were eroding the civic virtue necessary to preserve political independence. They looked back to the ideal of the armed and active freeholder, and prophesied decay if social and political reforms were not urgently enacted. Pocock has argued that these themes continued into the radicalism of the late eighteenth century, and so helps explain why it was imbued with backward-looking themes: the Anglo-Saxon constitution, the independent freeholder, worries about luxury and so on. He has also suggested that 'romantic radicalism, like other radicalisms before it, flowed from both a republican and a Tory source; this may help us to understand the movement of Coleridge, Southey, and Wordsworth from

---

[23] A. O. Lovejoy, 'On the discrimination of romanticisms', *PMLA* xxxix (1924), 232, 234. See also idem, 'The meaning of romanticism for the historian of ideas', *Journal of the History of Ideas* ii (1941), 257–78.

[24] R. Wellek, 'The concept of "romanticism" in literary history', *Comparative Literature* i (1949), 1–23, 147–72; J. McGann, *The romantic ideology: a critical investigation*, Chicago 1983; M. Butler, *Romantics, rebels and reactionaries: English literature and its background, 1760–1830*, Oxford 1981.

[25] See especially J. G. A. Pocock, *The Machiavellian moment: Florentine political thought and the Atlantic republican tradition*, Princeton 1975, and 'Cambridge paradigms and Scotch philosophers: a study of the relations between the civic humanist and the civil jurisprudential interpretation of eighteenth-century social thought', in I. Hont and M. Ignatieff (eds), *Wealth and virtue: the shaping of political economy in the Scottish Enlightenment*, Cambridge 1983, 235–52.

republican youth to Tory old age'.[26] He agreed with Cobban that Burke was important, but primarily because he proposed to reverse the 'modern' idea that commerce was the motor behind the growth of manners and instead argued that traditional ecclesiastical and chivalric manners stabilised commercial society. By so doing, Burke opened a space for the idea that commerce created a mechanical philosophy and a dismal science, and so led onto Coleridge's idea that a national Church or 'clerisy' was necessary to shore up the culture or manners that were being undermined. 'From now on', Pocock suggested of the early nineteenth century, 'there might be stern unbending Tories proclaiming the alliance of church and state as the only answer, and there might be Tory radicals castigating the existing church and state as quite incapable of providing it.'[27]

These arguments have been applied to Coleridge by a number of scholars.[28] Most recently, however, a study of that poet-philosopher has begun to challenge this approach, and also the broader assumptions about the apostasy of the lake poets. Pamela Edwards's *Statesman's science* is therefore of wider importance than its focus on Coleridge might suggest. There are two points of essential interest. The first is her belief that Pocock's arguments about the incompatibility of civic humanism and natural jurisprudence are largely unconvincing. It follows that if republicanism and liberalism are not conceptually distinct there is no reason to assume that radicals and Tories were somehow alien to the liberal tradition. She notes that John Stuart Mill believed that Coleridge contributed to a 'second school of liberalism' which differed from the 'prevailing school' of the Benthamites.[29] She also argues strongly for continuity in Coleridge's thought. His conviction was 'from first to last',

> that political liberty was secured by independence of conscience and reason, that this independence was undermined by party allegiance, that positive institutions and the Common Law rather than an encoded charter of natural rights was the best hope of a just and lasting polity, and that virtue and voluntarism were the prerequisites for a free and liberal society.[30]

Edwards's second point follows from this, because she is sceptical about the whole tradition of 'apostasy' which views the lake poets as passing from 'Jacobin radicalism' to 'Tory conservatism'. Whether it was Hazlitt in the nineteenth century or E. P. Thompson in the twentieth, Edwards believes

---

[26] Idem, *Virtue, commerce and history: essays on political thought and history, chiefly in the eighteenth century*, Cambridge 1985, 292.

[27] Ibid. 191.

[28] J. T. Miller, *Ideology and Enlightenment: the political and social thought of Samuel Taylor Coleridge*, New York 1988; J. Morrow, *Coleridge's political thought: property, morality and the limits of traditional discourse*, London 1990.

[29] P. Edwards, *The statesman's science: history, nature and law in the political thought of Samuel Taylor Coleridge*, New York 2004, 1, 3.

[30] Ibid. 8.

that these charges were politically motivated, and suggests that 'the romantics were ably and dramatically cast in the role of ... Judases'.[31] More substantially, the very political language which indicates 'apostasy' – radical, Jacobin, Tory, conservative – is itself open to question. Some of these terms are primarily labels of party affiliation, others are used anachronistically, and even those which are concerned with ideology are too often applied in an overly loose manner. In other words, the very idea that the lake poets were apostates is sustained by the terminology used to classify them. Edwards notes that it is striking that the best studies of Coleridge's social and political thought have been produced by scholars involved in editing his collected works: they have provided 'perceptive and subtle' accounts which 'remained scrupulously within the boundaries of the texts' and have eschewed attempts to locate Coleridge within 'broad ideological' streams.[32] This point serves as a warning not just about the paradigm of 'republicanism' but also that of 'romanticism'.

Why Robert Southey?

Robert Southey is the least known and least appreciated of the lake poets. While the reputations of Coleridge and Wordsworth weathered the charge of apostasy that of Southey suffered. By the end of the nineteenth century, when the list of romantic writers was being drawn up, his poetry was largely forgotten and he was rarely included. Being outside the canon of romantic literature ensured that for much of the twentieth century his literary output was relatively neglected.[33] Similarly, there has been less interest in his social and political thought compared to that of Wordsworth and Coleridge. Of course, there are important exceptions. In the nineteenth century Lord Shaftesbury and Thomas Carlyle were inspired by his criticisms of industrial society, and in 1905 Dicey argued that Southey was a major critic of individualism who hoped that the moral authority of the Church and the political action of the state could counteract the effects of *laissez-faire*. In his move from 'philanthropic Jacobin' to 'humanitarian Tory', he was also the anticipator of 'socialistic ideas' and the 'prophetic precursor of modern collectivism'.[34] Just over a decade later Max Beer commented in his *History of British socialism* that, among the lake poets, Southey possessed the most 'anti-capitalist spirit' and that *Letters from England* 'might have been written by a communist'. Beer

---

[31] Ibid. 14. See E. P. Thompson, 'Disenchantment or default? A lay sermon', in C. C. O'Brien and W. D. Vanech (eds), *Power and consciousness*, London 1969, 149–81.

[32] Edwards, *Statesman's science*, 7.

[33] A sample of recently published work includes M. Butler, *Literature as heritage: or reading other ways*, Cambridge 1988; C. Smith, *A quest for home: reading Robert Southey*, Liverpool 1997; L. Pratt (ed.), Special issue: 'Robert Southey', *RN* xxxii–xxxiii (2003–4), and L. Pratt (ed.), *Robert Southey and the contexts of English romanticism*, Aldershot 2006.

[34] A. V. Dicey, *Lectures on the relation between law and public opinion during the nineteenth century*, 2nd edn, London 1914, 223, 225.

thought that the lake poets reinvigorated conservatism with 'social righteous-ness and love of the people' which eventually flowered in 'Tory Democracy'.[35] Cobban, as we have seen, made similar points in the 1920s. Some commenta-tors – such as Walter Graham – were disinclined to concede much originality on this point, primarily because Southey's Toryism stuck in their throats and seemed incompatible with any serious commitment to social reform.[36] There have over the course of the twentieth century been some important studies of Southey's ideas, with Geoffrey Carnall's *Robert Southey and his age* of 1960 being the most thorough. But this remains a relatively thin stream when compared to the torrent of work devoted to Wordsworth and Coleridge.[37]

This neglect is an odd state of affairs. That fact that William Smith could wave copies of the *Quarterly Review* in parliament, and that William Hazlitt could declaim passionately about the apostasy of the poet laureate indicates that he was not an inconsequential figure in his own time. He has, however, been overshadowed by Coleridge, whose reputation as a profound philosopher makes it all too easy to dismiss Southey as a petty propagandist. Coleridge, it is true, was intellectually gifted with a rare thirst for abstract thinking, but while he did engage with contemporary social and political questions, his style meant that he was often viewed, as in Peacock's *Melincourt*, as 'Mr Mystic'. Southey was widely perceived as the typical Tory, and his essays in the *Quarterly Review* and works such as the *Book of the Church* were taken as vigorous defences of the establishment. Some more perceptive observers, however, realised that this was not the whole story. Hazlitt, in his more generous moments, noted that Southey was not a complete reactionary, and suspected that his radical past was not wholly forgotten. 'At the corner of his pen, "there hangs a vaporous drop profound" of independence and liberality', he wrote in the *Spirit of the age*. 'Once a philanthropist and always a philanthro-pist. No man can entirely baulk his nature: it breaks out in spite of him.'[38] Similarly, J. S. Mill thought Southey more a speculative than a practical Tory. He had become an 'aristocrat in principle' but rejected 'aristocratic vices and

---

35 M. Beer, *A history of British socialism*, London 1919, i. 122–3.
36 See W. Haller, 'Southey's later radicalism', *PMLA* xxxvii (1922), 281–92, and W. Graham, 'Robert Southey as Tory reviewer', *PQ* ii (1923), 97–111.
37 G. Carnall, *Robert Southey and his age: the development of a conservative mind*, Oxford 1960. Other influential works include E. W. Meachen, 'From an historical religion to a religion of history: Robert Southey and the heroic in history', *Clio* ix (1980), 229–52; S. Gilley, 'Nationality and liberty, Protestant and Catholic: Robert Southey's *Book of the Church*', in S. Mews (ed.), *Religion and national identity*, Oxford 1982, 409–32; D. Eastwood, 'Robert Southey and the intellectual origins of romantic conservatism', *EHR* civ (1989), 308–31; 'Robert Southey and the meanings of patriotism', *JBS* xxxi (1992), 265–87; and 'Ruinous prosperity: Robert Southey's critique of the commercial system', *WC* xxv (1994), 72–6; J. Majeed, *Ungoverned imaginings: James Mill's The history of British India and orien-talism*, Oxford 1992, ch. ii; D. Winch, *Riches and poverty: an intellectual history of political economy in Britain, 1750–1834*, Cambridge 1996, chs xi–xii; P. Harling, 'Robert Southey and the language of social discipline', *Albion* xxx (1998), 630–55; and Connell, *Romanti-cism*, ch. v.
38 W. Hazlitt, *The spirit of the age*, London 1825, in *Selected writings*, vii. 218.

weaknesses'. 'Consequently he is not liked by the Tories, while the Whigs and radicals abhor him.'[39]

It should now be clear that Southey's conservatism seems more unusual than some commentators have suggested, and that his intellectual development was more complex than his opponents implied. The purpose of this book is therefore to provide a comprehensive account of his social and political thought, and its relevance for the wider question of 'romantic apostasy'. It is not primarily concerned with his poetry but with his ideas. Of course, his verse provides evidence of these and it is perhaps easier in his case – for instance in *Wat Tyler* of 1794 and the *Poet's pilgrimage to Waterloo* of 1816 – to see his beliefs expressed in his literary productions. More generally it might be contended that as someone who had to support himself by his pen we should not expect too much penetration or consistency in what he wrote. This might seem especially true of the many reviews that he contributed to periodicals during his life. In fact, however, he often took this work seriously. His short pieces in the *Annual Review* in the 1800s included clear statements of his views on a range of issues, and by the 1810s he had come to view his work in the *Quarterly Review* as giving him the best possible access to the public. It might also be argued that Southey made no attempt to formulate a coherent philosophy. While he disliked 'metaphysics' and 'systems', he was adamant that he had always possessed a connected view of the world. The aim of this book is to unearth that world view, and to tease out the social, economic, religious and political elements of his thought rather than to rehearse his biography.[40] It is divided into three chronological sections which roughly match the supposed phases of republicanism, apostasy and conservatism and which provide a good basis from which to evaluate his own defence that 'I altered my position as the world went round.'

---

[39] J. S. Mill to J. Sterling, 20–2 Oct. 1831, in *The earlier letters of John Stuart Mill, 1812–1848*, ed. F. E. Mineka, Toronto–London 1963, 83.
[40] The most important biographical studies are W. Haller, *The early life of Robert Southey, 1774–1803*, New York 1917; J. Simmons, *Southey*, London 1945; K. Curry, *Southey*, London 1975; M. Storey, *Robert Southey: a life*, Oxford 1997; and W. A. Speck, *Robert Southey: entire man of letters*, New Haven 2006.

PART I

REPUBLICANISM

1

Revolutionary Progress

Six months before France was proclaimed a republic, Southey was engaged in his own minor act of rebellion. Between March and April 1792 he and his close friend Grosvenor Bedford were working on articles for a magazine at Westminster School that they provocatively published as *The Flagellant*. In the fifth number a paper appeared under the pseudonym of Gualbertus which argued that corporal punishment was the work of Satan.[1] Once the headmaster, William Vincent, learned that Southey was the author, he expelled him, and warned Christ Church, Oxford, about this unruly supporter of the French Revolution. Although Southey was instead admitted to Balliol College in 1793, his time at Oxford was not productive. He spoke warily of the 'conformity' and 'orthodoxy' of the university, and thought his tutors remarkable only for 'great wigs & little wisdom'.[2] The problem was that while his uncle, Herbert Hill, had supported his education so that he might take orders, his own faith was shaky. 'To obtain future support', he told Horace Bedford, 'to return the benefits I have received – I must become contemptible infamous and perjured.'[3] Despite this, he neglected his studies in favour of writing poetry, and wistfully imagined emigration as a means both of solving his personal problems and escaping a country which seemed to be sliding into despotism. Southey's life was transformed in June 1794 when he was introduced to Samuel Taylor Coleridge, and together they hatched a scheme to emigrate to America. During 1795 they lived together in Bristol, writing poetry and delivering lectures in the hope of financing their plan. Hill was worried by the radical company his nephew was keeping, and persuaded him to visit Portugal. Relations between the two young men were already strained, and they were broken by this: Coleridge believed Southey was going to take orders to secure an income, and in a damning letter severed their friendship.[4] In the three short but busy years between expulsion from Westminster and embarkation for Iberia, the seeds were sown for Southey's social and political thinking.

'O barbarous days!', he wrote in *The Flagellant*, 'but see a later age, | When

---

1   *The Flagellant*, 29 Mar. 1792, 79–89. See W. A. Speck, 'Robert Southey and *The Flagellant*', *Harvard Library Bulletin* xiv (2003), 25–8.
2   R. Southey to C. Collins, 12–13 Jan. 1793, in R. Baughman, 'Southey the schoolboy', *Huntington Library Quarterly* vii (1944), 266; Southey to G. Bedford, 16 Jan. 1793, Bodleian Library, Oxford, MS Eng. Lett. c. 22, fo. 45.
3   Southey to H. Bedford, 11 Dec. 1793, *NL* i. 37.
4   S. T. Coleridge to Southey, [13] Nov. 1795, *CL* i. 163–73.

Reason had diffus'd a cheering ray, | Say, could it calm the furious bigot's rage? | Or make him his Redeemer's words obey?'[5] Here, in one of his earliest surviving 'political' writings, there is a clear contrast between the barbarism of the present and the enlightenment of the future. After his expulsion, he revisited these themes in a verse letter. He imagined looking over the course of history:

> Climes – centuries – nations – go, inspect them all
> See them successive rise – successive fall
> Still will you find dull Ignorance maintains
> In state illiberal his drowsy reign.[6]

Together these two early extracts represent the main themes of Southey's thinking in the 1790s. He ascribed great importance to the enlightenment of the population in the truths of reason – or perhaps the 'redeemer' – for the progress of history. Initially viewed as the embodiment and catalyst of this process, the French Revolution had turned out to be gravely disappointing by 1801. 'A military despotism!', he exclaimed to Mary Barker, 'popery reestablished! the negroes again to be enslaved!'[7] Despite this, his broader convictions about political and social progress had not been radically eroded. The purpose of this chapter is to assess the development of his thinking, but this task poses certain difficulties. Whereas the historian of Coleridge's ideas has a rich body of political work from the 1790s to draw on, there is no corresponding material by Southey. Hence in the most formative decade of his life, his views must be accessed through his many letters and through his poetry, particularly *Wat Tyler* and *Joan of Arc*.

Politics and religion

For its first three years, Southey's attitude towards the French Revolution is difficult to discern. We know by his own admission that he was an enthusiast for events across the channel but little more. He wrote an essay opposing Burke's *Reflections* and it is likely that he was aware of the pamphlet debate that it generated.[8] There was no indication, however, that he labelled himself a republican. But with the massacres and subsequent establishment of republicanism in France during September 1792, he had to reconsider his position. Some reformers thought that the 1791 constitution had already established a great degree of freedom and that any further moves towards republicanism were unnecessary. Southey seems to have shared these concerns, telling a sceptical friend that 'Time has justified all your prophecies with regard to my

---

[5] *The Flagellant*, 1 Mar. 1792, 13.
[6] Southey to G. Bedford, 14 May 1792, Bodl. Lib., MS Eng. Lett. c. 22, fo. 13.
[7] Southey to M. Barker, [Dec.] 1801, SL i. 180.
[8] Speck, *Southey*, 20–1.

French friends.' Speaking of Jacobins, *sans-culottes* and the 'fishwomen', he commented that it was difficult to say to such a mob, 'thus far, no farther'. The French had effectively changed tyrants from the 'mild irresolute Louis' to 'the savage, the unrelenting Petion'. 'I have seen a structure raised by the hand of wisdom, and defended by the sword of liberty, undermind by innovation, hurled from its basis by faction, and insulted by the proud abuse of despotism.'[9] He blamed the horror of 'mobocracy' on the 'national ferocity' of the French.[10] These comments reveal an early fear about politics in the hands of the 'mob', and also show Southey's concern that the republic would annihilate the benefits of the 1791 constitution. This pessimism was short-lived, however. A month later he could tell Bedford that 'If France models a republic and enjoys tranquillity who knows but Europe may become one great republic and Man be free of the whole? You see I use Paines words.' This was the first time that Southey spoke in terms of republicanism, and it seems to mark an important development. It is possible that around this time he read and was converted by the *Rights of man* to the 'republic system'.[11] As late as 1795 he could still be found eulogising its author in one of his Bristol lectures. 'I cried O Paine! hireless Priest of Liberty! unbought teacher of the poor! Chearing to me is the reflection that my heart hath ever acknowledged – that my tongue hath proudly proclaimed – the truth and Divinity of thy Doctrines!'[12]

But what did he mean by 'republicanism'?[13] In Britain few writers recommended it: however much they admired it in theory, in practice they supported the mixed constitution their country had enjoyed for a century. This critical view was widely shared across Europe, where very few people thought resuscitating classical republicanism possible or desirable. The idea that citizens made their own laws and defended their own state was inappropriate. Republicanism, it was argued, required a strong love of the public good, a relatively equal level of wealth and a high degree of cultural homogeneity. To attempt to create this in the modern world was imprudent because of the size of states, the extent of commerce and the inequality of the people. If introduced it would only lead to political instability and economic poverty. Thomas Paine's *Rights of man* was one attempt to solve this problem.[14] But it was not the only one. Similar answers were being put forward in France in the 1780s by

---

9 Southey to T. Lamb, [c. Sept. 1792], *SL* i. 3–4.
10 Ibid. i. 7.
11 Southey to G. Bedford, 21 Oct. 1792, *NL* i. 10. See N. Roe, *The politics of nature: Wordsworth and some contemporaries*, Basingstoke 1992, 39–44.
12 Southey to T. Southey, 9 May 1795, *NL* i. 93–4.
13 For surveys of a vast literature see D. Wootton, 'The republican tradition: from commonwealth to common sense', in D. Wootton (ed.), *Republicanism, liberty and commercial society, 1649–1776*, Stanford 1994, 1–41, and M. Philp, 'English republicanism in the 1790s', *Journal of Political Philosophy* vi (1998), 235–62.
14 R. Whatmore, *Republicanism and the French Revolution: an intellectual history of Jean-Baptiste Say's political economy*, Oxford 2000, 18–31, 77–82, and '"A gigantic manliness": Paine's republicanism in the 1790s', in S. Collini, R. Whatmore and B. Young (eds),

Jacques Pierre Brissot and Étienne Clavière. They both defended representative government, which was increasingly seen as synonymous with republicanism. 'What is liberty?' Brissot asked. 'It is the most perfect state of society: it is the state in which man depends but upon the laws which he makes.'[15] However, both men were strongly influenced by Rousseau's insistence on the need for reformed manners among the entire populace. As Richard Whatmore has argued, 'This meant the quality of the *moeurs*, or manners, of the citizenry, their willingness to sacrifice private interest to the public good, and their capacity to resist egoism.'[16] One requirement was greater equality among the ranks, and for this reason these writers were deeply opposed to hereditary aristocracy. But they differed from Rousseau on commerce. While he thought wealth and virtue were antithetical, they sympathised with Richard Price's view that honest commerce created independence. This should not be confused with luxury, for even Price warned that unless Americans eschewed the inflation of artificial wants they would not be able to preserve their free republic. Commerce was only desirable if 'the luxury, the inequality, selfishness and avarice foster'd by trade' was checked by the asceticism of 'frugality [and] simplicity of manners'.[17] Brissot's position was similar. In his *New travels in the United States* he wrote of the intimate relationship between liberty and independence, insisted that 'the simplicity of wants and of pleasures may be taken as a sure sign of patriotism', and praised agricultural life as more suited to virtue than cities and trade.[18] Paine was less equivocal about commerce. The important point, however, was that if commerce could create more independence and equality it would do good, as well promoting stability, but that if it led to luxury it would be harmful.

The French took little interest in republicanism until the early 1790s. The circle around Clavière and Brissot was vocal in calling for abolition of the monarchy, but others, such as Emmanuel Sieyès, professed themselves puzzled by these arguments. Sieyès believed that the 1791 constitution ensured that law was made by the people, and that the king as the hereditary executive was subject to it. This was quite different from the *ancien régime*, in which the king's will had been sovereign. For Sieyès it did not fundamentally matter whether the executive was a hereditary king or a committee, but he believed that the latter was more likely to be indecisive and so potentially dangerous. In this case France before 1792 was already a republic in the modern sense. As one historian has commented, 'In 1792, the form of the executive power changed; there was a revolution *within* the republic.'[19] But for republicans such

Economy, polity and society: British intellectual history, 1750–1950, Cambridge 2000, 135–57.

15 J. P. Brissot, *New travels in the United States of America*, London 1792, p. x.

16 Whatmore, *Republicanism*, 80.

17 R. Price to J. Bowdoin, 25 Oct. 1785, in *The correspondence of Richard Price*, ed. W. B. Peach and D. O. Thomas, Durham, NC–Cardiff 1983–94, ii. 316.

18 Brissot, *New travels*, p. xvi.

19 P. Gueniffey, 'Cordeliers and Girondins: the prehistory of the republic?', in B. Fontana

as Brissot and Paine no polity could be described as republican that possessed hereditary features: all aspects of the political edifice must be representative, elective and removable. *Rights of man* differed from the arguments of most British reformers because it so clearly disparaged the mixed constitution, and abused monarchs and aristocrats as the causes of corruption and poverty. Once they were ousted, the burden of taxation would be lowered, commerce would thrive, and all ranks would partake in the prosperity and peace that followed. As Whatmore argues, 'Paine's aim was to regenerate humanity by reconstructing the social order. Ranks would not be associated with political or civil inequalities, and moderate wealth would protect this social constitution.'[20] Meanwhile in France, although Clavière's own reforms had failed by the early 1790s, there was a near universal consensus that manners needed to be reformed. Most revolutionaries were now convinced that earlier reforms which changed the shape of the constitution while ignoring the form of the wider culture were mistaken. While the Girondins fell from power in 1793, the Jacobins were arguing that a republic of virtue could only be created if liberty was curtailed, and more sweeping measures taken to reform a populace deeply corrupted by monarchy. There was widespread agreement that republican manners – frugality, industry, equality and patriotism – had to be inculcated if the revolution were to survive.[21]

By the beginning of 1793 Southey was confident of his republicanism. During the trial of Louis XVI in January he wrote to Bedford at length trying to vindicate his views. He argued that the toil of labourers sustained the extravagance of courtiers and blamed poverty on the existence of places and pensions. He also attacked the House of Lords because it enabled the aristocracy to shift the burden of taxation from themselves to the poor. Ultimately the monarchy had been established by force, and there was no 'superior strength or wisdom in crowned heads'. Indeed, he doubted the popularity of monarchy in Britain, and argued that even its defenders knew that republicanism was the best system in theory. It was, he believed, workable in practice, and the diverse examples of 'Thebes Sparta & Athens & Carthage', as well as America, were the proof. If Britain had become a republic centuries ago, he claimed, she would have avoided the many bloody wars that arose from monarchical and aristocratic ambition.[22] The language and arguments used here are consistent with *Rights of man*, particularly in ascribing poverty to the existence of monarchy and aristocracy, and in stating that republicanism was a peaceful system of politics. Southey was also supportive of the Girondins, as is evident in his comments on their execution in October 1793. This event 'completely harrowed up my faculties' and led him to think that 'virtue can only aspire to content in obscurity; for happiness is out of the question. I

(ed.), *The invention of the modern republic*, Cambridge 1994, 93.
[20] Whatmore, '"A gigantic manliness"', 154.
[21] Idem, *Republicanism*, 93–5.
[22] Southey to G. Bedford, 8 Jan. 1793, Bodl. Lib., MS Eng. Lett. c. 22, fos 43–4.

look round the world, and everywhere find the same mournful spectacle – the strong tyrannising over the weak, man and beast; the same depravity pervades the whole creation; oppression is triumphant everywhere. ... There is no place for virtue'.[23] To be so strongly affected suggests that he was following French politics closely. It also seems probable that he was aware of Brissot's *New travels*, because Coleridge used it while preparing for pantisocracy, and quoted it favourably in *Conciones ad populum*.[24] If Paine and Brissot are useful guides to Southey's politics at this time, it is likely that he saw republicanism in terms of a representative government and a reformed populace. As we shall see later, however, he was more sceptical about the effects of commerce on the populace.

Just as Southey was defining himself against the political establishment, so too he was expressing grave doubts about the religious establishment. The status of religion was a rather divisive issue among reformers: many came from within dissenting circles and viewed the open scepticism of Paine, Godwin and Thelwall with some concern. Coleridge's own thinking was deeply bound up with religion. The latitudinarianism of Cambridge, and the Unitarian contacts he made there, helped him develop his early interest in David Hartley and Joseph Priestley.[25] By 1795 he was sufficiently confident that true radicalism was the 'system of Jesus' that he attacked sceptical radicals in a series of lectures. But Southey's position is less clear. He was not especially exposed to dissenting ideas as a youth (although Bristol was a major centre of Quakerism), and if anything religion was neglected in his childhood and schooling.[26] Oxford was unlikely to have had any effect other than exacerbating his dislike of orthodoxy. When Thomas Poole met Southey in September 1794, he commented that 'In Religion, shocking to say in a mere Boy as he is, I fear he wavers between Deism and Atheism.' Early the following year, Coleridge told George Dyer that 'Southey is *Christianizing* apace'.[27] Taken together these statements imply that under Coleridge's influence the young Southey moved from something approaching atheism to something approaching Christianity. While these comments convey an impression of Southey as an extremist in matters of faith, they lack specificity. A rather different picture emerges when we attend to his letters.

In these we find a young man wrestling with his beliefs. In part this was because of the recent death of his father, but it was also because of his intended career in the Church. Whatever Poole might have claimed, there is little to indicate leanings to atheism, for Southey disdained the 'witty impiety' of

---

23 Southey to G. Bedford, 11 Nov. 1793, *LC* i. 189.
24 S. T. Coleridge, *Lectures, 1795: on politics and religion*, ed. L. Patton and P. Mann, London–Princeton 1971, 47–8. See R. Holmes, *Coleridge: early visions*, London 1989, 77.
25 N. Roe, *Wordsworth and Coleridge: the radical years*, Oxford 1988, ch. iii.
26 Simmons, *Southey*, 36.
27 T. Poole to J. Haskins, 22 Sept. 1794, in *Thomas Poole and his friends*, ed. M. E. Sandford, London 1888, i. 97; Coleridge to G. Dyer, [late Feb. 1795], *CL* i. 153.

Voltaire and the 'artful infidelity' of Hume.[28] 'The idea of meeting a different fate in another world', he told Bedford, 'is enough to overthrow every Atheistical doctrine', and the trials of life were best soothed by the consolations of religion.[29] Rather, he seemed to hold to a simple set of religious beliefs that fell somewhere between deism and Socinianism. He left Westminster, as he later admitted, with 'my religious principles shaken by Gibbon', and it seems that *Decline and fall* did much to undermine his faith in the status of biblical revelation.[30] One letter finds him arguing that 'the book of life of benevolence & simple truth' had been polluted by those 'damned monks' who monopolised Scripture and 'pieced them & patchd them' together from sources as diverse as 'Alexandrian Platonists – the Oriental fictions & Jewish Cabbala'.[31] Unsurprisingly, he rejected the doctrines of the Trinity and original sin. Humanity was not in a state of sin, and required no act of atonement to redeem it. Even though he had to subscribe to the Thirty-Nine Articles in order to matriculate, he proclaimed that 'of the sanctity of those mysteries I know nothing – their incomprehensibility is evident – Athanasius the reputed author of that stumbling block confessed he understood them not – Tillotson wished the creed expunged from the liturgy – yet the one was a Saint & the other an Archbishop'.[32] He also opposed all forms of establishment. If Christ was not divine, he could not have established a priesthood by apostolic succession, and nor could the Church possess any special mediatory powers. Establishments produced 'but a mulish kind of barren religion'.[33] The Church's main aim was to preserve its power and privilege, and he believed that most of its clergy were intolerant bigots who would happily resort to persecution when their arguments failed them. His own faith, he claimed, was very simple, and 'Were I a Legislator, I would build a temple to the One Eternal Universal God. My national creed should be God is one, Christ is the Saviour of Mankind.' He did not specify in what way Christ remained a saviour, though as we shall see he was probably referring to his moral teachings. He continued, stating that 'every man who acknowledged a deity might worship him unmolested under my establishment. The human race would soon be fraternized by a system so liberal and those atrocious animosities which prompt the orthodox to revile their dissenting brethren would soon be forgotten'.[34] Understandably a career in the Church of England presented problems for Southey. His virtually deistic faith found room for God's existence, the immortality of the soul, as well as the moral truth of Christ's teachings, but for very few 'speculative points of faith'.[35] He found little need for them.

---

28 Southey to G. Bedford, 26 Dec. 1792, *NL* i. 13.
29 Southey to G. Bedford, [14] Feb. 1793, *LC* i. 175.
30 Southey to C. H. Townshend, 5 June 1816, ibid. iv. 186.
31 Southey to G. Bedford, 29 Oct. 1793, Bodl. Lib., MS Eng. Lett. c. 22, fo. 72.
32 Southey to G. Bedford, 16 Jan. 1793, ibid. fo. 45.
33 Southey to G. Bedford, 31 July 1793, *NL* i. 31.
34 Ibid.
35 Southey to G. Bedford, 8 Feb. 1793, ibid. i. 17.

Against established beliefs and practices, he proposed a religion of nature. 'Written on Sunday morning', composed in 1795, made this clear enough. 'Go thou and seek the House of Prayer! | I to the Woodlands wend, and there | In lovely Nature see the GOD OF LOVE.'[36] In *Joan of Arc*, a lengthy section on religion was, as the *Analytical Review* noted, of more relevance to the eighteenth than the fifteenth century.[37] In the third book, Joan was tested for heresy by doctors of theology, who put forward the Catholic ecclesiology that the Church was the only means of reconciliation with God. Joan, like Southey, disagreed.[38] She shocked them by insisting that her religion was taught to her by nature. Since the fall, they argued, man's nature had been corrupt and therefore 'Nature can teach to sin' but it cannot 'tell thee that St. Peter holds the keys, | And that his successors' unbounded power | Extends o'er either world'. Only by belonging to the Church could a person be saved: 'Altho' thy life | Of sin were free, if of this holy truth | Ignorant, thy soul in liquid flames must rue | Transgression.'[39] The purest of lives, if lived outside the Church, was still a damned life. Joan rejected this: 'For sins confest | To holy Priest and absolution given | I knew them not; for ignorant of sin | Why should I seek forgiveness?'[40] Her sinlessness was natural:

> It is not Nature that can teach to sin:
> Nature is all Benevolence – all Love,
> All Beauty! …
> … Nature teach sin!
> O blasphemy against the Holy One
> Who made us all for Happiness and Love,
> Infinite happiness – infinite love,
> Partakers of his own eternity.[41]

Joan did not believe in the Trinity and the fall, and so had little need for a Church which insisted that degraded humanity required its absolution for salvation. The contrast between Church and nature in this epic poem is plainly stated. Joan explicitly rejected the forms of organised religion:

> In forest shade my infant years train'd up
> Knew not devotion's forms. The chaunted mass,
> The silver altar and religious robe,
> The mystic wafer and the hallowed cup,
> Gods priest-created, are to me unknown.
> Beneath no high-arch'd roof I bow'd in prayer,

---

[36] R. Southey, *Poetical works: 1793–1810*, ed. L. Pratt, London 2004, v. 96.

[37] *Analytical Review* xxiii (1796), 173–4, 176.

[38] See A. M. C. Waterman, 'The nexus between theology and political doctrine in Church and dissent', in K. Haakonssen (ed.), *Enlightenment and religion: rational dissent in eighteenth-century Britain*, Cambridge 1996, 193–218.

[39] R. Southey, *Joan of Arc*, Bristol 1796, in *Poetical works*, i. 52.

[40] Ibid.

[41] Ibid. i. 53.

No solemn light by storied pane disguis'd,
No trophied pillars, and no imag'd cross
Wak'd my young mind to artificial awe,
To fear the God I only learnt to love.[42]

These passages have sometimes been ascribed to the influence of Coleridge, because of their similarity to his own views, and because he helped Southey redraft the poem. In fact they were written a year before Southey met Coleridge, and, often in unaltered form, were retained in the later 1798 edition from which Coleridge's lines were removed.[43] But what then was the origin of Southey's religion of nature? The best guide is to be found not in rational dissent, but in the writings of Rousseau.

While Rousseau's political writings were not widely read in eighteenth-century Britain, books such as Emile, the New Eloisa and the Confessions were much more popular. Southey knew them well.[44] In 1792 he had written a short essay which argued that Rousseau was superior to Richardson, and in later life he stated that – along with Gibbon – he had left Westminster with 'a head full of Rousseau and Werter'.[45] Even in 1796 he could write an 'Inscription' praising Rousseau as a 'MAN of NATURE'.[46] While Southey was not the most astute reader of the Genevan, his influence is still very clear. In the 1790s Rousseau was identified as the philosopher of a 'radical' version of sensibility which conservatives felt was dangerous because it encouraged the pursuit of purportedly natural feelings which were felt to undermine the traditional social and sexual order.[47] Southey, too, was imbued with sensibility. In the spring of 1793 he was reading Henry Mackenzie's Man of feeling ('few works have ever pleased me so painfully or so much') and he later wrote that his 'mimosa sensibility' was heavily informed by Rousseau.[48] While reading the Confessions in the summer of 1793 he noted that one passage 'expresses my religious opinions better than I could do it myself'. In it Rousseau wrote of how contemplating the wonders of nature inspired reverence for the divinity,

---

42 Ibid. i. 51. See pp. 276–7 for revisions to the second edition.
43 See J. Wordsworth, 'Introduction' to the reprint of Joan of Arc, Oxford 1993, unpaginated; Southey, 'Joan of Arc' (1793), British Library, London, MS RP 1222, bk 5, lines 332–44; Joan, 277.
44 Southey to G. Bedford, 16 Mar. 1793, LC i. 178; Southey to G. Bedford, 5 May, 14 July 1793, NL i. 21, 27; R. Southey, Letters written during a short residence in Spain and Portugal, Bristol 1797, 47. See G. Dart, Rousseau, Robespierre, and English romanticism, Cambridge 1999.
45 Southey to Townshend, 5 June 1816, LC iv. 186.
46 Southey, Poetical works, v. 67.
47 See M. Butler, Jane Austen and the war of ideas, Oxford 1975; J. Todd, Sensibility: an introduction, London 1986; and C. Jones, Radical sensibility: literature and ideas in the 1790s, London 1993.
48 Southey to G. Bedford, 4 Apr. 1793, LC i. 181; Southey to W. Taylor, 12 Mar. 1799, in A memoir of the life and writings of the late William Taylor of Norwich, ed. J. W. Robberds, London 1843, i. 262.

and that he could not understand how it could be otherwise.[49] Southey identified closely with this. As he told Bedford, 'Rousseau in the present proscription of his opinions has been branded an Infidel. he was not one. the Savoyard curate speaks his faith – it is the creed of rational Xtianity.'[50] By the middle of 1793 Southey had found a system of beliefs to which he could assent.

He was referring to the 'profession of faith' of the Savoyard vicar in *Emile*. Although he was a deist, Rousseau owed a lot to Genevan Calvinism's liberalisation in the early eighteenth century. The stress on sin, predestination and justification by faith had been eroded in favour of a more Pelagian ethical activism.[51] For the Savoyard vicar any religion that damned those who lacked knowledge of revelation without reference to the worth of their lives was simply 'iniquitous and cruel'.[52] A moral life was the means of salvation, and Rousseau saw the life of Christ as perhaps the supreme example of this. At the same time, however, the Gospel also contained many 'unbelievable things' that were 'repugnant to reason'. The lesson to be taken was that humanity possessed moral freedom and the capacity to reform itself.[53] In this we have already seen Southey's close agreement. But Rousseau was concerned not just with religion here, but also the nature of morality. He wanted a moral theory which was neither relativist nor consequentionalist, and he also wanted it to be readily available to all people so that we 'can be men without being scholars'.[54] The solution was not in the complexities of reason but in the simplicities of feeling. There was an inner sense which enabled people to recognise right from wrong. 'There is in the depth of souls', he wrote, 'an innate principle of justice and virtue according to which, in spite of our maxims, we judge our actions and those of others as good or bad. It is to this principle I give the name *conscience*.'[55] Although he tried to steer a middle way between those who located morality in reason and those who rested it on the passions, he did at times seem to fall closer to the latter position. 'Conscience, conscience! Divine instinct, immortal and celestial voice, certain guide of a being that is ignorant and limited but intelligent and free; infallible judge of good and bad which makes man like unto God; it is you who make the excellence of his nature and the morality of his actions.'[56] If this 'infallible judge' was available to all humans why did they not always listen? It was because it spoke to us in 'nature's language' and liked 'refuge and peace'. It could not be heard among the vices and prejudices of the modern world. 'It flees or

---

[49] Southey to G. Bedford, 4 Aug. 1793, *NL* i. 33. See J. J. Rousseau, *Confessions*, ed. J. M. Cohen, London 1953, 593.

[50] Southey to G. Bedford, 25 July 1793, Bodl. Lib., MS Eng. Lett. c. 22, fo. 64.

[51] H. Rosenblatt, *Rousseau and Geneva: from the* First discourse *to the* Social contract, *1749–1762*, Cambridge 1997, 11–17.

[52] J. J. Rousseau, *Emile: or, on education*, ed. A. Bloom, Harmondsworth 1991, 297.

[53] Ibid. 308.

[54] Ibid. 290.

[55] Ibid. 289.

[56] Ibid. 290.

keeps quiet before them. Their noisy voices stifle its voice and prevent it from making itself heard. ... It finally gives up as a result of being dismissed. It no longer speaks to us. It no longer responds to us.'[57] Wicked men had 'icy' hearts because they listened to the passions of their bodies rather than the feelings of their souls.[58] Rousseau was not saying, however, that the conscience only operated in a state of nature but rather that it was the voice of nature as experienced by social beings.[59] It was available to all in the modern world, but would only be heard if people stopped and listened.

Joan of Arc was first written in the summer of 1793, when Southey was immersed in Rousseauvian themes, and so it is not surprising to find them in the poem. Joan had been raised from infancy in a forest far removed from civilised life, and this ensured that she had learned to see and feel the 'GOD OF LOVE' all around her. In the 1793 draft the hermit that educated her tells her that he has 'traind thee in the path that leads to bliss' and asks her to 'firmly still proceed | Unmov'd by all the noisy crowd that throng | The painted road of vice'.[60] Joan's upbringing provided her with a firm basis for a virtuous life, as long as she continued to hold herself above the vices and passions of modern life. This required a firm and steady commitment to the inner voice. She explained this to the king,

> Charles – tho Fortune sit
> Above thy reach yet virtue as mild as good
> Unwillingly departs – recurring still
> In contemplative hour with many a pang
> Of conscience, oft despis'd.[61]

In the 1793 manuscript this speech is crossed out, and the version that was published in 1796 is written in the margin.

> In the human heart
> Dwells VIRTUE; milder form! and templed there
> Loves her meet altar; and, tho' oft dislodg'd,
> Reluctantly she quits her lov'd abode,
> And oft returns, and oft importunate
> Reclaims her empire.[62]

The conscience, which was central to the practice of a virtuous life, was best understood in moments of solitude and contemplation. As with Rousseau, those people whose consciences no longer spoke to them lacked feeling and

---

[57] Ibid. 291.
[58] Ibid. 287.
[59] C. Taylor, *Sources of the self: the making of modern identity*, Cambridge 1989, 359. See also Rosenblatt, *Rousseau*, 177.
[60] Southey, 'Joan' (1793), bk 1, lines 311–13.
[61] Ibid. bk 6, lines 314–18.
[62] Idem, *Joan*, 68.

pity.[63] In *Joan of Arc*, the character Bertram described how during the siege of Rouen it had been necessary to release the women and children to the mercy of the English: 'What is man I That he can hear the groan of wretchedness I And feel no fleshy pang!' 'I did think I There was not on this earth a heart so hard I Could hear a famish'd woman cry for bread, I And know no pity.' King Henry was also guilty, said Bertram: 'every moment [I] thought that Henry's heart I Hard as it was, must feel'.[64] These were natural responses to suffering, and only the very depraved had no such feelings. Indeed, much of Southey's early poetry was infused with the themes of sensibility, in which figures of virtue and innocence are contrasted with those of inhumanity and indifference.

Southey also used his epic to present a case for ethical activism, which brings us back to his Pelagian conception of Christianity. Joan defended the duty of benevolence and rejected the idea that individuals should focus their energies on preparing for the next world. In the first draft she resisted those who counselled her to retire to a convent, saying that she would not wear out her life in the 'tiresome path' of devotion. It was not in prayer or mass or 'duly counted beads' that God looked for piety. The 'tree' of life was 'judgd only by the fruits' and an abundant crop was better than 'the ivys joyless arms I that clasp the antique cloisters wall I In barren indolence'.[65] This idea was developed in the ninth book of the published version, which consists of an allegorical dream where Joan was tempted by the figure of Despair to give up on the world. He stated that life was miserable and purposeless for most people, and that God was indifferent to them. Joan insisted that there was an afterlife, and duties to be performed in this life. There was pleasure to be found in looking back on a life of duty, and knowing the joys to come:

> A dawn of glory, a reward in Heaven,
> He shall not gain who never merited.
> If thou didst know the worth of one good deed
> In life's last hour, thou would'st not bid me lose
> The power to benefit; if I but save
> A drowning fly, I shall not live in vain.[66]

Hence, in the clearest terms, Southey – speaking through Joan – was stating the centrality of living a benevolent life, and that good works were necessary for salvation. There was a duty to resist oppression and to help those suffering. He was, however, aware that an epic based on a war of national liberation would sit uneasily with this appeal to universal benevolence, and so he inserted a speech where Joan told her troops to refrain from unnecessary cruelty against the English. Even though God was on their side, they would

---

63 Idem, 'Joan' (1793), bk 11, lines 762–71, makes explicit reference to Rousseau and sensibility.
64 Idem, *Joan*, 39, 40.
65 Idem, 'Joan' (1793), bk 10, lines 505–13.
66 Idem, *Joan*, 143.

lose that favour if they acted unjustly.[67] In *Joan of Arc*, then, Rousseau's influence is at its clearest, and even if the published edition had erased some of the trail there seems little doubt that the Genevan's thinking about religion and morality had a strong effect on Southey.

Godwin and the critique of political society

Towards the end of 1793 Southey's intellectual world was shaken by a new work. In November and December he read Godwin's *Enquiry concerning political justice* and 'all but worshipped'. 'I am studying such a book!' he hurriedly told Bedford, 'Talk of morality … Democracy, real true democracy is but another word for morality – they are like body and soul.'[68] This enthusiasm would be intense for around two years, but even afterwards the general themes of *Political justice* were important to him. Coleridge, however, was rather less impressed. Initially intrigued by Southey's praise, he had by October 1794 concluded that 'I think not so highly of him as you do – and I have read him with the greatest attention.'[69] In 1795 he was openly attacking Godwin's thought in his lectures, and by late 1796 was promising to write a volume exposing the critical flaws in it.[70] This is ironic, because there was much in *Political justice* that Coleridge agreed with. Both he and Godwin developed their thinking from the materials of rational dissent, and particularly the necessitarianism of Hartley and Priestley. Peter Mann has suggested that Coleridge also agreed with Godwin in his 'analysis of the role of property in society, his criticism of "luxury" and superfluities, his belief that the social institutions built upon the system of unequal property produced all other evils, political, moral, and intellectual, and his advocacy of social and moral change by non-violent progressive "illumination"'.[71] But what Coleridge disliked, he disliked intensely. This included Godwin's defence of stoicism, his views on sex and marriage, and his notorious atheism. Southey, however, was not overly bothered by Godwin's religious views. Indeed, he saw that the germ of *Political justice* was compatible with religion. 'I have talked to Seward of the eternal & immutable Laws of Justice', he told Bedford, 'he tells me of the eternal & immutable laws of Religion. the difference exists only in terms.'[72] It is worth noting, however, that he picked out elements that suited him most, and so perhaps did not fully understand the work. This was Coleridge's view in 1811 when he told Godwin – perhaps uncharitably – that 'When he was young, he just looked enough into your books to believe that

---

67 Ibid. 126.
68 Southey to G. Bedford, 26 Nov. 1793, Bodl. Lib., MS Eng. Lett. c. 22, fo. 80.
69 Coleridge to Southey, 21 Oct. 1794, *CL* i. 115.
70 Coleridge to B. Flower, 11 Dec. 1796; Coleridge to J. Thelwall, 21 Dec. 1796, *CL* i. 267, 293.
71 P. Mann, 'Editors' introduction II', in Coleridge, *Lectures, 1795*, p. lxxii
72 Southey to G. Bedford, 26 Nov. 1793, Bodl. Lib., MS Eng. Lett. c. 22, fo. 81.

you taught Republicanism and Stoicism – ergo, that you were of his opinion, & he of yours and this was all.'[73]

Political justice was published in 1793 as a philosophical work aimed at an educated audience. At its core was a development of the claims of rational dissent with the theology removed. Following Price's arguments about the existence of objective laws of justice, Godwin argued that the full and free exercise of the private judgement was the means of discovering those laws. We were obliged to act morally not because of the feelings we might have or the interests we served, but because 'Truth' – the substitute for God – obliged us to. It was this which encouraged Godwin's reputation for stoicism, because it implied that feelings of love, loyalty, honour and gratitude were subordinate to the claims of justice.[74] *Political justice* also featured a revised version of the necessitarianism of Hartley and Priestley, which showed how the mind responded to external stimuli and how the individual built up complex patterns of behaviour which, while seemingly voluntary, were in fact necessitated. Godwin added to this the idea that as the mind compared ideas it was moved most powerfully to act by those which were true. Hence, necessitarianism was the mechanism of perfectibility. Much of the rest of *Political justice* argued that the inherited institutions of politics and property produced the vices which they were purported to control. The progress of enlightenment had removed some of these abuses, but much more remained possible. Hence Godwin's argument was teleological and perfectibilist: the exercise of our judgement in pursuit of the truth enabled us to liberate ourselves from the constraints in which we existed. 'As we develop greater autonomy from these constraints and become more perfectly directed by reason and truth, our conduct increasingly promotes the greatest good and society gradually improves. The process is a gradual one and a long one – indeed it is an infinite process.'[75] This argument meant that Godwin set little store by constitutional amendment or violent revolution as motors of change. Only by private judgement and open discussion would progress occur, and only then when individuals were convinced of the uselessness of their existing institutions: attempting to force opinion was self-defeating.[76]

There was much in *Political justice* that Southey found supportive and stimulating. Its stoicism was one important element which he later claimed weaned him from sensibility, although his interest in this went back to early 1793 when he was encouraged by Edward Seward to make Epictetus his 'manual' for 'many months'.[77] Undoubtedly there were personal reasons why the rigours of a stoical life might appeal, but it is the implications it

---

[73] Coleridge to W. Godwin, [c. 29 Mar. 1811], *CL* iii. 316.
[74] M. Philp, *Godwin's political justice*, London 1986, 23–34. See ch. vii for an account of revisions to this stoicism.
[75] Ibid. 94.
[76] W. Godwin, *An enquiry concerning political justice*, London 1793, in *The political and philosophical writings of William Godwin*, ed. M. Philp, London 1993, iii. 470–3.
[77] Southey to Townshend, 5 June 1816, *LC* iv. 186.

had for his moral thinking which concern us here. He certainly believed that there was an absolute moral order by which the rightness of an act was judged, and also that such actions were to be performed because they were right and not because of any rewards that might flow from them. Southey had once told Seward that 'If our tutors would but make our studies interesting we should pursue them with pleasure. Certainly we should he replied; but I feel a pleasure in studying them because I know it is my duty.' This advice was 'true philosophy, of that species which tends to make mankind happy, because it first makes them good'.[78] It is commonly assumed that the stoic urge to live a life according to nature and reason required the ruthless suppression of emotions. But, as A. A. Long has argued, this is not quite right, for the stoic was not 'impassive' to pleasures and pains, but rather not overly moved by them: 'his disposition is characterized by "good emotional states". Well-wishing, wishing another man good things for his sake; joy: rejoicing in virtuous actions, a tranquil life, a good conscience; and "wariness", reasonable disinclination'.[79] Little in this would have conflicted with Southey's interpretation of Rousseau. He did not believe that Godwin demanded the suppression of emotion, only that partial feelings did not override the duty to act justly. 'Bedford because I hold gratitude a vice', he wrote in explanation, 'does my heart beat less warmly to affection. Think you that Brutus loved not his children when he abandoned them?'[80] Southey admired Romans like Brutus and Cato because they could act justly in spite of the interests and feelings which prompted otherwise. But it was this which annoyed Coleridge in his personal relations with Southey. While at times he admired his friend's 'moral Excellence' and '*perpendicular Virtue*', he could also find it too harsh.[81] 'Your undeviating Simplicity of Rectitude has made you too rapid in decision', he commented, 'having never erred, you feel more *indignation* at Error, than *Pity* for it. There is *Phlogiston* in your heart.'[82] No doubt this reflects Coleridge's leanings towards self-pity, but it does also convey a sense of how strongly stoicism affected Southey.

The idea of a stoic as the embodiment of virtue is most evident in *Wat Tyler*. The key characters of the drama, Tyler and John Ball, were both presented as figures of moral rectitude who generally bore the injustices heaped upon them without anger. They commanded admiration and deserved emulation, and personally derived pleasure only from knowing that they had done the right thing. After his release from prison, Ball tells Tyler how much he had suffered while languishing there, 'but I bore it cheerily – I My heart was glad – for I had done my duty'. In preaching the virtues of a benevolent Christian life he had fulfilled his responsibilities, and so his pain was a matter of indifference. Indeed, all he could think of was the suffering of others: 'I pitied my

78 Southey to G. Bedford, [c.] 2 Feb. 1793, *NL* i. 16.
79 A. A. Long, *Hellenistic philosophy: stoics, epicureans, sceptics*, London 1974, 207.
80 Southey to G. Bedford, [27 Sept. 1794], *NL* i. 80.
81 Coleridge to Dyer, [late Feb. 1795], *CL* i. 152–3.
82 Coleridge to Southey, 19 Sept. 1794, ibid. i. 106.

oppressors, and I sorrow'd | For the poor men of England.'[83] Here then we can see Southey fusing Godwinian stoicism with Christian fortitude. The former comes out more strongly when, after Tyler's murder, Ball explained that he did not mourn the death of 'an honest virtuous friend' for himself, but because of what he had been as a leader of the peasants:

> he was one
> Gifted with the strong energy of mind,
> Quick to perceive the right, and prompt to act
> When Justice needed: he would listen to me
> With due attention, yet not yielding lightly
> What had to him seem'd good: severe in virtue,
> He awed the ruder people, whome he led,
> By his stern rectitude.[84]

The influence of Godwin seems undeniable in the references to the needs of justice and the perception of right. It is noticeable, however, that this 'energy of mind' was possessed by only a few, while the 'ruder' people needed a stern leader to guide them. Without Tyler 'the giddy multitude' were 'blind to their own good'.[85] For Southey there was not yet an equality in ability to discern the truth. A letter written before he had read Godwin is suggestive in this regard: 'Deism will do well for the philosopher whose cool calm passions may be governed by principles of Reason & Morality, but the minds of the million require a more powerful tie. they must be activated by hope & fear – two master springs admirably touched by religion.'[86] Here it is important to note that, first, Southey understands that religion might have a central role to play in the reformation of character, an idea which Godwin played down, and that second, even while he was enthused by Rousseau, he stressed the need for the 'philosopher' to control his emotions. This would suggest that the conflict in his mind between 'sensibility' and 'stoicism' was not as sharp as it might have been.

Coleridge was deeply opposed to Godwin's stoicism. In their refusal to be moved by love or pity, he saw the stoics not as upright exemplars of virtue, but as conceited and selfish men who disdained vice because it was beneath them.[87] The problem was that *Political justice* attempted to 'inculcate benevolence while it does away every home-born Feeling' and so Godwin 'builds without a foundation, proposes an end without establishing the means'.[88] This view arose because Coleridge held to a Hartleyan account of the origins of benevolence in which the affection a child felt for those close to him

[83] R. Southey, *Wat Tyler*, London 1817, 26.
[84] Ibid. 52.
[85] Ibid. 53.
[86] Southey to G. Bedford, 25 July 1793, Bodl. Lib., MS Eng. Lett. c. 22, fo. 64.
[87] Coleridge, *Lectures*, 1795, 156–7.
[88] Ibid. 162, 164.

expanded by association until eventually he came to love all humanity. As Coleridge insisted to Southey,

> The ardour of private Attachments makes Philanthropy a necessary *habit* of the Soul. I love my *Friend* – such as *he* is, all mankind are or *might be*! The deduction is evident –. Philanthropy (and indeed every other Virtue) is a thing of *Concretion* – Some home-born Feeling is the *center* of the Ball, that, rolling on thro' Life collects and assimilates every congenial Affection.[89]

This point was restated in his 'Lectures on revealed religion', where he even claimed that 'Jesus knew our Nature – that expands like the circles of a Lake – the Love of our Friends, parents and neighbours lead[s] us to the love of our Country to the love of all Mankind. The intensity of private attachment encourages, not prevents, universal philanthropy.'[90] Coleridge's position, then, remained the same during his close relationship with Southey. He could not accept Godwin's argument that feelings must be subordinate to the pursuit of benevolence because the latter arose from the former. Wollstonecraft is also interesting for her arguments that humans could not achieve an elevated and impartial approach to justice. Like Southey, she had once been favourably inclined to Rousseau's idea of the conscience, but moved away from it because of a growing scepticism about sensibility. This had become 'the manie of the day, and compassion the virtue which is to cover a multitude of vices, whilst justice is left to mourn in sullen silence, and balance truth in vain'.[91] Instead, Karen Green has suggested, she used the idea of the 'imagination' as a bridge between natural motives and rational calculations. As humans grew they experienced a wide range of feelings, and learned that other people also experienced them. These were then examined and controlled by the understanding, and so virtue emerged in dialogue between feeling and reason.[92] Southey was deeply affected by Wollstonecraft's writings, although his fragmentary comments are insufficient to draw any conclusions about whether he identified with her approach to moral judgement.[93]

Southey was also profoundly impressed by Godwin's account of existing institutions which seemed to show that they were the cause of most social ills. Vice was the product of circumstance rather than the result of an irredeemably corrupt human nature. For this reason Southey claimed to embrace necessitarianism. He excitedly told Bedford that 'now admitting the human mind to be blank of original ideas, it follows that every thing is the object

---

89 Coleridge to Southey, 13 July [1794], *CL* i. 86.
90 Coleridge, *Lectures*, 1795, 163.
91 Cited in K. Green, 'The passions and the imagination in Wollstonecraft's theory of moral judgement', *Utilitas* ix (1997), 274.
92 Ibid. 284.
93 He read the *Rights of woman* in December 1793, and wrote a sonnet 'To Mary Wollstonecraft' in 1795: *Poetical works*, v. 35–6.

of education, & of example'.[94] People were necessitated to act as they did because of the way their minds had been formed and so 'the Necessarian will not look upon the instrument of a bad deed with anger or abhorrence, he will pity him'.[95] It followed that crime was caused by the inequalities of political society, as were the emotions that led people into conflict. 'The passions are not vicious', Southey insisted, ''tis society that makes the indulgence of them so.'[96] The social order was 'depraved' because it created the artificial distinctions which caused misery. Indeed, 'there is scarcely one crime in the old Bailey calendar which does not originate in the inventions of political society' he wrote while reading *Political justice*. 'Would man thieve did not want tempt him? ... Sin is artificial – it is the monstrous offspring of government and property.'[97] This idea was enshrined in the 'Botany Bay eclogues' of early 1794, in which the crimes of various transportees were traced to political society: William was caught killing his landlord's game in order to protect his own crops, while Elinor was forced into prostitution to feed herself.[98] When Coleridge met Southey in June that year, it seems that necessitarianism was one of the issues they discussed, because Southey borrowed one of Coleridge's favourite works, Hartley's *Observations on man*, from Bristol Library on 8 July.[99] Coleridge evidently hoped to wean his new friend from Godwinian to Hartleyan necessitarianism, and although this new work reignited Southey's zeal – evident in a lengthy letter written to Bedford on 20 July – there is no evidence of a more fundamental sea-change in his thinking. Indeed, Southey's interest in necessitarianism was more lightly worn than Coleridge's. The main attraction was that it reinforced his belief that vicious behaviour was not natural to humanity but was a product of circumstance, and that in a changed environment it could be removed and mankind ultimately perfected. 'Man cannot act without motives', he explained, 'Give him the strongest motives for virtue and take away all motives for vice and Man would approach very near perfection.'[100]

The critique of property offered by *Political justice* was to prove particularly important to Southey. 'It is unjust', Godwin wrote, 'if one man labour to the destruction of his health or his life, that another may abound in luxuries. It is unjust, if one man be deprived of leisure to cultivate his rational powers, while another man contributes not a single effort to add to the common stock.'[101] Not only did the luxury of the idle rich necessitate the physically exhausting labour of the poor, but it also denied them time for the intellectual develop-

94 Southey to G. Bedford, 26 Nov. 1793, Bodl. Lib., MS Eng. Lett. c. 22, fo. 81.
95 Southey to G. Bedford, 6 June 1794, ibid. fo. 113.
96 Southey to G. Bedford, 12 June 1794, *NL* i. 57.
97 Southey to H. Bedford, 12 Dec. 1793, ibid. i. 40.
98 Southey, *Poetical works*, v. 4–8, 73–83.
99 P. Kaufman, 'The reading of Southey and Coleridge: the record of their borrowings from the Bristol library, 1793–1798', *Modern Philology* xxi (1924), 318.
100 Southey to G. Bedford, 20 July 1794, *NL* i. 61.
101 Godwin, *Political justice*, 423.

ment necessary for progress. Godwin stressed the Christian contribution to arguments about the immorality of property accumulation, but insisted that charity was a feeble solution to the problem, and instead argued that justice demanded that everyone give all that they could to those in greater need than themselves.[102] In time this would lead to an equality of property. In such a rational state of society individuals would labour to fulfil basic human needs rather than to provide luxuries – which were in any event born of a love of distinction – and so because everyone would work, it would take little time to satisfy those needs.[103] Godwin stressed the equality of individual ownership, however, and rejected arguments about communal property-holding, an important point with which Coleridge disagreed. In his 'Lectures', he argued that once nomadic peoples became settled, claims to exclusive ownership of land emerged.[104] As commerce and manufacture developed they created new artificial wants which worsened inequality. Clashing interests, jarring passions and seething envy became so common that government arose as a solution. In fact, however, it was only a quack medicine which worsened the very ills it was supposed to cure. To support growing political and religious establishments, the lower orders were overworked and overtaxed, and kept in ignorance to prevent them from questioning their exploitation. Indeed, they accepted this 'unnatural Toil' because they were spurred on by the hope of attaining 'unnatural Luxuries' for themselves.[105] Coleridge noted that under Mosaic Law the Jews had ensured equality by re-equalising the ownership of land every fifty years. This was not an ideal solution, however, and he insisted that all the while anyone possessed anything exclusively as theirs, the 'selfish Passions will have full play', and governments and priesthood had their legitimation.[106] 'An abolition of all individual Property', he argued, 'is perhaps the only infallible Preventative against accumulation, but the Jews were too ignorant a people, too deeply leavened with the Vices of Ægypt to be capable of so exalted a state of Society.'[107] Only when true Christianity reigned in the hearts of everyone would communal ownership become possible and government cease to be necessary.[108]

Southey strongly sympathised with Godwin's views, even if he chose to express them in a rather different idiom. In *Joan of Arc*, an idyllic past was imagined in which equality had existed, but this had been supplanted by the 'artificial boundaries that divide | Man from his species'. This 'fall' occurred 'when Cain's stern son | Delved in the bowels of the earth for gold, |

102 Ibid. 425–6.
103 Ibid. 440. See G. Claeys, 'The origins of the rights of labor: republicanism, commerce and the construction of modern social theory in Britain, 1796–1805', *Journal of Modern History* lxvi (1994), 277.
104 Coleridge, *Lectures*, 1795, 219–29.
105 Ibid. 223.
106 Ibid. 228.
107 Ibid. 128.
108 Ibid. 228–9. See Morrow, *Coleridge's political thought*, 21–7.

Accursed bane of virtue'. Instead of paying homage to 'JUSTICE' man instead worshipped 'WEALTH and POWER, the Idols he had made'.[109] These passages show the influence of the idea of the golden age, and particularly Dryden's famous translation of the first book of Ovid's *Metamorphoses*, which dealt with the transition from an age of simple equality to a time when the greed for gold and the passion for iron dominated.[110] Southey was also referring to a popular interpretation of Genesis in which Enoch, the son of Cain, was thought to have founded the first city, and his offspring were said to be responsible for developing civilisation, including the mining of copper, iron and gold. He was using these traditions to underline his view that the earth had been 'framed for happiness' by God but that man had made it a 'theatre of woe'.[111] This theme was dealt with most explicitly in *Wat Tyler*, which fused the critique of monarchy and aristocracy offered by Paine with Godwin's attack on property. There Hob thought that the peasants were mere instruments for the desires of the rich:

> Sweated for them the wearying summer's day,
> Wasted for them the wages of our toil;
> Fought for them, conquer'd for them, bled for them,
> Still to be trampled on, and still despis'd.[112]

If they were not taxed so extensively the labour of the peasants would be sufficient to support them comfortably. Tyler considered the lives of animals that did not need artificial distinctions:

> No fancied boundaries of mine and thine
> Restrain their wanderings: Nature gives enough
> For all; but Man, with arrogant selfishness,
> Proud of his heaps, hoards up superfluous stores,
> Robb'd from his weaker fellows, starves the poor,
> Or gives to pity what he owes to justice![113]

This passage reveals the influence of Godwin's views about charity, but more important, it also shows Southey's sympathy for the idea that God gave the earth to mankind in common, and that nature was abundant enough for all.[114] The argument was continued by Ball, who told King Richard and his courtiers

---

[109] Southey, *Joan*, 157.
[110] Idem, 'Joan' (1793), bk 3, lines 244–5, used the phrase 'teeming earth', which had appeared in Dryden's translation of the first book of *Metamorphoses*: *John Dryden*, ed. K. Walker, Oxford 1987, 385.
[111] Southey, *Joan*, 158. See J. G. A. Pocock, *Barbarism and religion*, IV: *Barbarians, savages and empires*, Cambridge 2005, 90, 100.
[112] Southey, *Wat Tyler*, 20.
[113] Ibid. 10.
[114] See I. Hont, *Jealousy of trade: international competition and the nation state in historical perspective*, Cambridge, MA. 2005, 389–443, and T. A. Horne, *Property rights and poverty: political argument in Britain, 1605–1834*, Chapel Hill 1990, 9–41.

that 'all mankind are equal' and that there was no need for 'vain distinctions'. Ball must have read his Godwin when he asked why it was that

> Your larders hung with dainties; while your vassal,
> As virtuous, and as able too by nature,
> Tho' by your selfish tyranny depriv'd
> Of mind's improvement, shivers in his rags
> And starves amid the plenty he creates.[115]

Southey's point was simply that if the poor were able to enjoy the fruits of their own labour there would be no poverty. There is a strong Godwinian flavour to much of this, although he did not explain whether property was to be held in common, or whether a greater equality of individual ownership was desirable. *Wat Tyler*, however, was not a manifesto, and we must turn to pantisocracy for further clues.

The idea of pantisocracy, meaning equal government of all, was the fruit of conversations between Southey and Coleridge in the weeks after they first met.[116] Coleridge invented both the terms pantisocracy and aspheterism, meaning the generalisation of individual property, but it is probable that the idea of emigrating originated with Southey given that he had entertained such fantasies for over a year. In early 1793 he imagined an island utopia peopled with 'Xtians not Philosophers' where virtue would be honoured and vice and luxury rejected: it would 'introduce the advantages and yet avoid the vices of cultivated society'.[117] By the end of the year this yearning had become stronger. He thought of himself living a simple and agricultural life, wielding an axe and cultivating ground that had not been touched since its creation. 'I should be pleased to reside in a country where men's abilities would ensure respect', he told Horace Bedford, 'where society was upon a proper footing, and man was considered as more valuable than money.'[118] All he asked for was 'honest independence' for 'the wants of man are so very few ... they must be attainable somewhere'.[119] The 'Botany Bay eclogues' also conveyed a sense of this simple life in a new land: 'The realm of Nature! for as yet unknown | The crimes and comforts of luxurious life.'[120] It was not surprising, then, that Southey and Coleridge developed a taste for emigration. The plan they

115 Southey, *Wat Tyler*, 65, 66.
116 See E. Logan, 'Coleridge's scheme of pantisocracy and American travel accounts', *PMLA* xlv (1930), 1069–94; J. R. MacGillivray, 'The pantisocracy scheme and its immediate background', in M. W. Wallace (ed.), *Studies in English at University College, Toronto*, Toronto 1931, 131–69; N. Leask, 'Pantisocracy and the politics of the "Preface" to *Lyrical ballads*', in A. Yarrington and K. Everest (eds), *Reflections of revolution: images of romanticism*, London 1993, 39–58; and J. C. McKusick, '"Wisely forgetful": Coleridge and the politics of pantisocracy', in T. Fulford and P. J. Kitson (eds), *Romanticism and colonialism: writing and empire, 1780–1830*, Cambridge 1998, 107–28.
117 Southey to G. Bedford, 8 Feb. 1793, *NL* i. 19.
118 Southey to H. Bedford, 13 Nov. 1793, *LC* i. 193–4.
119 Southey to H. Bedford, 22 Dec. 1793, ibid. i. 198.
120 Southey, *Poetical works*, v. 7–8.

developed, however, was considerably more involved than simply retiring to America. The idea was for twelve men and their wives to emigrate, and to establish a community near the Susquehanna River in Pennsylvania where political and religious views would be freely held, subject to the wider laws of the United States. The fruits of their labour would be held in common and leisure hours were 'to be spent in study, liberal discussions, and the education of their children'.[121] Only a small amount of labour time would be needed to provide all the community's wants. As Southey explained to Horace Bedford,

> According to the computation of Adam Smith one man in twenty is employed in providing the necessities and comforts of life. He works ten hours a day and in consequence cannot enjoy his mental faculties, but divide that labour among the whole twenty and the sum of work is half an hour to each individual. Allmighty God! the comforts of life may be procured by the daily toil of half an hour![122]

This idea was lifted directly from *Political justice*, and was fully supported by Coleridge.[123] Hence pantisocracy was based on Godwin's views about creating the space for rational education by reducing labour time, which would be possible because of the eschewal of luxury production in favour of real wants. Added to this scheme was the ideal of communal ownership, which probably derived from Coleridge.

Differences soon began to emerge. While Southey was concerned with practicalities in Bristol, Coleridge spent his time in Cambridge and London fretting about the way the plan was changing. He was not happy about the idea of bringing along servants because it undermined the equality integral to the scheme. He disagreed with Southey's claim that their children 'will be educated as ours – and the Education we shall give them will be such as to render them incapable of blushing at the want of it in their Parents'. Nor did he think servants necessary to help raise the children of the community, because that was the duty of the mothers. He told Southey that '*this is not our* Plan – nor can I defend it'.[124] Southey probably thought that he was accommodating practicalities, but these differences reflected underlying disagreements over how the scheme would work. Because Coleridge approached matters as a Hartleyan necessitarian, he had strong ideas about the character of those who emigrated, and the education of the children once in America. He wrote of the emigrants – before Southey changed the plan – that 'they have each a sufficient strength of head to make the virtues of the heart respectable; and that they are all highly charged with that enthusiasm which results from strong perceptions of moral rectitude, called into life and

---

121 Poole to Haskins, 22 Sept. 1794, in *Thomas Poole*, i. 98.
122 Southey to H. Bedford, 22 Aug. 1794, *NL* i. 70.
123 Godwin, *Political justice*, 439; Coleridge, *Lectures, 1795*, 223.
124 Coleridge to Southey, 21 Oct. [1794], *CL* i. 114.

action by ardent feelings'.[125] It was essential that all those who travelled were 'saturated with the Divinity of Truth' else they would 'tinge the Mind of the Infants with prejudications'.[126] Following Hartley he insisted that 'Wherever Men *can* be vicious, some *will* be. The leading Idea of Pantisocracy is to make men *necessarily* virtuous by removing all Motives to Evil – all possible Temptations.'[127] Coleridge berated Southey for his lack of understanding of the principles of pantisocracy, and felt that it had now become 'necessarily imperfect'.[128] Southey clearly believed that such an altered scheme would work. He either did not understand or did not share Coleridge's concerns. After all, he had imagined schemes of emigration before in which necessitarianism did not play any role. He seemed to think that once the community was established, the labour and study of its members would meet their social needs. Living in a simple environment there would be no need for vicious behaviour, and such habits would, in effect, melt away. Whatever the explanation, by the end of 1794 Coleridge knew that Southey saw the scheme differently, as evidenced in his lament that 'I would ardently, that you were a Necessitarian'.[129] The idea lingered on into 1795, but its practicality faded from view.

While it is now apparent that Southey followed Godwin's assessment of political society, it is also necessary to consider whether he followed Godwin's gradualist solutions. In private the author of *Political justice* was sceptical about the trajectory of the French Revolution, and the methods used by its leaders. Southey, by contrast, was still openly enthusiastic. Certainly he possessed a strong sense of the inevitability of progress, which for him was bound up with the providential plan that lay behind history. Although there is a Godwinian feel to the following passage from *Wat Tyler*, the biblical and apocalyptic language is also evident.

> the destin'd hour must come,
> When it shall blaze with sun-surpassing splendour,
> And the dark mists of prejudice and falsehood
> Fade in its strong effulgence. Flattery's incense
> No more shall shadow round the gore-dyed throne;
> The altar of oppression, fed with rites,
> More savage than the Priests of Moloch taught,
> Shall be consum'd amid the fires of Justice;
> The ray of truth shall emanate around,
> And the whole world be lighted![130]

The same hopes for the future were also clear in *Joan of Arc* where it was stated that God had ordained all things for the best, and that man would eventually

---

125 Coleridge to C. Heath, 29 Aug. 1794, ibid. i. 97.
126 Coleridge to Southey, [c. 23 Oct. 1794], ibid. i. 119.
127 Coleridge to Southey, 21 Oct. 1794, ibid. i. 114.
128 Coleridge to Southey, [c. 23 Oct. 1794], ibid. i. 120.
129 Coleridge to Southey, [c. 29 Dec. 1794], ibid. i. 145.
130 Southey, *Wat Tyler*, 69.

burst the fetters that were 'only strong whilst strong | Believed'. In this future paradise 'VIRTUE and EQUALITY' would preserve the 'reign of LOVE ... whilst WISDOM shall secure | The state of bliss which IGNORANCE betrayed'.[131] This implies that while an initial 'golden age' of man was one of innocence, in the future it would be knowledge of the truth that would set man free. But whereas Godwin stressed that truth would only emerge slowly by the promotion of free discussion, Southey remained sympathetic to the idea that society could be revolutionised by virtuous leaders. It was for this reason that he was initially inclined to think that the actions of Robespierre 'must not be judged by common laws' and that he was 'the benefactor of mankind' whose death was 'the greatest misfortune Europe could have sustained'.[132] Coleridge thought Robespierre 'possessed a glowing ardour that still remembered the *end*, and a cool ferocity that never either overlooked, or scrupled, the *means*. What that *end* was, is not known: that it was a wicked one, has by no means been proved'.[133] Indeed, in the *Fall of Robespierre* Coleridge and Southey seemed unsure about whether the central protagonist was an exalted visionary or a despicable monster.[134] In *Wat Tyler*, Southey was similarly ambivalent about whether violent means could justify the ends of freedom and equality. Piers asked Ball, 'Are we not equal all? – have you not told me, | Equality is the sacred right of man, | Inalienable, though by force witheld?' Ball replied:

> Even so: but Piers, my frail and fallible judgment
> Knows hardly to decide, if it be right
> Peaceably to return, content with little,
> With this half restitution of our rights,
> Or boldly to proceed through blood and slaughter,
> Till we should all be equal, and all happy
> I chose the milder way: – perhaps I err'd.[135]

Godwin would have argued that the milder way was the correct one, and there is some evidence that Southey was coming to this view, for he told Bedford in late 1794 that 'revolutions should take place in the mind'.[136] In an anonymous 'Inscription' of 1798 for the erection of a column at the site of Tyler's death, he revisited his earlier work. He asked the citizen to accept that 'not by tumult and mad violence' could peace, order and reform be achieved, 'But by calm, collected public voice – | Marking our fathers' errors, be we wise'.[137] This suggests that by the end of the 1790s there was a mellowing in Southey's views about the means if not the ends to be pursued.

131 Idem, *Joan*, 158.
132 Southey to H. Bedford, 22 Aug. 1794, *NL* i. 73.
133 Coleridge, *Lectures, 1795*, 35.
134 Idem [and R. Southey], *The fall of Robespierre*, Cambridge 1794, passim.
135 Southey, *Wat Tyler*, 57.
136 Cited in Storey, *Southey*, 64.
137 Southey, *Poetical works*, v. 170–1.

Disenchantment?

After returning from Portugal in 1796, Southey remained unpersuaded about the merits of joining the Church. Instead, he decided upon the law, and enrolled at Gray's Inn in 1797. Although he was still keeping term in 1799, it is clear that he spent most of his time writing. Indeed his output in these years is striking, and suggests that he was thinking about making literature his career if it could pay. In terms of his politics, he had written in 1796 of the reception of *Joan of Arc* that if the aristocracy 'will favour me by forgetting that I have ever meddled too much with public concerns, I will take care not to awaken their memories'.[138] He did not in fact try that hard. The *British Critic* thought his *Letters written during a short residence in Spain and Portugal* revealed 'the innovating spirit of the present times' and were written with 'the true spirit of Illuminism', while the *Anti-Jacobin* famously attacked his poetry for being subversive in both politics and taste.[139] Still, he did begin to reappraise some of his enthusiasm of the earlier 1790s. At times he expressed pessimism about how easy it might be to reform the people, suggesting that a year spent trying to help them would soon cure one of 'prejudices in their favour'.[140] 'I detest the mob of mankind', he told Bedford, 'the mobility as well as the nobility', but, nevertheless, they were still capable of virtue and happiness. They might now be a 'blackguard mob – but remember that God made them for young Angels.'[141] The progress of revolution in France and reaction in Britain had made him realise that 'in the ardent perception of the end I glanced rapidly over the means'.[142] Despite this, he still held close to his core convictions: when asked in 1799 if he agreed with Coleridge's political recantation in 'France: an ode', he claimed that the very question hurt him.[143] The real problem was that the French Revolution and the British radicals had ceased to express the ideals he continued to hold.

The drift of philosophical opinion in the Godwin circle was troubling. Southey became convinced that necessitarianism, materialism and atheism were linked together, and he began to define his own position against them. He 'declared war' against metaphysics, and announced that 'I think it may be proved, that all the material and necessarian controversies are "much ado about nothing"; that they end exactly where they began; and that all the moral advantages said to result from them by the illuminated, are fairly and more easily deducible from religion, or even from common sense.'[144] By the summer of 1796 he had firmly retracted whatever earlier support he had for

138 Southey to C. Wynn, 24 May 1796, *SL* i. 30.
139 *British Critic* xi (1798), 366; G. Canning and others, *The poetry of the anti-Jacobin*, London 1799, 5–11, 18–23, 235.
140 Southey to G. Bedford, 26 July 1796, *NL* i. 113.
141 Southey to G. Bedford, 26 June 1796, Bodl. Lib., MS Eng. Lett. c. 22, fos 198, 199.
142 Southey to H. Bedford, 12 June 1796, ibid. fo. 191.
143 Southey to E. Southey, 16 May 1799, *NL* i. 191.
144 Southey to G. Bedford, 12 June 1796, *LC* i. 277.

necessitarianism, and was now opposed to the idea that the mind was a simple product of circumstance. He even replied to a short article by Mary Hays which had eulogised Helvétius. She had argued that 'Man is born, simply, a perceptive being, or a creature capable of receiving sensation. The nature of these sensations must depend upon the external circumstances by which he is surrounded. ... All knowledge is conveyed through the medium of the senses.'[145] Because humans were not born with different aptitudes, the application of the correct stimuli during education could create virtue. Southey replied that, while Helvétius was currently 'very fashionable', it remained the case that the organisation of the brain varied among individuals, and experience showed that there were gradations of intellect. The education of two children might be exactly the same, but they would still possess different talents and abilities: 'I have known a child catch a tune before he could articulate a sentence, though his brother never discovered the least inclination for music. Now the *education* of their *ears*, had been precisely the same; for their mother had sung the same songs to both in their infancy.'[146] People were born with different degrees of perfection in the brain, just as they might differ in the quality of their sight. The following year Southey continued this thought when he told Bedford that 'I am no believer in the Helvetian system. Development is the term to apply to the progress of the human character, and it explains my opinions on the subject. I think I can trace it in myself – I was born stubborn-obstinate – by the blessing of God I have continued so.'[147] His rejection of the view that humans could be engineered by manipulating their sensory input was consistent with his doubts about the ease of reforming human character.

Atheism was another trend Southey despised, especially as it seemed to have taken hold of friends such as Robert Allen and Anthony Carlisle. He believed that Godwin's own announcement of his atheism would do good by enabling people to see how absurd the arguments were once rehearsed in print. First, atheism could not explain the origins of humanity: 'if man were made by the casual meeting of atoms', he asked, 'how could he have supported himself without superior assistance? The use of the muscles is only attained by practice, – but how could he have fed himself? how know from what cause hunger proceeded? how know by what means to remedy the pain'.[148] Atheism rested on the idea of an 'eternal series' but arguments for an intelligent first cause were 'impregnable'.[149] A second reason was offered in a letter to the Unitarian minister John P. Estlin, who had written a pamphlet on the *Nature and causes of atheism*. For Southey, the central reason why people became atheists was the difficulty of reconciling physical and moral evil with a benevolent and powerful God.

145 [M. Hays], 'On the philosophy of Helvetius', *Monthly Magazine* ii (1796), 386.
146 [R. Southey], 'On the philosophy of Helvetius', ibid. 629.
147 Southey to G. Bedford, 30 Sept. 1797, *NL* i. 149.
148 Southey to G. Bedford, 26 June 1796, *LC* i. 282.
149 Southey to J. P. Estlin, 9 Apr. 1797, *NL* i. 124.

Many of my friends and acquaintances believe these difficulties insuperable. I find them Atheists or Sceptics not because they are vain and conceited, not because the texture of their mind is coarse, but because there is evil in the world. The contemplation of the miseries of others, or the endurance of their own ... induces them to doubt or disbelieve the existence of that Being, who if he exists must be benevolent and powerful, and whose power could execute what his benevolence must prompt.[150]

Although he was aware of difficulties with the argument, Southey – like Coleridge – defended the idea of optimism, which claimed that the evils of the present would be comprehensible if humans possessed full knowledge of the providential plan.[151] Elsewhere he claimed that the best defence of optimism was to be found in Rousseau's *Letter to Voltaire*, which argued that there was nothing in the constitution of the universe that made evil inevitable.[152] Moral evils were always the result of man's free actions and could not be imputed to God, while physical evils could be lessened if humanity learned the lessons of nature. Thus, *contra* Voltaire, the deaths in the Lisbon earthquake of 1755 did not indicate that God was cruel, but that humans had foolishly built unsound houses.[153] Southey's own religious opinions had not changed much since the early 1790s. He now styled himself a Socinian, but he continued to harbour doubts about many parts of the Bible. Concerning the Old Testament, for example, he wrote that 'I know too little to do anything but doubt. but it is possible for a Socinian to believe Xtianity & reject Judaism.'[154]

Politically, Southey also found little from which to draw comfort. The establishment of the Directory in France signalled a new phase in the republic, which, in an effort to end the revolution and create political stability introduced a new constitution on 5 Fructidor (22 August 1795) that consisted of two legislative assemblies and a drastically reduced electorate. The benefits of the 1793 constitution, such as the right to work and to education, were not renewed. Southey was not impressed by this change of affairs. 'At present the politics of France puzzles me', he wrote, and commented that there was little ability among leaders and that 'the decree of 5th Fructidor is an oppressive one'.[155] He had little to say about French affairs until Napoleon returned from Egypt in late 1799 and overthrew the Directory. The new constitution that came into force on 25 December was analysed in the *Morning Post* by Coleridge, who now argued for a propertied basis to government.[156] Southey,

---

150 Ibid. i. 123.

151 Ibid. i. 124; Coleridge, *Lectures, 1795*, 103ff.

152 Southey to J. May, 6 Apr. 1798, *SL* i. 54.

153 J. J. Rousseau, *Letter to Voltaire*, in J. J. Rousseau, *The Discourses and other early political writings*, ed. V. Gourevitch, Cambridge 1997, 232–46.

154 Southey to May, [24 Apr.] 1799, in *The letters of Robert Southey to John May, 1797 to 1838*, ed. C. Ramos, Austin 1976, 44.

155 Southey to G. Bedford, [Oct. 1795], *NL* i. 102.

156 J. Colmer, *Coleridge: critic of society*, Oxford 1959, ch. iii; Morrow, *Coleridge's political thought*, ch. ii.

meanwhile, had no faith in the 'rascally constitution' of Sieyès and Napoleon, and even suggested that the former ought to have been executed by Robespierre.[157] Such 'cursed complex governments' could not compare with the simple system of the early 1790s: 'one house of representatives, lodging the executive in committees' was 'the plain and common system of government'. He also suggested that after Robespierre the country had needed a Lycurgus, 'a man loved for his virtue, and bold, and inflexible and who should have levelled the property of France, and then would the republic have been immortal, and the world must have been revolutionized by example'.[158] Babeuf, he thought, might have been such a man.[159] So, even in 1800, Southey could express a lingering faith that a virtuous and stoical legislator could have driven through the reforms which were necessary to ground republicanism. Failure to do this had ruined the revolution. His conclusion – which he never subsequently deviated from – was that the French were 'children' who were incapable of freedom because the 'base of morality was wanting'.[160] He felt that his 'Jacobine corns' had been trodden on, and now he was 'a thorough English republican'.[161]

Whatever he meant by this, he was certainly an implacable opponent of Pitt. In his quest to destroy his internal and external enemies, Pitt was undermining British liberty, and Southey even suspected that the prime minister was behind the attack on the king's coach in late 1795 'so to alarm the people that they might gladly submit to any of his measures'.[162] Three years later, he thought Britons had become so paranoid about the threat of France, that they would accept any measure justified by the name of necessity. The danger for Britain was the re-establishment of despotism, even as Europe was freeing herself from it. He told Charles Wynn that

> The old systems of government I think must fall; but in this country the immediate danger is on the other hand, – from an unconstitutional and unlimited power. Burleigh saw how a parliament might be employed against the people, and Montesquieu prophesied the fall of English liberty when the legislature should become corrupt. You will not agree with me in thinking this prophecy fulfilled.[163]

It was this corruption which allowed Pitt to continue a war that was unpopular and expensive, and could only end in the destruction of Britain's commerce.[164] The repression of government and the cost of war were exemplified in Southey's eyes by the outcome of the debate between Richard

---

157 Southey to J. Rickman, 9 Jan. 1800, *LC* ii. 46.
158 Southey to Coleridge, 23 Dec. 1799, *NL* i. 211.
159 Southey to Coleridge, 16 Jan. 1800, ibid. i. 215.
160 Southey to Rickman, 9 Jan. 1800, *LC* ii. 46
161 Southey to Coleridge, 16 Jan. 1800, *NL* i. 215.
162 Southey to Wynn, 23 Apr. 1796, *SL* i. 26.
163 Southey to Wynn, 15 Aug. 1798, *LC* i. 340.
164 Southey to T. Southey, [1796], and 16 Mar. 1797, BL, MS Add. 30927, fos 13, 15.

Watson, bishop of Llandaff, and Gilbert Wakefield in 1798.[165] Watson had recommended in his *Address to the people of Great Britain* that an income tax be introduced to help pay off the national debt. If everyone paid an equal percentage, he suggested, no-one would be richer or poorer in relative terms. Wakefield published a critical response to this (Southey recalled him saying that 'all parts of the building may sink together – and the gentlemen up stairs still have their comfortable prospect, but where is the ground floor sunk to?') and was successfully prosecuted for his efforts. Income tax was introduced the following year, and although Southey agreed with Turgot that in principle it was an 'open and fair' tax, the plan proposed by Pitt hit lower income groups too harshly.[166] Southey's disgust with the government was evident in his anonymous 'Ode, to a pig, while his nose was boring'. It described how the 'social Pig' had resigned his natural rights to live in a more comfortable and 'safer stye', only to discover that it was to have its nose bored and eventually be slaughtered. The point was clear: government was supposedly instituted to protect and support its people, but in fact they were starved and exploited by it.[167] In February 1801 Pitt's resignation offered some consolation, and allowed Southey – who was again in Portugal – to hope that 'England has mended – is mending – will mend.'[168]

It is illuminating to examine a letter Southey wrote to John May in June 1797.[169] He had recently finished reading Madame Roland's *Appeal to impartial posterity* in which the famous Girondin reflected on the revolution, her life and her friends. Southey felt that it was a book that made him love individuals but detest the mass of mankind. 'There was a time when I believed in the persuadability of man & had the mania of man-mending; experience has taught me better.' The mind grew 'stiff and unyielding' after a certain age, making it difficult for individuals to change their opinions and actions. Thinkers like Helvétius and Godwin, he suggested, were too optimistic about the ease with which humans could change. Even the 'ablest physician' could do little in 'the great lazar-house of society' and the individual was best advised to seek retirement if he wanted to avoid corruption. But Southey could not yet reconcile himself to the inequality of the world. Of the rich he commented that 'you will scarcely find one who has ever felt shocked at the reflection that God has given to the poor mental capabilities that might infinitely benefit mankind & given them in vain – only to be stifled by society'. 'The savage & civilized states are alike unnatural, alike unworthy of the origin & end of man', he insisted. While scepticism and atheism were under-

---

[165] R. Watson, *An address to the people of Great Britain*, London 1798, and G. Wakefield, *A reply to some parts of the bishop of Llandaff's address to the people of Great Britain*, London 1798.

[166] Southey to Wynn, 30 Mar. 1799, *NL* i. 182.

[167] Southey, *Poetical works*, v. 360–1. See *CPB* iv. 198.

[168] Southey to Barker, [Dec.] 1801, *SL* i. 180.

[169] Southey to May, 26 June 1797, in *Letters to May*, 25–6.

standable responses to this state of affairs, they only contributed to the very vices the perfectionist hoped to eradicate. Nor was secular 'social science' of any use. Southey did not agree, however, with millenarians such as Priestley, who argued that '*another revelation*' was necessary to overcome the current wickedness of humanity. He felt instead that 'with the right exertions of our own reasoning faculties' what had already been given by God was sufficient. Written in the life of Christ and the heart of man were the necessary precepts of 'true Christianity'. If these were followed the evils of contemporary society would wither away. Southey had not lost his faith in both progress and republicanism, but he had become more sceptical about the methods by which they could be achieved. He may in 1801 have felt himself a very different man from the boy who was expelled from Westminster, but at heart his hopes and beliefs remained remarkably similar.

PART II
APOSTASY?

2

The Imperatives of War

After a fifteenth-month sojourn in Portugal, Southey returned to England in July 1801 with mixed feelings. The warm environment had improved his health and he had been deeply absorbed in his research on Portuguese history, but the declaration of war by France and Spain on Portugal made return prudent. Once again he was faced with the problems of what to do with his life and how to support his family. He abandoned the idea of returning to legal studies, and even lacked a home. After much prevarication, in August 1803 he accepted Coleridge's offer to share a house in Keswick. Greta Hall was inconveniently far from London, but he slowly settled in. He remained there for the rest of his life, responsible for both his family and effectively Coleridge's. His decision to be a poet, however, did not prove entirely viable financially. *Thalaba the destroyer*, *Madoc* and the *Curse of Kehama* received hostile reviews and sold poorly. In any event, Southey came to think himself less a poet and more an historian. His cherished project was the 'History of Portugal', the plan for which had swollen by 1804 to include twelve volumes covering its empire, religion and literature.[1] He began extensive research into these areas, but financial need prevented him from proceeding far. Increasingly his means were met – and so also his time was occupied – by reviewing. Between 1802 and 1808 he contributed around 150 articles to the *Annual Review*, and in 1809 he began writing for the *Quarterly Review*, which by 1816 was paying £100 an article. He also provided the contemporary 'History of Europe' in the *Edinburgh Annual Register* between 1809 and 1812 for £400 a year.[2] Although he often complained about this work, he took it as an opportunity to develop his thoughts about various subjects. The range of these was evident in *Letters from England*, which purported to be the correspondence of a Spaniard travelling in England. The guise of Don Espriella did not fool many people for long but it did show that Southey was not content to be a lonely poet hidden in the folds of Cumberland. By 1815 he was reasonably comfortable: if he spent, as Bagehot later put it, morning, noon and night in his library, living a life of 'no events, no experiences', it was partly because he had to, but also because he thought he was being useful.[3]

[1] Southey to T. Southey, 12 Sept. 1804, *LC* ii. 305–6.
[2] L. Madden (ed.), *Robert Southey: the critical heritage*, London 1972, 24–6; K. Curry, 'Southey's contributions to the *Annual Review*', *Bulletin of Bibliography* xvi (1939), 195–7; K. Curry and R. Dedmon, 'Southey's contributions to *The Quarterly Review*', *WC* vi (1975), 261–72.
[3] Cited in Madden, *Southey*, 448.

'Evil was his Good': resisting Napoleon

On 27 March 1802 the peace of Amiens was signed, ending nearly a decade of war with France. It was widely welcomed, and many people hoped that it marked a permanent return to peace and prosperity. During the 1790s opponents of the war had claimed that Britain had no right to interfere in the affairs of a sovereign nation, sometimes arguing that only defensive wars were justified, and always stressing the social and economic costs of war.[4] Southey and Coleridge remained opponents of the war even after they had lost faith in France. While Southey was in Portugal, Coleridge wrote a number of essays on France for the *Morning Post*, arguing that Jacobinism had been replaced by despotism. Although France had 'fallen back into its antient character, of an ambitious, intriguing military Power' with a constitution 'founded on the most tyrannous Oligarchy', he insisted that this was no reason not to negotiate.[5] He attacked the ministerial view that France was not serious in desiring peace and argued that for strategic reasons Napoleon required it. Once this was secured, the revival of manufacturing and commerce would help cool French military ambition and lead to a modification of her government.[6] Southey later advanced the same view in *Letters from England*, where he stressed that France wanted peace in order to develop her commerce, while England needed it to recover financially. '[T]hey are miserable politicians', he went on, 'who suppose that any new grounds of dispute can arise, important enough to overpower these considerations.'[7] In 1802, then, Southey and Coleridge both hoped that the peace would be permanent.

As the year progressed, however, both men began to reassess their attitudes to peace and to the Foxite opposition that supported it. Fox was reluctant to be sucked back into war, and hoped that diplomacy could solve the continuing problem of French occupation across Europe.[8] Coleridge, conversely, thought France showed no signs of 'cooling', so he grew sceptical about whether peace could last. His growing dislike of the Foxite opposition was made apparent in November 1802, in two letters which attacked Fox's flattery of Napoleon during his visit to France. 'One sentiment of pity or indignation at the iron despotism which this upstart Corsican had reduced forty millions of your fellow creatures?' Coleridge raged. 'Not a syllable! Not a breathing! You *exulted*, Sir, that the war had *ended* as it *ought* to end, gloriously for France, ignominiously for Great Britain!!'[9] Southey was clearly surprised by this tirade, and suspected that Daniel Stuart, the editor of the *Morning Post*, was responsible for the articles. Coleridge corrected this error in early 1803. 'If I have erred',

---

4 J. E. Cookson, *The friends of peace: anti-war liberalism in England, 1793–1815*, Cambridge 1982, ch. ii.
5 *EOT* i. 70–1.
6 Ibid. i. 75, 79.
7 *LE* i. 131. Espriella was supposedly writing during the peace between 1802 and 1803.
8 L. G. Mitchell, *Charles James Fox*, Oxford 1992, 199–202.
9 *EOT* i. 386.

he remarked, 'how gladly should I have it pointed out to me! ... & what am I to understand by your remark, my dear Southey? – Have you heard any thing from France, which inclines you to think favourably of Bonaparte, of the French Government, or of Fox's apparent adulation?'[10] Southey was under no illusions about France, but he did not yet believe that a return to war was necessary. He execrated the 'all-sacrificing and all-pliable ambition' of Napoleon, but did not think that war with Britain would be risked.[11] By contrast, Coleridge insisted that Napoleon was flattering some powers while deceiving others, so that he could pursue his goals without reawakening the continent against him. This could not be endured for long.[12] By March there was a growing realisation that war was likely. Napoleon's territorial ambitions meant that Britain was unwilling to give up Malta (despite this being a stipulation of Amiens). Southey supported this, and told Coleridge that 'You were a clearer-sighted politician than I.'[13] War was declared in May, with Fox blaming Britain for re-entry, and darkly hinting that it was a plot to allow George III to restore the 'despotism' of the 1790s.[14] Southey, however, thought war was perfectly justified, and believed that France 'must suffer by war, or she will war on all eternity'.[15] He also believed, as he later expressed it in *Letters from England*, that the English were united in supporting this war and were now 'decidedly Anti-Gallican'.[16] By the summer of 1803 Southey had become one of the most vigorous supporters of the war.

The lake poets had initially viewed Napoleon as a great military leader whose Egyptian campaign of 1798–9 would spread freedom, science and the arts to the backward and despotic peoples of the east.[17] The events of late 1799 shattered these hopes and led to a growing conviction that the hero was in fact a despot. Coleridge argued in late 1802 that France was following the pattern of republican Rome and degenerating into an empire founded on a 'masked and military despotism'. In both cases the commercial spirit was partly responsible for corrupting morals and for breeding contempt of religious and political establishments. In such turmoil the people turned to a military leader for stability, providing the pretext Napoleon needed to concentrate power into his own hands.[18] Both Coleridge and Southey saw France as a military despotism which had 'no other rule than the will and pleasure of its lord and master' who was an 'absolute Tyrant' pursuing universal monarchy. While some continued to think generously of Napoleon, Southey doubted

---

10 Coleridge to Southey, [8] Jan. 1803, CL ii. 912.
11 Southey to C. Danvers, 2 Dec. 1801, NL i. 260.
12 EOT i. 419–22.
13 Southey to Coleridge, 14 Mar. 1803, LC ii. 202.
14 Mitchell, Fox, 202.
15 Southey to Wynn, 7 June 1803, NL i. 313.
16 LE iii. 131.
17 S. Bainbridge, *Napoleon and English romanticism*, Cambridge 1995, 24–5.
18 EOT i. 314. See also p. 338.

that he could ever be trusted.[19] Britain should distinguish between the French ruler and the French nation, and refuse to deal with the former, but offering to make peace with the latter if the people overthrew their emperor. Southey's belief that Napoleon was a Satanic figure, the enemy of continental peace and liberty, was nicely summarised in an ode written in 1814: 'Evil was his Good', 'Himself in Hell's whole panoply he clad; | No law but his own headstrong will he knew, | No counsellor but his own wicked heart.'[20]

Although Southey and Coleridge were now vigorous defenders of the war, they should not be labelled 'Tories'. The political landscape in the 1800s was unstable, and it is not possible to identify coherent Whig or Tory parties and principles. While the Foxite Whigs formed the 'old' opposition, the governing coalition of the 1790s had collapsed into a number of factions after Pitt's resignation in 1801. Canning followed his mentor out of office, while the Addingtonians remained, overseeing the peace and then the resumption of war. The 'new' opposition was led by Grenville and was opposed to the peace from the outset. Southey and Coleridge were initially sympathetic to Addington's ministry because they believed the 'suspicion, and alarm, and plots' of the 1790s were over, and the liberty of the press was returning.[21] Once war resumed, however, Southey found himself in agreement with William Windham and the Grenvillites, although 'they got right by sticking in the wrong'.[22] As Addington failed to pursue the war with vigour, Southey hoped that the 1804 coalition between 'old' and 'new' oppositions would prove fruitful. Pitt's second ministry sickened him, and he rejoiced that the hated minister's death necessitated the formation of the ministry of 'All the Talents'.[23] Despite his disagreements with their stance on the Catholic question, he regretted their fall, and thereafter became more disillusioned with politics for some time, arguing that 'there must always be a lack of talent in a House of Commons so chosen'.[24] In 1808 he read Fox's posthumously published *History of the early part of the reign of James the second*. It prompted him to reject Whig myths about the perpetual threat of Toryism, insisting that 'In spite of all Mr. Fox can say, Whigs and Tories have never meant much more than Ins and Outs, or Outs and Ins; a fact upon which the last year of his life set the great seal.'[25]

Southey's growing distaste for the Whigs was exacerbated by their association with supporters of peace. After 1805 pressure grew to end the war. Some took the principled view that offensive wars were simply unjustified, but Southey thought them inconsistent, because 'while they admit that the principle of war must be allowed in just cases, they, at all times, and in all

19 [Southey], 'Europe, 1808', 24; Southey to J. Montgomery, 29 Nov. 1811, *NL* ii. 13.
20 *The Times*, 21 Apr. 1814.
21 *LE* i. 133. See *EOT* i. 368.
22 Southey to G. Bedford, 12 June 1803, *LC* ii. 215.
23 Southey to G. Bedford, 21 Apr. 1807, ibid. iii. 82.
24 Southey to G. Bedford, 22 Mar. 1807, *SL* i. 427.
25 Southey to May, 11 Nov. 1808, ibid. ii. 105.

cases, cry out against the practice, setting their compassionate feelings in array against the manlier virtues'.[26] The other argument put forward was more pragmatic, and suggested that Britain's lack of allies meant that she could not destroy the French army, just as France could not destroy the British navy. The war was an expensive stalemate and so peace was essential. These arguments grew louder after 1807, when the Orders in Council were blamed for creating recession in the export industry. Southey and Wordsworth believed the 'peace-mongers' harboured sympathies towards Napoleon because they still viewed him as a liberator: they 'looked with complacency now upon the progress which oppression was making in the world, because France was the oppressor!'[27] The *Edinburgh Review* was persistently attacked by Southey for its pacifism. In 1809 he complained to Bedford that

> Jeffrey has been trying to unite the opposition and the Jacobins, as they are called. He *hurts* the Opposition, and he wrongs the Jacobins; he hurts the former by associating them with a name that is still unpopular, and he wrong the friends of liberty by supposing they are not the deadliest enemies of Bonaparte.[28]

This suggests that Southey was both pro-war and pro-reform. How could he think this in the same year that he became a reviewer for the conservative *Quarterly Review*?

The *Quarterly Review* was established to counteract the *Edinburgh Review*, which was moving from its early political agnosticism to a stronger anti-war and pro-reform agenda. In October 1808 the infamous 'Don Cevallos' review appeared, which was co-written by Francis Jeffrey and Henry Brougham. It took a pessimistic view about the war, and insisted that peace was necessary. Brougham went further, however, in suggesting that domestic interest in Spanish patriotism would provoke demands for political reform at home. Some 'radical improvements' in the constitution were necessary and 'there is now a better prospect of reform in England, than that which the French revolution, for a moment held out to us, and then seemed to hide for ever'.[29] For opponents of reform, this finally revealed that the true colours of Jeffrey's magazine were, as one pamphlet put it, 'Jacobinical'. This was too much. Famously, Lord Buchan was reported to have kicked the offending number into the street, while Sydney Smith told of people fumigating their library shelves.[30] Walter Scott was indignant and left the *Edinburgh* for a new review to be published

---

[26] [Southey], 'Europe, 1808', 23.
[27] Ibid. See CC, 226; Cookson, *Friends*, ch. ix.
[28] Southey to G. Bedford, 6 Jan. 1809, *LC* iii. 205.
[29] [F. Jeffrey and H. Brougham], 'Don Pedro Cevallos on the French usurpation of Spain', *ER* xiii (Oct. 1808), 223. See also [H. Brougham], 'Mr. Whitbread's letter on Spain', *ER* xii (July 1808), 433–48.
[30] S. Smith to Lady Holland, 10 Jan. 1809, in *The letters of Sydney Smith*, ed. N. C. Smith, Oxford 1953, i. 152; J. Clive, *Scotch reviewers: the* Edinburgh Review, *1802–15*, London 1957, 111.

by John Murray.[31] It was to be edited by the staunchly orthodox William Gifford, who had overseen the *Anti-Jacobin* ten years earlier, but Scott hoped it would preserve some degree of independence from the ministry.

Southey's reasons for joining this review were different from those of other contributors. His main concern was not the pro-reform but the anti-war stance of the *Edinburgh*. He believed that the purpose of the *Quarterly* was to counter the 'base politicks, which would make us betray Spain and Portugal, and lay us at the feet of Bonaparte'.[32] Tellingly, he refused to write an article on the Spanish question because he thought a pro-ministerial review would have little sympathy with his opinions. Murray, at least, was grateful for this. Although Southey knew much about Spain, '*his* is not the kind of knowledge which we want, and it is, moreover, trusting our secret to a stranger, who has, by the way, a directly opposite bias in politics'.[33] Southey was vigilant for signs of anti-Jacobinism in the *Quarterly*. In May 1809 he heard from James Ballantyne that a number of reviewers had talked of '"unmuzzling Gifford," that is setting up the old cry of Anti-Jacobinism'. Southey's reply was curt. 'I simply told him … I should withdraw from the journal, "being of any party than the Anti-Jacobine".'[34] Indeed, Southey often complained that Gifford edited his articles, altering or removing passages that were deemed insufficiently orthodox. It therefore appears that when Southey joined the *Quarterly* he did not strongly identify with its politics other than its pro-war stance. He even found it amusing that his opinions coincided with it, telling his brother that 'as long as this government caravan was travelling my road I was content to travel with it; and that, although my opinions hang together, all the hanging which they imply does not immediately appear'.[35]

An armed nation

The war against Napoleon was no less than 'a war of virtue against vice, Light against Darkness, the Good Principle against the Evil One'.[36] It needed to be fought with vigour: a 'defensive war will not do' because it 'would break the spirit of the nation'.[37] Southey believed that it was essential that Britain become an armed nation with a military spirit in order to defend her liberty and to defeat France. This required, as far as he was concerned, a readjustment of eighteenth-century blue-water assumptions about imperial and foreign

---

[31] See S. Smiles, *A publisher and his friends: a memoir and correspondence of the late John Murray*, London 1891, 91–154, and *The letters of Sir Walter Scott*, ed. H. J. C. Grierson, London 1932–7, ii. 100–53.

[32] Southey to H. Hill, 10 Nov. 1808, *NL* i. 490.

[33] J. Murray to W. Scott, 15 Nov. 1808, in Smiles, *A publisher*, i. 111.

[34] Southey to G. Bedford, 19 May 1809, *NL* i. 508.

[35] Southey to T. Southey, 22 Nov. 1808, *LC* iii. 194–5.

[36] Southey to H. Senhouse, 19 Oct. 1808, *NL* i. 484.

[37] Southey to Wynn, 7 June 1803, ibid. i. 313.

policy. Although these views had been popular throughout the period, in the first half of the century court Whigs had insisted that the security of Hanover and Britain required that considerable resources be committed to maintaining the balance of power in Europe. By the 1750s, however, politicians were arguing that shoring up the balance of power was expensive and ineffective. The blue-water approach, advocated by Tories such as Bolingbroke, increasingly appealed to patriot Whigs like the elder Pitt. By dominating the seas and acquiring new territories it would be possible to make Britain commercially 'great' and at the same time drain her competitors of the sinews of power. Although blue-water policy did not preclude continental alliances and subsidies, it advocated using them sparingly. It was also a popular policy because the role of the navy was elevated above that of a standing army, which remained an object of suspicion. But it did require expansion of home defence as the country was more susceptible to attack from the continent, and so the militia was accordingly remodelled in the late 1750s. Blue-water thinking remained central to British policy in the second half of the eighteenth century, even after 1792 when there was growing awareness that it was less appropriate given Europe's very different political situation.[38]

From Southey's point of view, this approach had to change if the war were to be won. There were widespread concerns about the difficulties of raising sufficient numbers for the army, while the militia was also thought problematic. It had expanded during the 1790s, but its recruits were still chosen by ballot and subjected to the gentry's leadership. This accounted for some of its unpopularity among the middling and lower orders, and helps explain why many preferred the volunteers instead. This body grew rapidly during the late 1790s, but the government viewed its members with suspicion, partly because they were deemed inefficient, and partly because they fell outside the control of the authorities. In 1804 the Volunteer Consolidation Bill unsuccessfully attempted to remedy this, but Whigs such as Fox and Whitbread countered that those who had volunteered their services were entitled to choose their own leaders. Southey agreed that the attempt to deprive volunteers of their right to elect officers was 'rascally and abominable', claiming that they usually chose men of 'property, character or talents'. He was, however, no defender of the volunteers and expressed a hope that they would lay down their arms.[39] A more radical reorganisation of the national military system was necessary if it were to operate effectively.

As war minister under 'All the Talents', Windham got a chance to do just that. He believed that the existing military system was counter-productive,

[38] See D. A. Baugh, 'Maritime strength and Atlantic commerce: the uses of "a grand marine empire"', in L. Stone (ed.), *An imperial state at war: Britain from 1689 to 1815*, London 1994, 185–223; D. A. Baugh, 'Withdrawing from Europe: Anglo-French maritime geopolitics, 1750–1800', *International History Review* xx (1998), 1–32; and E. H. Gould, *The persistence of empire: British political culture in the age of the American Revolution*, Chapel Hill 2000.
[39] Southey to T. Southey, 31 Jan. 1804, LC ii. 255.

because its various branches starved the others of manpower. Within weeks of taking office his plans were produced. He stressed the needs of the army, and argued that it was essential to channel manpower into it from home defence. This was to be done, first, by introducing limited service to make the army more attractive, second, by reducing both the volunteers and the militia, and third, by training some 200,000 men a year, who could be formed into an 'armed peasantry' for home defence, and who could also provide a basis for army recruitment. Windham never found out if his plans would have worked, because after the 'Talents' resigned, Castlereagh put forward a new set of measures in 1808. The idea of universal training was abandoned because he feared entrusting military power to the populace, and home defence was assigned to local county-based militia which could draw in the remaining volunteers. The ending of substitution went some way towards creating a system of personal service and the localist nature of the proposals were also attractive to the lower orders who did not wish to serve away from home. This system was to remain in place until the end of the war.[40]

Southey, however, preferred Windham's proposals. He had been critical of the traditional militia for the same reasons as various radical writers, particularly in their hostility to the balloting system. Those who could afford to could buy a substitute to serve for them, but the cost of these varied considerably. Others might choose to pay the £10 fine. In effect, Southey argued, the ballot operated as a 'tax by lottery', but the poor man had no choice but to serve for the required number of years, only to find his 'place in society filled up' when he returned to his former occupation.[41] Southey followed Windham's reforms carefully, and lamented that the fall of the 'Talents' meant their loss. He attacked Castlereagh's proposals because they did not introduce limited service or martial reform, and agreed with the 'venerable patriot' John Cartwright who had petitioned against them. Cartwright argued that the country could not rely on the navy, volunteers and a standing army for national defence and that the solution lay (unsurprisingly) in the mists of the Saxon past. Under King Alfred, England had enjoyed a vigorous military branch of the constitution that made it the duty of all people to defend the state by arms, and thereby preserve their freedom. Ideally the militia should be reconstituted in this form. Southey thought that Cartwright's proposals would 'unite the characters of the soldier and the citizen, each liable to be degraded when they exist apart, and it will for ever secure us against even the threat of invasion'.[42] In Letters from England, therefore, he proposed that every schoolboy be trained in the use of arms to ensure that within a genera-

[40] J. W. Fortescue, The county lieutenancies and the army, 1803–1814, London 1909, 159–73; The Windham papers, ed. [A. P. Primrose], earl of Roseberry, London 1913, ii. 285–8, 295, 301–6; J. E. Cookson, The British armed nation, 1793–1815, Oxford 1997, 80–8.
[41] LE i. 114–15.
[42] [Southey], 'Europe, 1808', 90. See The life and correspondence of Major Cartwright, ed. F. D. Cartwright, London 1826, i. 316–36, 353–6, 396–400.

tion every man would also be a soldier.[43] Like Windham, he believed that this was ideal for national defence, but could also serve as a basis for military recruitment.

As for the army, Southey was insistent that it be made more attractive so that people chose to serve their country rather than enlisting because they were unemployed or inebriated. The solution was limited service. Like many critics, Southey portrayed the army as a barbaric system of servitude. In an unpublished passage from *Letters from England* he likened an English soldier to an American slave, for 'he continues in slavery, nay the better he performs his duty the more hopeless is his condition; it is vain for him then to expect discharge, till age or accident shall have disabled him'.[44] However, if service were for a minimum of seven years it would be a much more appealing prospect, and would also provide men with useful skills when they returned to civilian life. If they chose to serve longer their pay would be increased, and they should be entitled to honorary awards such as medals for excellence. It was also necessary to overhaul the 'barbarous' martial laws and punishments which made a mockery of Britain's claim to be a civilised nation.[45] Finally, during peacetime soldiers should live in military villages where they might cultivate gardens and perform public works. These proposals stemmed from Southey's view that it was better to treat soldiers as humans rather than as beasts. Not only was this morally superior, it also made them better soldiers. Indeed, he believed that the enthusiasm for volunteering proved that the love of military life was a natural passion, but thought that it had been destroyed by Britain's wretched military system. This enthusiasm for the 'armed nation' accorded with those radical writers who thought it was a strong national spirit that lay behind the successes of the Americans in the 1770s and the French in the 1790s.[46] An armed nation of patriots was the best way to conduct a just war, but it was also essential for home defence: 'England might ... defy', Southey proclaimed, 'not France alone, but the whole continent leagued with France, even if the impassable gulph between this happy island and its enemies were filled up.'[47]

Understandably, Southey also attached great importance to naval and military leaders. He was hardly unique in eulogising naval heroes, but tried to resist the bellicose sentiments lying behind enthusiasm for figures such as Admiral Vernon. This is most evident in his interest in Nelson, whose death in 1805 had so moved him that he was tempted to write a funeral hymn.[48]

---

43 *LE* i. 117.
44 Ibid. i. 111 continues in Southey, 'Letters of D. Manuel Alvarez Espriella on England', Chetham's Library, Manchester, MS Mun. A.4.2, sect. 7.
45 *LE* i. 109–18; [Southey], 'Europe, 1808', 5–6; [idem], 'The history of Europe, 1810', *EAR* iii (1812), i. 161–2.
46 *LE* i. 112–15.
47 Ibid. i. 117.
48 Southey to G. Bedford, 13 Nov. 1805, *LC* ii. 353. See G. Jordan and N. Rogers, 'Admirals as heroes: patriotism and liberty in Hanoverian England', *JBS* xxviii (1989), 205–6.

In 1813 he published his famous *Life of Nelson* which developed a *Quarterly Review* essay of 1810.[49] This popular work presented Nelson as a national patriot, but did so without turning him into an establishment lackey. Indeed, the orthodox *British Critic* praised the book but had little sympathy with Southey's 'private and political opinions'.[50] The *Life of Nelson* was written as the story of a patriot martyr whose life was worthy of emulation because of its selflessness and benevolence. In order to present Nelson in this way, it was necessary to explain away one or two 'stains' on his character, which Southey did by arguing that his 'infatuated attachment' to Lady Hamilton occasionally corrupted his judgement.[51] Nelson's career from relatively humble beginnings was traced, with particular stress on his ill health and early sense of dejection about his profession. Southey emphasised a mental transformation that occurred after one period of prolonged depression. Nelson himself wrote that 'a sudden glow of patriotism was kindled within me, and presented my king and country as my patron. "Well, then," I exclaimed, "I will be a hero! and, confiding in Providence, brave every danger!"'[52] From this crucial moment, Nelson put country before self without compromising his humanity. In particular, Southey noted his reputation for treating his sailors with respect and kindness and praised him for governing men by 'their reason and their affections'. Nelson possessed an 'an active and watchful benevolence', demonstrated in his concern to improve the conditions of naval life and in his commitment to promoting men of talent.[53] For Southey, he bore all the hallmarks of enlightened patriotism, in which devotion to country was blended with Christian benevolence. These worthy characteristics made his declining health and eventual death even more moving. They also explained the extent of public grief: 'men started at the intelligence and turned pale; as if they had heard of the loss of a dear friend. An object of our admiration and affection, of our pride and of our hopes, was suddenly taken from us'.[54] This national grief stood in contrast to the government's behaviour towards Nelson, which Southey thought demonstrated an unwillingness to confer the highest honours on him in life. Indeed it is the account of Nelson as a national patriot, rather than a political functionary, which makes the biography striking. Southey was angered when he heard that the death of Pitt was to be accorded the same status as Nelson's, for Pitt's greatness had been the mere 'trick of a party' while Nelson's was supported by 'the feelings of the whole people'.[55]

---

[49] [R. Southey], 'Lives of Nelson', *QR* iii (Feb. 1810), 218–62, and *The life of Nelson*, London 1813. See D. Eastwood, 'Patriotism personified: Robert Southey's *Life of Nelson* reconsidered', *Mariner's Mirror* lxxvii (1991), 143–9.

[50] Cited in Madden, *Southey*, 173.

[51] Southey, *Nelson*, ii. 46, 52.

[52] Cited ibid. i. 24.

[53] Ibid. ii. 186, 187.

[54] Ibid. ii. 272.

[55] Southey to T. Southey, 5 Mar. 1806, *SL* i. 362. See Southey, *Nelson*, i. 246–7; ii. 153.

By contrast, Southey's treatment of Wellington was a little more muted. He lacked biographical material to give a personal flavour to his two *Quarterly Review* articles of 1815, and so most of the narrative was devoted to military campaigns. Perhaps for this reason he refused Murray's offer to develop a book-length 'Life'. Furthermore, he was enraged when he heard that Wellington had tried to persuade John Wilson Croker to alter various passages in the second article to accentuate Wellington's pivotal role in the victory at Waterloo. At Southey's insistence the passages were restored, but the incident hardly showed the commitment to truth and impartiality expected from a patriot.[56] Wellington also came from an aristocratic background, and held an ensign's commission from his teens (a practice, Southey was pleased to note, that had since been abolished).[57] There could be no narrative of social struggle as with Nelson. Nevertheless, Southey did praise Wellington as an inspiring leader who possessed significant military ability, particularly in the peninsular campaign. He also hoped that Wellington took more satisfaction from liberating an oppressed people than from the many honours which were conferred upon him, suggesting, perhaps, ambivalence about Wellington's motives. The most important reason why Wellington was admired, however, was that he had helped raise Britain's military reputation from a century of decline, and restore it to the excellence of the days of Marlborough.[58]

The importance of this was evident in Southey's views about British war policy. For much of the period after 1793 Britain avoided continental campaigns in the hope that France could be defeated in the global arena. When occasions presented themselves, Pitt, and subsequently Addington, formed alliances with continental powers such as Russia and Austria, and subsidised their engagements, but these coalitions reaped few rewards. Southey was deeply critical of this policy, arguing that Britain's should actually utilise her fearsome naval and military power. He also believed that his country was the 'only supporter of morals, intellect, and freedom' in the war.[59] The policy of alliances was propping up continental regimes that he loathed, and thereby making Britain subservient to their interests. He fervently believed that the old state system was doomed because it could not muster the patriotic forces which were necessary to defeat Napoleon's armies. Rather than subsidising these countries, Britain should instead encourage popular resistance to both Napoleon and the old regimes. This was a just aim, but it was also necessary if the war were to be won. The traditional policy that had served for decades could do little when soldiers under Napoleon's command were enthused by patriotic fervour. As Wordsworth wrote in one sonnet, 'O'erweening

---

[56] [R. Southey], 'Life of Wellington', *QR* xiii (Apr., July 1815), 215–75, 448–526. See Southey to Hill, 6 Dec. 1815, *SL* iii. 5–6, and Southey to Wynn, 15 Dec. 1815, *NL* ii. 125–7.

[57] [Southey], 'Wellington', 216.

[58] Ibid. 271–4. These passages were re-used in his *History of the peninsular war*, London 1823–32, iii. 921–7.

[59] [Southey], 'Europe, 1808', 27.

Statesmen have full long relied | On fleets and armies, and external wealth: | But from *within* proceeds a Nation's health.'[60]

Southey found hope in the publication of Captain Charles Pasley's *Essay on the military policy and institutions of the British empire*, which went through four editions between 1810 and 1812. Pasley was a lieutenant in the Royal Engineers, and had met Coleridge in Malta in 1805.[61] Southey thought his book a 'political Bible' which ought to be 'in the heart of every Englishman' and an inspiration to a great statesman. Wordsworth, similarly, was deeply impressed with the *Essay*, and wrote Pasley a lengthy reflective letter in 1811.[62] To make its arguments more widely known, Southey asked to review the volume for the *Quarterly*, although he told Bedford that 'I shall be somewhat crippled by G[ifford].s Pitt-idolatry'.[63] He was right. Gifford was so concerned about Southey's review that he engaged Croker to rewrite most of it. Southey disowned the article because of these alterations, and especially because it directly contradicted some of the ideas he had advanced.[64] Croker wished to defend existing military policy and believed that the *Essay* was full of 'dangerous principles'.[65] Pasley was mistaken, for instance, in his views about the need for a stronger martial spirit: the British were an ocean-loving people who had no liking for extensive standing armies. He was also mistaken in advocating a policy of aggrandisement, for this would be deeply unpopular among European allies.[66] The substance of the article hardly fitted the conclusion (which was certainly Southey's) that the *Essay* was the most important book to have fallen under the reviewer's observation.[67] While the response to the *Essay* will be fully examined in a later chapter, it is important to stress here that both Southey and Wordsworth took it as a plea for the abandonment of the expensive and ineffective system of alliances and for a more vigorous prosecution of the war, especially through a commitment to campaigns on land as well as at sea. Only in this way would Britain prove herself worthy to deliver Europe from the tyranny of France.

Southey's move to a pro-war position should not be viewed as a capitulation to the establishment. Although he distanced himself from the Whigs, this was primarily from those 'pessimists' who believed peace was necessary. An

---

[60] W. Wordsworth, *Poetical works*, ed. T. Hutchinson and E. de Selincourt, Oxford 1936, 254.

[61] See R. Holmes, *Coleridge: darker reflections*, London 1998, 39, 51–2. They also collaborated on some articles: *EOT* iii. 92–5, 187–214.

[62] Southey to W. S. Landor, 11 Jan. 1811; Southey to E. Elliott, 7 Feb. 1811, *LC* iii. 295, 298; Wordsworth to C. Pasley, 28 Mar. 1811, in *The letters of William and Dorothy Wordsworth*, ed. E. de Selincourt and others, Oxford 1967–93, ii. 473–82.

[63] Southey to G. Bedford, 14 Jan. 1811, *NL* ii. 4.

[64] Southey to Wynn, 19 July 1811, *SL* ii. 228.

[65] [J. W. Croker and R. Southey], 'Capt. Pasley on the military policy of Great Britain', *QR* v (May 1811), 431.

[66] Ibid. 404, 416–18, 429–31.

[67] Ibid. 437.

offensive war to destroy the 'Corsican' was not driven by a narrow-minded desire to elevate British interests for their own sake, but to rid Europe of an ambitious tyrant who threatened universal monarchy and the subversion of liberty. Southey believed that it was necessary to embrace a military spirit because it was essential both to preserve the nation from attack, and also to prosecute the war in a successful manner. This certainly gave a strong patriotic flavour to his views, but even as an early contributor to the *Quarterly Review* he was no simple 'Tory' supporter of the incumbent ministry.

3

Riches and Poverty

In the first issue of the *Edinburgh Review*, Francis Jeffrey launched a scathing
– and subsequently famous – attack on the new 'sect' of poets. While purportedly a review of Southey's *Thalaba*, it was clear that he also had Wordsworth
and Coleridge in his sights, and particularly the preface to the 1801 edition
of *Lyrical ballads*. Among many other faults, Jeffrey insisted that the 'sect'
followed Rousseau's 'discontent with the present constitution of society'.
'Instead of contemplating the wonders and the pleasures which civilization
has created for mankind, they are perpetually brooding over the disorders by
which its progress has been attended.' All the sufferings of the lower orders
were blamed on the 'vicious constitution of society' and none on their own
'excesses'.[1] Some six years later, Jeffrey was at it again in his unflattering
review of *Letters from England*. Southey, he thought, persisted in attacking the
'present constitution of society' and especially the commercial and manufacturing establishments. Rather than expressing admiration for the exertions of
industry he chose instead to paint a gloomy picture of the misery and the vice
of townspeople, and to predict ruin to the nation. Yet, Jeffrey proclaimed,
'he goes to the bottom of nothing'. His treatment of political economy was
'superficial and declamatory', and ultimately he belonged 'rather to the sentimental than to the reasoning class of composers'.[2]

Jeffrey's assault on Southey's social and economic thinking was among the
first, and established the tone of such criticisms thereafter. While little notice
was taken of these opinions in the 1800s, after Waterloo they became the
subject of interest and controversy across the political spectrum. Southey has
often been claimed as one of the 'romantic' founders of the 'Condition of
England' question who showed that the lamentable condition of the poor was
caused by the impact of the industrial revolution and the vogue for *laissez-
faire*. There are, however, good reasons for challenging this argument. It is
now customary to emphasise the protracted and gradualist nature of indus-
trialisation, and so attention has therefore turned to identifying the origins
of the 'myth' of the catastrophic view of the 'industrial revolution'. D. C.
Coleman and Gareth Stedman Jones both see Engels as the chief architect of
this view, and conclude that English writers were of little importance.[3] Even
if the lake poets cannot be seen as parents of this 'myth' they may have acted

---

1 [F. Jeffrey], 'Southey's Thalaba', *ER* i (Oct. 1802), 64, 71.
2 [Idem], 'Don Manuel Espriella's letters from England', *ER* xi (Jan. 1808), 372.
3 D. C. Coleman, *Myth, history and the industrial revolution*, London 1992, 1–42;
G. Stedman Jones, 'National bankruptcy and social revolution: European observers on

as its midwives. Similarly, their opposition to political economy needs further reconsideration. Southey certainly had a loathing of this 'science'. Adam Smith's *Wealth of nations*, he wrote in 1812, was 'a tedious and hard-hearted book' which estimated man's importance 'by the gain which can be extracted from him'. It was a bitter defence of the 'brute, denuded, pitiable animal, the man of the manufacturing system!'[4] This was a woeful (perhaps even wilful) misunderstanding which may have helped to damage Smith's reputation, but it was not the result of sustained intellectual engagement. Instead, the negative attitude to political economy must be seen as a product of Southey's encounter with Thomas Malthus' *Essay on the principle of population*, and particularly the debate about poverty to which it was a contribution.[5]

'Malthouses rascally metaphysics':[6] nature and the *Essay on population*

The relationship between 'nature' and 'society' was a recurring motif at the time Malthus was composing his *Essay*. These arguments were fraught with contradictory impulses. Among radical writers, the critical value of 'nature' was still retained by the end of the eighteenth century. Paine, for instance, used nature as a way of showing how far existing social and political structures were unjust. In this radicals were careful to distinguish their usage of 'nature' from the mid-century fashion for 'primitivism'. Although Rousseau's thinking was considerably more complicated than many of his readers assumed, his *Discourse on inequality* was nevertheless associated with the view that only in the state of nature was happiness possible. David Stack has argued that radicals instead invoked an Aristotelian concept of nature in which 'the juristic and abstract state of nature was dropped in favour of an historical and sociological view'.[7] Not only was change acceptable, it was desirable because it was part of the nature of man to use his intellect to progress and to develop. In effect the invocation of nature became bound up with a vision of progress: a golden age in the future rather than in the past. What radicals wished to retain was a sense that some changes that had occurred – such as the usurpation of the rights of the poor and the political dominance of a king and his court – were contrary to the laws of nature.

Southey's thinking in this period, as we have seen, fluctuated uncertainly between a pseudo-Rousseauvian evocation of a past golden age, and a broadly Godwinian faith in the future of progress. In *Letters from England*

Britain, 1813–44', in D. Winch and P. O'Brien (eds), *The political economy of British historical experience, 1688–1914*, Oxford 2002, 61–92.

4   [R. Southey], 'Inquiry into the poor laws', *QR* viii (Dec. 1812), 337. Southey had borrowed the *Wealth of nations* from Bristol Library in November 1794.

5   See Winch, *Riches*, ch. xi.

6   Southey to Rickman, 12 Sept. 1803, *NL* i. 327.

7   D. Stack, *Nature and artifice: the life and thought of Thomas Hodgskin*, Woodbridge 1998, 11.

he insisted that it was 'high treason against human nature, and blasphemy against Omniscient Goodness' to prefer the savage state to the social, but he also lauded the perfection of nature as created by God.[8] This was evident in his appreciation of a little known book by Jacques Henri Bernardin de Saint-Pierre called *Studies of nature*.[9] 'I hesitate not to pronounce it one of the most interesting works ever produced', Southey told Bedford, and 'that heart must be a bad one that is not deeply moved by its perusal'.[10] Saint-Pierre, who was a friend and supporter of Rousseau, designed his work to show the harmonies of nature and to refute those who denied the attributes of God. There would not have been 'a single unwholesome spot on the Earth, if men had not put their hands to it'. Man himself was born good but it was 'society that renders him wicked'.[11] Southey was strongly sympathetic to a view that stressed the beauty and perfection of the natural world because it was God's creation, yet in making this case he was not advocating a return to nature.

The difficulty of the radical position in contrasting 'nature' with 'artifice' was exactly this. Either they were accused of primitivism, or they were told (especially in the 1790s) that if nature developed through society, then existing forms of society were in fact natural. Nature and artifice in effect became the same thing: 'Twas *nature* gave religion's rule, | And bade the wise conduct the fool.'[12] This was most common in the tradition of natural theology which dominated in the eighteenth century. It appealed to moderate Anglicans because it provided a means of scientific investigation into the nature of the world without having to resort to the incessantly debated mysteries of revelation. It therefore became essential to show that the state of the world was compatible with a wise and benevolent creator.[13] William Paley's *Natural theology* may be viewed as a summary of eighteenth-century English thinking on this problem of the existence of evil. He believed that on balance 'the common course of things is in favour of happiness' and 'misery the exception'.[14] Many supposed evils arose from the existence of multiple and general laws of nature that inevitably criss-crossed in ways that could harm humans. A person blown over a cliff, for example, suffered the effects both of wind and gravity. It was better that such fixed laws existed, and were known, than that God constantly intervened to prevent such accidents. As for 'moral' evil, that was an inevitable product of human freedom. In a state of probation, individuals experienced the rewards and punishments which the world

---

[8] *LE* i. 306.

[9] J. H. B. de Saint-Pierre, *Studies of nature*, trans. H. Hunter, London 1796.

[10] Southey to G. Bedford, 17 Nov. 1796, *NL* i. 118. See also Southey to T. Southey, 2 Feb. 1800, ibid. 223.

[11] Saint-Pierre, *Studies*, ii. 40, 134.

[12] Cited in Stack, *Nature*, 12.

[13] F. M. Turner, *Contesting cultural authority: essays in Victorian intellectual life*, Cambridge 1993, 101–27.

[14] W. Paley, *Natural theology*, London 1802, 497. Boyd Hilton describes this as 'cosmic optimism' in *The age of atonement: the influence of evangelicalism on social and economic thought, 1795–1865*, Oxford 1988, 4.

meted out as a consequence of their free will, and would so learn to alter their moral behaviour in the hope of a future state of happiness. The inequality of property was inevitable and intended by God. In *Reasons for contentment* Paley tried to show that the lack of riches was not an evil, because the poor were blessed with the advantages of innocence, industry and frugality which were causes of happiness.[15] In Paley's theological utilitarianism, 'nature' simply meant the physical and human world. It was to be judged according to how far it produced temporal and spiritual happiness, and not by whether it accorded with some fictive and pre-social laws of nature.

Southey had not read the original 1798 edition of Malthus' *Essay on population*, but Coleridge was familiar with it. While he attacked it as 'illogical' and unoriginal, he no longer accepted the arguments of Godwin and Condorcet, its chief targets. 'No!' he told Josiah Wedgwood, 'God knows – I am sufficiently sceptical & in truth more than sceptical, concerning the possibility of universal Plenty & Wisdom but my doubts rest on other grounds.'[16] Godwin himself confronted the population issue in his *Thoughts occasioned by the perusal of Dr. Parr's Spital sermon*, suggesting that 'The advocates of old establishments and old abuses, could not have found a doctrine, more to their hearts content, more effectual to shut out all reform and improvement for ever.'[17] While Godwin accepted Malthus' ratios that showed how population growth would outstrip food supply, he was not convinced that they undermined perfectibility. To highlight this point he wondered whether the misery of all humankind was preferable to abortion and infanticide, which would sufficiently reduce the population to enable perfectibility. While Coleridge and Southey reacted warmly to Godwin's pamphlet, they found these passages offensive. Coleridge told Southey that 'I was so much delighted with all the rest of the Pamphlet that I could have myself pulled his nose for that loathsome & damnable passage.'[18] Southey believed that Malthus was a threat to his thinking because he, like Godwin, saw the *Essay* as a capitulation to the *status quo*. Therefore, when in 1803 he was asked to review the second edition for the *Annual Review*, he announced that 'It is my heart's desire to put this rascally book to death and damnation', and hoped that Malthus would be crushed as a 'mischievous reptile'.[19] Coleridge declined to collaborate, and warned Southey 'to be exceedingly temperate & courteous & guarded in your Language'.[20] It was too late, however, and Southey's tone offended friends like William Taylor, who had reviewed the *Essay* for the *Critical Review*. 'I do not like your article', he told Southey. 'A clergyman who is heterodox, a Cantab who is a Foxite, a constitutionalist who treated Godwin with urbanity, was

---

15 W. Paley, *Reasons for contentment*, London 1793.
16 Coleridge to J. Wedgwood, 21 May 1799, CL i. 518.
17 W. Godwin, *Thoughts occasioned by the perusal of Dr. Parr's Spital sermon*, London 1801, in *Political and philosophical writings*, ii. 198.
18 Coleridge to Southey, 11 Aug. [1801], CL ii. 751.
19 Southey to Rickman, 27 July 1803, SL i. 225.
20 Coleridge to Southey, [25 Jan. 1804], CL ii. 1039. See Connell, *Romanticism*, 37–41.

entitled to politer hostility. I think I have shaken the two main pillars of his system more effectually than you, and without the absence of reverence.'[21] Taylor understood better than Southey that Malthus was politically liberal. Educated at the dissenting academy in Warrington, and thereafter at Jesus College, Cambridge, Malthus' tendencies were Foxite. He remained sympathetic to moderate reform throughout his life, and supported the repeal of the Test and Corporation Acts, and the implementation of Catholic emancipation. He was not therefore a Tory.[22] What was distinctive, however, was that his 'discovery' seemed to make the case for perfectibility untenable, and it was this that made Southey's blood boil. Four points need to be stressed.

First, Malthus was committed to the Newtonian method of inducing general laws from observable evidence. The second edition of the *Essay* detailed at great length his belief that the population principle was scientifically verifiable, and had implications for social speculation. Godwin and Condorcet were unscientific in reasoning from (unproven) causes to possible effects, rather than from observed effects to possible causes. This led them into the quagmire of perfectibilist speculation, evident in Godwin's suggestions about achieving immortality. Such opinions, Malthus thought, encouraged false optimism about the removal of social ills. In the first *Essay* he presented a devastating account of how the population principle would cause a propertyless utopia to collapse back into a propertied system. This was not, as earlier proponents of population crises had suggested, a likelihood in the distant future when the globe had become overpopulated. Rather, it was a current problem that was evident in the 'perpetual oscillation' between population levels and the means of subsistence. The pressures on living standards caused by over-population were ever present until positive or preventive checks operated and brought population back within the means of subsistence and provided a more reasonable standard of living for the populace. The inevitability of this oscillation was stressed in the first *Essay*, giving it a very pessimistic cast. The less gloomy second edition suggested that with moral restraint it was possible for population to remain within the means of subsistence. If people could control their reproductive urges then social improvement was possible.

The second point concerns Malthus' rejection of a society animated solely by benevolence. Although he conceded the beauty of the idea, it would collapse if ever achieved. 'Benevolence had established her reign in all hearts', he imagined

> and yet in so short a period as within fifty years, violence, oppression, falsehood, misery, every hateful vice, and every form of distress, which degrade and sadden the present state of society, seem to have been generated by the

21 Taylor to Southey, 20 May 1804, in Taylor, *Memoir*, i. 505. See [W. Taylor], 'Malthus on the principle of population', *Critical Review* i (1804), 11–25.
22 Winch, *Riches*, 253–5.

most imperious circumstances, by laws inherent in the nature of man, and absolutely independent of all human regulations.[23]

In other words human self-love was not a product of social institutions, but arose in nature. A social system based on equality of property and benevolence was not sustainable, and as population pressures increased humans would revert to a system of individuated property animated by self-love. Malthus' point was to show that property, self-love and hence inequality were natural and necessary. And, following Smith, this was not to be lamented because it was socially beneficial. For both thinkers self-love was the motor of society that was capable of producing the wealth to liberate nations from want. Godwin, by contrast, could not accept that self-interest was necessary, and saw it as one of the many social passions that would wither away with the progress of truth. For Malthus those passions were natural. As Donald Winch writes, 'Considered abstractly, all the passions, impulses, and wants with which God had endowed man were natural: their satisfaction brought happiness and thereby played an essential part in a beneficent design.'[24] Hence Malthus and Godwin had different conceptions of the nature that God had given man, with the former seeing the 'low' passions as consequentially beneficial, while the latter saw them as social corruptions which progress would render irrelevant.

The third issue was the problem of evil. In the first *Essay* Malthus wanted to elaborate an alternative theodicy to the Anglican orthodoxy of earthly life as a state of trial. His controversial argument was that God had introduced evil because human intellectual and spiritual potential evolved under its stimulus.[25] A Godwinian utopia would simply make men indolent. Evil was necessary 'as the mighty process of God, not for the trial, but for the creation and formation of mind, a process necessary to awaken inert, chaotic matter into spirit, to sublimate the dust of the earth into soul, to elicit an ethereal spark from the clod of clay'.[26] Although the first *Essay* did not impugn the wisdom or benevolence of God, it nevertheless incensed orthodox Anglicans. By 1799 Malthus was persuaded that his theodicy required some rethinking.[27] The second *Essay* of 1803 embraced a more conventional theological utilitarianism that was borrowed from Paley's *Natural theology*. Malthus also removed his earlier, gloomy conclusions and suggested that moral restraint was now possible. This drastically reduced the problem of evil that the population principle posed. Moreover, it allowed Malthus to argue that life was a state of trial in which vice was punished by natural laws. This paved the way for

---

[23] T. R. Malthus, *An essay on the principle of population*, 1st edn, London 1798, ed. A. Flew, London 1970, 138.

[24] Winch, *Riches*, 263.

[25] See A. M. C. Waterman, *Revolution, economics and religion: Christian political economy, 1798–1833*, Cambridge 1991, 97–112.

[26] Malthus, *Essay*, 1st edn, 202.

[27] Waterman, *Revolution*, 112.

evangelical political economy: the population principle could be interpreted as 'scientific confirmation of God's purpose in creating an educative world in which the struggle with scarcity taught the duty of prudential restraint over the passions'.[28]

Finally, the *Essay* had implications for discussions about the poor laws. In their current form, Malthus argued, they provided incentives for families to produce children they could not support, and so helped keep a large proportion of the population at subsistence level. If people understood this new law of nature they would see that general human happiness depended on controlling that population and that narrowing the supply of labour would raise its price. A single man would save until he could afford to marry, and in doing so he would also acquire the knowledge and habits to support his family comfortably. 'As the wages of labour would thus be sufficient to maintain with decency a large family, and as every married couple would set out with a sum for contingencies', Malthus believed, 'all squalid poverty would be removed from society; or would at least be confined to a very few, who had fallen into misfortunes against which no prudence or foresight could provide.'[29] The future might not be as bright as Godwin imagined, but it was none the less brighter than most of Malthus' critics thought.[30] However, if individuals were to obey the laws of nature they had to know them, so Malthus advocated a scheme of national education to instruct the poor in their moral duties. In the meantime artificial interference in natural laws – poor relief – was to be abolished. Once this was established, if a person married while being unable to provide for their family, they were knowingly committing an immoral act and should be left to carry the consequences. '[T]he punishment provided for it by the laws of nature falls directly and most severely upon the individual who commits the act, and, through him, only more remotely and feebly on society. … To the punishment, therefore, of nature he should be left, the punishment of severe want.'[31] The poor did not have a right to subsistence, and even acts of benevolence were best restricted. The ideal objects of charity were those who were suffering in spite of their efforts to avoid poverty. 'In relieving these, we exercise the appropriate office of benevolence, that of mitigating some of the partial evils arising from general laws.' As for charity to the 'idle and improvident' this should be scanty at best. 'We may perhaps take upon ourselves, with great caution, to mitigate in some degree the punishment which they are suffering from the laws of nature, but on no account to remove them entirely.'[32] In other words it was essential that the laws of nature should not be distorted: only if they were obeyed was there hope of material and moral improvement.

[28] Winch, *Riches*, 238.
[29] T. R. Malthus, *An essay on the principle of population*, 2nd edn, London 1803, ed. D. Winch, Cambridge 1992, 218.
[30] See ibid. 325–32.
[31] Ibid. 262.
[32] Ibid. 286.

By considering Southey's review with reference to these issues the differences between the two writers can be brought to the fore. First of all it should be noted that Southey did not fully understand the *Essay*, and so a number of his rebuttals were misplaced. He saw it as a defence of a pessimistic Panglossianism which had only achieved fame because of the anti-Jacobin moral and political climate of the late 1790s. This reaction had gone too far. Until the French Revolution, 'No wise man ever doubted, and no christian had ever disbelieved, that the general condition of mankind could be improved.' A firm belief in progress was a staple ingredient of pre-revolutionary assumptions, Southey thought, and it was 'rendered probable to the good by reason' and was fully backed up by religious faith. But the revolutionary period produced excessive optimism in men who had 'no faith and little reason' and who dreamed of immortality. Malthus arose to dispel the wild visions of Godwin and Condorcet and 'to prove that no material improvement can ever be expected in the state of society'.[33] The backlash against progress had gone too far. Moreover Southey, like Coleridge, denied that Malthus had made a discovery. Coleridge's annotated copy of the second *Essay* suggested that even if one underestimated the speed of population growth and wildly exaggerated the productivity of agriculture a time would still arise when the population could not be sustained.[34] Coleridge told Southey that 'I put it seriously to Mr. M's good sense, whether or no, if he had simply stated this in one sentence of half a dozen or half a score of Lines, any one individual in Europe would have felt the least inclination to contradict the statement.' Southey evidently agreed, because he directly inserted Coleridge's notes into his review.[35] His conclusion was that no one had ever disagreed that at some future point the earth would become overpopulated. He did not think that this law of nature was currently in operation, and therefore misunderstood Malthus' essential point about 'perpetual oscillation'.

This misunderstanding had implications for the problem of evil. Southey either did not understand or could not accept Malthus' theodicy, and argued that the population principle defamed the nature of creation. God had commanded man to 'Increase and multiply', and so if Malthus was right, God was not only wrong, but was issuing orders that harmed mankind.[36] Southey therefore believed that until the earth was fully peopled, any checks on population must be artificial and remediable:

> If a country be over-peopled, and crowded, and distressed, in regard to its system of society, before it be half peopled in proportion to its size and power of production; the fault lies in that system of society, not in the

---

[33] [R. Southey], 'Malthus's essay on population', *AR* ii (1804), 292.

[34] S. T. Coleridge, *Marginalia*, ed. H. J. Jackson and G. Whalley, London–Princeton 1980–2001, iii. 805–9. A number of these passages were used in Southey's review.

[35] Coleridge to Southey, [11 Jan. 1804], *CL* ii. 1026; [Southey], 'Malthus's essay', 293.

[36] [Southey], 'Malthus's essay', 297. Malthus replied to this in his 'Appendix, 1806', in *Essay*, 2nd edn, 334–5. See Coleridge to S. Coleridge, [9 Oct. 1806], *CL* ii. 1191.

system of nature. If, while not a tenth, nay not a hundredth part of the habitable world be cultivated, mankind be every where in want, the fault is their own.[37]

It followed that existing social evils were the result of human 'error and ignorance', but that once wisdom had 'perfected virtue' such suffering would cease.[38] This was the central theme of the review. Southey argued that the issue was not whether humanity could be perfected in a Godwinian fashion but 'whether or not there were any hopes' for mankind, 'whether wisdom would be progressive with knowledge, and virtue with wisdom, and happiness with virtue'.[39] His perfectionism clearly remained undented by the *Essay*, and he continued to think that a world free from vice and evil was possible.

Once the world was fully peopled to its productive capacity, humanity would have acquired the knowledge and virtue to restrain its passions, thus preventing a crisis in subsistence. Southey claimed that Malthus seemed to be in two minds about this issue. The first *Essay* offered a gloomy account of the human emotions, assuming that 'lust and hunger are alike passions of physical necessity, and the one equally with the other independent of the reason and the will'. Southey found this deeply disturbing, because it implied that every unmarried man was a 'brotheller', every unmarried woman a 'strumpet'. If this view of humanity were true then no moral progress could ever occur. In the second *Essay*, however, Malthus admitted that chastity was possible. For Southey this meant that the whole argument against improvement collapsed.[40] He asked how Malthus differed from the defenders of perfectibility, for if humanity could restrain its passions, nothing could stop its improvement. Southey and Coleridge both thought that the revisions in the second *Essay* undermined the anti-perfectibility case of the first. To an extent this was true, but it overlooked the very different intellectual frameworks within which Southey and Malthus were working. Southey relied on a free will moral perfectionism, in which mankind progressed towards pure benevolence. This account was a rechristianised version of Godwinism. Indeed, in his review Southey commented that Godwin had attempted a fusion of stoicism and sensuality, thus diluting 'the wisdom of the antients with his own folly'.[41] It was this 'sensuality' which made Godwin's utopia untenable for Malthus. Southey, however, wanted 'sensuality' removed from his 'utopia', ensuring that population pressures could be avoided when they finally occurred. His own view of the future echoed Godwin's *telos* because 'every man shall enjoy as much happiness as his physical and moral powers are capable of enjoying; that happiness being regulated by and subservient to the general welfare'.[42]

37 [Southey], 'Malthus's essay', 297–8.
38 Ibid. 298, 295.
39 Ibid. 295.
40 Ibid. 296.
41 Ibid. 295.
42 Ibid. 299.

This point is important, because it helps to explain why Southey found Malthus' attitude to the poor laws extremely offensive. 'Perpetual oscillation' meant that there was a need for immediate moral restraint to prevent subsistence crises. For Malthus only the fear of starvation would impel people to restrain their sexual desires. Moreover, his fidelity to Smith's natural liberty meant that the demand for moral restraint fell upon the poor because their lower wages made supporting a family difficult. Unsurprisingly Southey took a different view. The existing evils of society, he wrote in disgust, were to be remedied by abolishing the poor rates and starving the poor into celibacy. Malthus expected them to exercise 'that virtue, which as he had reasoned, could only exist in men highly enlightened and highly virtuous, he expects and demands from the ignorant, degraded, brutalized, miserable, poor people of England!'[43] It was absurd to expect the most ignorant to be the most enlightened. Moreover, because the condition of the poor was neither natural nor just, it was immoral to remove what little relief they were afforded. In Southey's mind Malthus was simply an apologist for the selfishness of the wealthy: 'This reformer calls for no sacrifice from the rich; on the contrary, he proposes to relieve them from their parish rates: he recommends nothing to them but that they should harden their hearts.'[44] The wickedness of the *Essay* was fully revealed in the famous table of nature metaphor, which Southey quoted as proof that Malthus' aim was to turn the English constitution into an oriental despotism.

Southey's antagonism to Malthus was lifelong, and he often restated his objections in his major publications. He also supported anti-Malthusian works such as Thomas Jarrold's *Dissertation on man* and, much later, Michael Sadler's *Law of population*.[45] His growing antagonism to political economy as a selfish system evolved from his stereotype of Malthusianism rather than from engagement with Smith. This was exacerbated by the sense that the *Essay* was becoming influential: in 1807 Samuel Whitbread's bill for reform of the poor laws sparked off an extensive debate about the growth of poverty and the applicability of Malthus' ideas.[46] Southey was preparing *Letters from England* for the press at the time, and could not resist inserting some sarcastic comments. Espriella noted that philosophers and politicians were in a 'state of alarm':

It has been discovered that the world is over-peopled, and that it must always be so, from an error in the constitution of nature – that the law

---

[43] Ibid. 300.

[44] Ibid. 300–1.

[45] See [idem], 'Jarrold's dissertation on man', AR v (1807), 607–15; 'Inquiry', 320–7; STM ii. 260–2; and Southey to Rickman, 1 May 1830, SL iv. 180. The main passages from the *Annual Review* essay were silently incorporated into the reprint of 'Inquiry' in R. Southey, *Essays moral and political*, London 1832.

[46] See J. R. Poynter, *Society and pauperism: English ideas on poor relief, 1795–1834*, London 1969, 207–22.

which says 'Increase and multiply', was given without sufficient consideration; in short, that He who made the world does not know how to manage it
properly, and therefore there are serious thoughts of requesting the English
parliament to take the business out of his hands.[47]

This succinctly captures the core of Southey's opposition to the *Essay*. He
simply believed that the population principle impugned the wisdom and
benevolence of God, and absolved humanity from solving the problems
of poverty that it had created. It seemed to advise the rich to harden their
hearts, and the poor to be damned. To Southey this seemed like an eschewal
of morality and an abandonment of progress. The growth of virtue would
ensure that a more egalitarian state of society was sustainable, and so 'the
farthing candle of [Malthus's] fame must stink and go out'.[48]

Poverty amidst plenty

It was a striking irony to many in the late eighteenth century that in the
wealthiest of nations poverty was increasing. Since the 1780s there had been
heightened anxiety about the moral health of the nation, and this brought
with it an accumulation of 'knowledge' about the lower orders, especially
in the form of agricultural reports and influential surveys such as Frederick
Eden's *State of the poor*. A more down-to-earth concern was the growing cost
of the poor laws. Official returns for 1802–3 seemed to show that the rates had
reached £5.2m., double what they were in 1783, and triple the sum for 1776.[49]
It appeared that there were more than a million paupers, although in practice
only 200,000 able-bodied men and women were in receipt of permanent relief.
The fact that these figures were inaccurate should not disguise the widespread
unease they produced. Southey certainly shared these worries. In *Letters from
England* he wrote that the laws were the 'disgrace of the statutes' because
– following the 1802–3 figures – a 'tenth part' of the population claimed
relief.[50] The point was repeated at greater length in 'Inquiry into the poor
laws' in 1812, where he also noted that the official figures took no account of
the uncertain nature of employment in the manufacturing districts. By this
time, he commented, nearly every one 'has his reason ready for the increase
of the poor'.[51] More religiously inspired moralists either invoked the traditional claim that 'ye have the poor with you always', or blamed a breakdown
in the moral fibre of the nation for creating dissolute manners and ultimately

---

47 *LE* iii. 316–17.
48 [Southey], 'Malthus's essay', 137.
49 Poynter, *Society*, 187–8. See also G. Himmelfarb, *The idea of poverty: England in the early
industrial age*, London 1984, chs i–v.
50 *LE* i. 297.
51 [Southey], 'Inquiry', 320.

increased poverty. This latter claim could easily be fused with Malthusianism to set the stage for the evangelical political economy of the post-war years.

Conversely the 1790s also saw the flowering of more radical approaches to the question of poverty.[52] These were attacked by 'loyalist' writers for advocating a return to classical republican simplicity and equality which was unsuited to the modern world. Hierarchy, it was argued, was essential to prosperity, and any attempt at 'levelling' would create poverty for all.[53] In fact the ideas of radicals about commercial society were a good deal more complex. Paine and Thelwall rested their case on a radical version of the jurisprudential view of society that turned imperfect rights to charity into perfect rights of justice to be enforced by government.[54] Neither wished to return to a state of equality or to undermine the existence of property. In the second part of *Rights of man*, Paine had argued that while the riches acquired by commerce were just, the distribution of land originated in robbery and lack of access to it was a major cause of poverty. A progressive tax on inherited property could be used to reduce the power of the landed interest and to set up various basic welfare provisions. In *Agrarian justice* he went further, arguing that no one in a state of civilisation ought to be worse off than in a state of nature. Land had originally been given to humanity in common, and a right to compensation for its loss was retained after the establishment of society. Thelwall developed similar ideas, opposing the accumulation of landed property, and insisting that everyone retained a right to a share of the natural inheritance of land which had been taken from them. It has also been suggested that the innovative point about Thelwall was that he went beyond the 'static welfare-oriented' approach of Paine to suggest that labour had a right to a share of the progress of commercial society.[55] Therefore as commerce advanced it would bring higher living standards to the poorer members of the community. Paine and Thelwall were seeking to compensate for past injustices in the distribution of land and to ensure that the wealth of commercial society was distributed more widely and evenly.

Godwin, by contrast, had somewhat different preoccupations which have led some historians to see him as an 'agrarian radical' who eschewed commercial society.[56] As we have seen, he believed that the idleness and luxury of the rich doomed the poor to excessive labour and disabled them from pursuing rational improvement. The solution was the eventual eradication of political society and luxury production. In *The enquirer*, Godwin departed from the 'primitivism' of *Political justice*, and offered more practical remedies for the inequalities of society. He reasserted his belief that labour itself was not an

---

[52] G. Stedman Jones, *An end to poverty? A historical debate*, London 2004, chs i–iii.

[53] See G. Claeys, 'The French Revolution debate and British political thought', *History of Political Thought* xi (1990), 59–80.

[54] Idem, 'Origins', 257–74; I. Hampsher-Monk, 'John Thelwall and the eighteenth-century radical response to political economy', *HJ* xxxiv (1991), 1–20.

[55] Claeys, 'Origins', 270.

[56] Ibid. 275.

evil, but rather its quantity. The poor lived in a state of 'negative happiness', and because they lacked leisure they were predestined to be 'victims of ignorance and prejudice'. Even if they had some education, the drudgery of their lives disabled them from using it. All these problems were compounded by periodic lack of employment and the absence of welfare provision.[57] The 'genuine wealth of man' was leisure, and Godwin suggested some ways in which it might be promoted. He rejected the idea of a community of goods because it was a system of 'servility and imbecility' that destroyed 'independence and individuality'. It followed that some degree of inequality was inevitable, but the extremes could be prevented if everyone – rich and poor – took their share of labour and so reduced the overall burden. 'Those hours which are not required for the production of the necessaries of life, may be devoted to the cultivation of the understanding, the enlarging of the stock of knowledge, the refining our taste, and thus opening us to new and more exquisite sources of enjoyment.'[58] Scaling down the level of luxury production would also create more leisure time. For this reason the avaricious man was less harmful than the luxurious man: at least he did not increase the need for labour by creating greater demand for luxuries. Godwin's intention was to attack the established belief (the 'curse' of 'civilized nations') that profusion was socially beneficial, and he claimed that these thoughts contained the 'germs of a code of political science' which would extend liberty and happiness if enacted.[59]

Southey would have been familiar with these arguments. A further source for his ideas may be found in Saint-Pierre's *Studies of nature*. Interestingly, while this work was critical of the existing social structure, it was largely indifferent to political forms. Saint-Pierre had no desire to 'disturb, much less destroy, the different orders of the State', claimed that '[t]he people is no idol of mine' and hoped that a Christian patriot monarch would govern justly and equitably.[60] The English translator was clearly troubled by this, and told his readers to ignore the final part of the work because it contained a lengthy homage to Louis XVI.[61] On social issues, however, Saint-Pierre was more appealing. He opposed the monopolisation of land by the nobility in France and Britain, and believed that this was the main reason for the growth of the poor. While large farms turned vast tracts of land into 'solitudes' and encouraged farmers to indulge in luxury, smaller holdings were actually more productive as well as socially beneficial. He recommended agrarian laws to counteract luxury, curb the accumulation of land and reduce landed domination of politics.[62] Similarly, the moneyed aristocracy should also be denied

---

[57] W. Godwin, *The enquirer: reflections on education, manners, and literature*, London 1797, in *Political and philosophical writings*, v. 151

[58] Ibid. v. 153, 156.

[59] Ibid. v. 160.

[60] Saint-Pierre, *Studies*, iv. 100–1. See also p. 108.

[61] Ibid. iv. 402.

[62] Ibid. ii. 56–7, 98, 108–9; iv. 117, 130.

their monopoly of office, and such positions thrown open to all orders of the state. More competition in commerce would also prevent the rich from artificially suppressing the wages of the poor to feed their own luxury, although, Saint-Pierre warned, commerce should not become over-dominant. Agriculture was central, partly for reasons of self-sufficiency, but also because it was 'the great support of morals and religion'.[63] Alongside all this, Saint-Pierre also insisted that a national rather than a private system of education be introduced to ensure the inculcation of true virtue in the population.[64] Whether Southey was influenced by these ideas cannot be known, but nevertheless the similarities with his own are striking.

The nature of poverty remained a central theme in his writings. As in his poetry of the 1790s, he was prone to indulge in sentimental vignettes of the lives of the poor, and especially women and children, as a means of exciting sympathy. In *Letters from England*, for instance, there were accounts of pregnant women dying on the roadside because they had been cast out by the parish, and of children growing up without love or care in workhouses.[65] Most vivid were descriptions of poor women raking through ashes in the hope of finding some 'half burnt cinders' or 'the old cowering over a few embers – the children shivering in rags, pale and livid – all the activity and joyousness natural to their time of life chilled within them'.[66] This language drew attention to the helplessness of the poorest members of society and underlined the idea of a country which could not support itself during food scarcities or trade fluctuations.[67] This was bad enough, but what made it worse was that while the condition of the higher classes had improved over the centuries – the gentry enjoyed better housing and education than ever – that of the poor had been 'stationary'. It was not clear that they had benefited much from being in the social state:

> The best conceivable state for man is that wherein he has the full employment of all his powers, bodily and intellectual. This is the lot of the higher classes in Europe; the poor enjoys neither – the savage only the former. If, therefore, religion were out of the question, it had been happier for the poor man to have been born among savages, than in a civilised country, where he is in fact the victim of civilisation.[68]

The comparison between the savage and social states was used to highlight the imperfections of existing society. Godwin was echoed in the assertion that society prevented the unfolding of the human *telos*, and Paine and Thelwall in the idea that the poor were materially worse off in the social state. There

63 Ibid. iv. 129. See also pp. 111–12, 115.
64 Ibid. ii. 115, 131.
65 *LE* i. 299.
66 Ibid. i. 304.
67 [Southey], 'Inquiry', 319.
68 *LE* i. 307–8.

was, then, agreement amongst these writers that such poverty was unacceptable, but why had it worsened?

The typical answer to this question led back to the critique of 'old corruption'. Whether advanced by Paine's reasoning or Cobbett's rhetoric, the focus was on the way that an unrepresentative elite abused the wealth of the nation for its own ends. In *Letters from England*, Southey was inclined to agree, citing the 'ruinous wars of the present reign, and the oppressive system of taxation pursued by the late premier' as among the main reasons for the growth of poverty.[69] But by the 1810s his defence of the war and opposition to reform meant that he could no longer blame old corruption. It was Coleridge, however, who dealt with the issue fully in *The Friend* in 1809. He agreed that legitimate questions could be asked about the timing and purpose of a tax but not its amount. Instead, the real issue was how rich a people was after it had been taxed. The Americans were lightly taxed yet lacked the comforts of the British. 'What matters it to a Man', Coleridge asked, 'that he pays six times more Taxes than his Father did if, notwithstanding, he with the same portion of exertion enjoys twice the Comforts which his Father did?'[70] He also argued that government expenditure was an economic stimulant, and adopted the metaphor of evaporated water returning as refreshing rain to make his point.[71] The real problem was that opponents of taxation believed that 'a nation in Debt represented as the same both in Kind and Consequences, as an individual Tradesman on the brink of Bankruptcy'.[72] This was not true, because the debtor and the creditor were the same – the nation. It followed that the national debt was not as ruinous as Hume had gloomily predicted. Since his time it had grown further, and yet the country was richer still. Adopting the optimistic arguments of earlier defenders of the debt, Coleridge believed that it contributed to political strength and material prosperity because it welded all the diverse elements of the state together, and ensured that they all had an interest in preserving it. A creditor could punish a debtor, but the nation would not punish itself. Hume was wrong because he assumed that only a part of the nation was interested in preserving public credit, whereas it was in the true interest of everyone.[73]

Southey did not yet adopt such arguments, but he too was looking for explanations of poverty that did not invoke 'old corruption'.[74] In *Letters from England*, and more fully in his 'Inquiry into the poor laws', he began to suggest that the Reformation period marked the beginnings of the growth of

[69] Ibid. i. 306.

[70] *TF* ii. 165.

[71] Ibid. ii. 160. This metaphor was repeated in *LS*, 156, and recycled in Southey, *William Smith*, 40, and *STM* i. 182. It was criticised in T. De Quincey, *Recollections of the lakes and the lake poets*, ed. D. Wright, Harmondsworth 1970, 242–5.

[72] *TF* ii. 159.

[73] Ibid. ii. 162–6. See Morrow, *Coleridge's political thought*, 93–6, and Pocock, *Virtue*, 125–41.

[74] But see *STM* i. 177–92.

poverty.[75] While the end of feudalism had been largely desirable, the lower orders had benefited little from the rise of free labour, and the dissolution of the monasteries meant that there was nothing for the indigent to fall back upon. By the middle of the eighteenth century the independent yeomanry – 'a race of men above the labourers, though labourers themselves' – were being squeezed out of the small farms that they had once held. There was hence 'one gradation the less in society' making the differences between the ranks more rigid and harder to overcome.[76] This had increased the number of day labourers dependent on wages to support themselves, but their incomes remained limited because of the long-held view that low wages were the only way to keep the poor industrious.[77] This theory, Southey surmised, was the principle behind the poor laws: wages were just adequate to support the labourer, and low enough to prevent his wasting them in the alehouse, and so relief would be provided in times of distress. Southey believed, however, that this idea assumed that an entire class could not be trusted with higher wages, and so the prudent and industrious labourer was denied the opportunity to save because of the spendthrift. No one had the chance to become independent, and sooner or later all would be obliged to seek relief. Furthermore, he thought that overseers of the poor laws were often corrupt, and ruthless in preventing settlement. Indeed the laws of settlement were a restriction on the mobility of the poor. 'They are no longer sold with the soil, it is true', he noted, 'but they cannot quit the soil, if there be any probability or suspicion that age or infirmity may disable them.'[78] There was a disincentive to move to places where work was available or provisions were cheaper. As with Smith, the laws of settlement were viewed as an attack on liberty, a cause of inadequate wages and a major reason why the poor were unable to improve themselves.[79]

A 'main cause' of poverty was the manufacturing system. Southey claimed in *Letters from England* that 'it is the inevitable tendency of that system to multiply the number of the poor, and to make them vicious, diseased, and miserable'.[80] The result was that the poor rates were high and the hospitals and workhouses were overflowing.[81] John Rickman was initially puzzled by this argument, and, after reading 'Inquiry into the poor laws', he pointed out that manufacturing workers were well paid, and that in fact the rates had been increasing most in agricultural counties. He was in effect questioning Southey's linkage of manufacturing with poverty. In reply, Southey pointed out that he ought to have distinguished between the 'poor' generally and

75 *LE* i. 296–7; [Southey], 'Inquiry', 328–37.
76 *LE* iii. 117, 118.
77 See Himmelfarb, *Idea*, 51–3, and Hilton, *Age of atonement*, 100.
78 *LE* i. 298.
79 A. Smith, *An enquiry into the nature and causes of the wealth of nations*, ed. R. H. Campbell and A. S. Skinner, Oxford 1976, i. 152–7.
80 *LE* i. 306.
81 Ibid. ii. 142–3.

'paupers' specifically. He added that manufacturing employment was precarious because of its dependence on uncertain foreign markets and the caprice of fashionable demand.[82] It is worth stressing that Southey was hardly unique in his concerns about manufacturing. As Winch has shown, Malthus also worried about the health and virtue of workers, and about unstable demand in the sector.[83] On the other hand, Southey also accepted that manufacturing was a major factor in Britain's wealth and power, and he had no desire to destroy it 'root and branch'. He was not an agrarian who wished to see the end of manufacturing, only that it occupy a relative place within the economy. Just as a nation could be 'too warlike', so also it could be 'too commercial'.[84]

Jeffrey was at least partially correct in seeing in Southey a strong aesthetic response to manufacturing. The lake poets had already indicated their views on the classic contrast between town and country: Wordsworth's preface to *Lyrical ballads* stated that the passions and manners of rural folk were closer to nature, while towns encouraged social vanity and the smothering of genuine emotions.[85] Southey developed this contrast in a slightly different way when he presented manufacturing centres as polluters of the senses and perversions of nature. In *Letters from England*, Birmingham makes Espriella's head ache with the 'multiplicity of infernal noises': 'the hammering of presses, the clatter of engines, and the whirling of wheels'. But it was not just the ears that were offended. Espriella's eyes were hurt by the 'light of infernal fires', and his vision sullied by the smoke over the city.[86] 'Every where around us, instead of the village church whose steeple usually adorns so beautifully the English landscape; the tower of some manufactory was to be seen in the distance, vomiting up flames and smoke, and blasting every thing around with its metallic vapours.'[87] The dirt 'fills the whole atmosphere and penetrates every where, spotting and staining every thing, and getting into the pores and nostrils'.[88] The eyes of labourers were red, and their hair was turned green by the brassworks. Meanwhile, in Manchester, people lived crowded together in damp and dark cellars, beyond the reach of light or air. They worked long hours in the heat and noise of cotton factories, the constant motion of which made Espriella giddy.[89] In effect, the human body and its very senses were twisted and distorted by these hellish towns. This point was underlined when

---

[82] Rickman to Southey, 12 Mar. 1813, in O. Williams, *Lamb's friend the census taker: life and letters of John Rickman*, London 1912, 167–8; Southey to Rickman, Mar. 1813, *LC* iv. 28. See also [Southey], 'Inquiry', 343–4.

[83] S. Collini, D. Winch and J. Burrow, *That noble science of politics: a study of nineteenth century intellectual history*, Cambridge 1983, 55, 73–5, 78.

[84] [Southey], 'Inquiry', 343. He rejected the neo-physiocracy of William Spence in 'Europe, 1808', 27, and 'The history of Europe, 1811', *EAR* iv (1813), i. 189.

[85] W. Wordsworth, 'Preface' to *Lyrical ballads*, London 1800, in *The prose works of William Wordsworth*, ed. W. J. B. Owen and J. W. Smyser, Oxford 1974, i. 124.

[86] *LE* ii. 114–15.

[87] Ibid. ii. 129–30

[88] Ibid. ii. 117.

[89] Ibid. ii. 141.

one of Espriella's travellers told him that a number of the mines in the region around Birmingham were on fire. 'If you were to travel this road by night … you would see the whole country a-fire, and might fancy you were going to hell!' Similarly, when contemplating child labour in Manchester, Espriella 'thought that if Dante had peopled one of his hells with children, here was a scene worthy to have supplied him with new images of torment'.[90]

It was not simply a matter of aesthetics. Southey's point was that the perversity of the environment had grave consequences for the health and character of the workers. Children were deprived of fresh air, natural sleep and healthy exercise: they suffered either from being mangled by machines or by inhalation of particles of metal or dust.[91] But the moral effects of manufacturing were ultimately graver. The 'virtues and comforts of inferior life wither away in such atmospheres, like flowers transplanted from the field to pine at a street-window'.[92] Here the contrast was with the effects of rural life. In the countryside the peasant 'cannot grow up without receiving some of the natural and softening impressions of religion' even if formally such education was neglected. Sunday was a day of rest, and the bells of the church present a 'sweet and tranquillizing sound':

> [T]he church and the church-yard are to him sacred things: there is the font in which he was baptized, the altar at which his parents became man and wife, the place where they and their fathers before them have listened to the word of God, the graves wherein they have been laid to rest in the Lord, and where he is one day to be laid beside them.[93]

The idea was that traditional rural life involved the ordinary man and woman in a web of familial and social connections. They were attached to those they worked for: 'the remembrance of kind offices received, and faithful services performed, – an inheritance transmitted from parent to son'. These local attachments were destroyed in manufacturing towns where workers were far away from their families and lacked any strong attachment to their employers.[94] They were 'utterly uninstructed in the commonest principles of religion and morality' and so were 'as debauched and profligate as human beings under the influence of such circumstances must inevitably be'.[95] 'When his diviner part has never been called forth', Southey believed, 'the mere animal is all that remains, and mere animal gratification must be the natural end and aim of his blind desires.'[96] The manufacturing system, by its long hours and harsh conditions, denied workers even the most basic education in religion and morality,

---

90 Ibid. ii. 130, 141.
91 Ibid. ii. 141–7.
92 [Southey], 'Inquiry', 337.
93 Ibid. 338.
94 Ibid.
95 *LE* ii. 142.
96 [Southey], 'Inquiry', 340.

and so prevented them from developing as human beings. Their income was not the issue because their environment created the vices which ensured that it was wasted. 'However high the wages may be', Southey claimed, 'profligacy of every kind keeps pace and draws after it its inevitable punishment of debility, disease, poverty, want, and early death.'[97]

In *Letters from England*, Espriella commented that Spaniards were amazed that they could purchase goods such as cloths, muslins and buttons so cheaply from Britain, but that these riches were ultimately built on the misery and poverty of the lower classes. 'Wealth flows into the country, but how does it circulate there?', he asked. 'Not equally and healthfully through the whole system; it sprouts into wens and tumours, and collects into aneurisms which starve and palsy the extremities.'[98] This medical imagery conveyed a picture of a diseased body politic because of the concentrations of both riches and poverty. The riches of one man had been made possible by the labour of many. 'The hundred, human beings like himself, as wonderfully fashioned by Nature, gifted with the like capacities, and equally made for immortality, are sacrificed body and soul.'[99] Whether consciously or not, Southey was restating Godwin's arguments about the luxurious lifestyles of the few resting on the excessive labour of the many. Both men were attacking what they saw as the systematic and deliberate attempt to keep the lower orders in poverty and ignorance. 'The poor must be kept miserably poor', Southey lamented,

> or such a state of things could not continue; there must be laws to regulate their wages, not by the value of their work, but by the pleasure of their masters; laws to prevent their removal from one place to another within the kingdom, and to prohibit their emigration out of it.[100]

All these regulations effectively prevented the lower orders from being able to improve themselves. This suggests that what Southey was attacking was a system of 'artifice'. Since the sixteenth century trade had increasingly become a reason of state, and he believed that since then the interests of the bulk of the population had been subordinated to the pursuit of wealth. In other words, Southey was criticising the features of what was later to be known as 'mercantilism', and not, as often assumed, the system of *laissez-faire*, which in any case did not yet exist.[101]

97 Ibid.
98 *LE* ii. 147.
99 Ibid. ii. 145.
100 Ibid. ii. 150.
101 See D. C. Coleman, 'Mercantilism revisited', *HJ* xxiii (1980), 773–91; L. Magnusson, *Mercantilism: the shaping of an economic language*, London 1994, chs i–ii; and Hont, *Jealousy*, 365–8.

Jeffrey had commented that Southey, 'after having exerted himself to show the darkness of the dungeon which we have dug for ourselves, he very humanely leaves us to grope our way out of it, the best way we can'.[102] There is some truth in this, and only from the mid-1810s did Southey begin to develop his social and economic thoughts. Still, some points were clear. There was a duty to support a growing population, and so if men could not find work it ought to be provided for them. Employment on useful public works – naval stations, new roads, draining fens – and even projects of 'ostentatious convenience', such as monuments to Nelson and Wellington, were better than that 'men who have hands, and are willing to work, should hunger for want of employment'.[103] Ideally, however, economic independence was preferable, and Southey wondered if some way could be found to create small holdings of land, possibly through using the land tax to break up large estates and counteract the effects of primogeniture.[104] He also hoped that wages would be increased. In *Letters from England*, Espriella advised 'leaving the price of labour to find its own level: the higher it is the better'. 'High wages are a general benefit, because money thus distributed is employed to the greatest general advantage. The labourer, lifted up one step in society, acquires the pride and the wants, the habits and the feelings, of the class now next above him.'[105] Thelwall had made the same point when he argued for a social system of 'imperceptible gradations of rank, where step rises above step by slow degrees'.[106] But the most important change of all was to introduce national education, the 'superstructure of prosperity and happiness':

> Lay but this foundation, poverty will be diminished, and want will disappear in proportion as the lower classes are instructed in their duties, for then only will they understand their true interests: they will become provident, and the wages of labour may be greatly advanced to the unequivocal benefit of all persons; thus will the poor rates be diminished, and thus only may they be ultimately abolished. Thus also should we render ourselves less dependent upon the foreign consumer; the labourer being better taught and better paid, would acquire a taste for the new comforts which would then be placed within his reach, and by raising this class of the community a step in civilization, we create a new and numerous class of customers at home.[107]

A system of education would create a revolution in manners: manufacturing workers would be less likely to spend their wages in a dissolute fashion, and

---

102 [Jeffrey], 'Espriella', 373.
103 [Southey], 'Inquiry', 352–3.
104 *LE* ii. 152. See also [R. Southey], 'The history of Europe, 1809', *EAR* ii (1811), i. 292.
105 *LE* ii. 151, 152.
106 Cited in Claeys, 'Origins', 265.
107 [Southey], 'Inquiry', 354. Southey was inspired by [W. Taylor], 'Reports on the condition of the poor', *AR* i (1803), 419–26, which formed 'one of the ablest chapters upon this branch of political economy that has ever been written': *LE* ii. 152.

would be more likely to save, while the propertied classes would grow to trust the poor enough to raise their wages. The increase of consumption among the lower orders would soak up some of the manufacture currently sent abroad, as well as inspiring them to improve their lot further. It would also mean that they would finally be sharing – like other classes – in the improvement of civilisation.

4

The Uses and Abuses of an Established Church

In November 1811 the young Percy Shelley arrived in Keswick, intent on meeting his poetic idol. During his three-month visit he discussed his political and social views with Southey, and gradually but firmly became disillusioned with his former hero. He found someone who hated the Irish, opposed Catholic emancipation and distrusted parliamentary reform: in short someone who was 'corrupted by the world, contaminated by Custom'. But he also discovered that the poet did not believe in the inspiration of the evangelists, the Trinity or original sin, prompting Shelley to write that 'if ever there was a definition of a Deist I think it could never be clearer than this confession of faith'. There seem to be continuities with Southey's views from the 1790s, raising the question of how his theological beliefs were compatible with his staunch defence of the established Church. This chapter looks at the development of his private and public religious convictions in the early nineteenth century, and suggests that he retained his earlier heterodox beliefs, but defended the religious establishment on the grounds of utility. It was the best means of promoting morality, education and order. This was evident to Shelley when Southey told him that 'Expediency ought to be made the ground of politics but not of morals'.[1] This grounding of politics in expediency was also being defended by Coleridge in *The Friend* between 1809 and 1810, and there are certain similarities in their thinking that bear closer scrutiny. First, however, it may be useful to take a broad overview of the debate about the establishment as it developed in the eighteenth century.

Until the middle of the eighteenth century the ascendancy of latitudinarianism was broadly accepted. At one extreme there remained a robust tradition of High Church thought, which viewed Church and State as a unity, and, at the other extreme, those dissenters who, in arguing that the kingdom of Christ was not of this world, were increasingly critical of the established Church. The moderate latitudinarian position tried to reach out to both extremes by accepting the right to private judgement, but insisting that an established Church with articles of faith was essential to social order.[2] These

---

[1] P. B. Shelley to E. Hitchener, 26 Dec. 1811, 2, 7 Jan. 1812, in *The letters of Percy Bysshe Shelley*, ed. F. L. Jones, Oxford 1964, i. 210, 212, 216, 223.

[2] See J. G. A. Pocock, 'Clergy and commerce: the conservative Enlightenment in England', in R. Ajello and others (eds), *L'età dei Lumi: studi storici sul settecento europeo in onore di Franco Venturi*, Naples 1985, i. 523–62; J. Gascoigne, 'Anglican latitudinarianism and political radicalism in the late eighteenth century', *History* lxxi (1986), 22–38; and J. C. D. Clark, *English society, 1660–1832: religion, ideology and politics during the ancien régime*, Cambridge 2000.

matters became more pressing in the 1770s: the Feather's Tavern Association aimed for a more comprehensive establishment by abolition of the requirement that clergymen subscribe to the Thirty-Nine Articles. Opponents saw this demand against the background of rational dissent, and feared that the ultimate aim was the subversion of the establishment. Josiah Tucker did not see the wisdom of 'demolishing the present venerable Structure, even before we know, what *Kind* of Building, or whether *any* Building is to be erected in its Place'. He argued that the establishment was the bulwark of the Reformation and prevented the advance of infidelity and superstition. As far as the High Churchman William Jones was concerned, 'All that can be done is to establish one, and tolerate the rest; and this is done already.'[3] Toleration of those outside the establishment was preferred to wider comprehension within the Church. Burke was concerned that the abolition of subscription would enable clerics to promote dangerous ideas. 'In their closets', he stated in February 1772, 'they may embrace what tenets they please, but for the sake of peace and order, they must inculcate from the pulpit only the religion of the state.'[4] The idea that a state religion was necessary for 'peace and order' was the sort of utility-based defence which extreme dissenters opposed. They believed that the right of private judgement was infringed by the existence of any established Church. This was increasingly evident in some of the arguments offered by those campaigning for repeal of the Test and Corporation Acts in the 1780s. This, in part, explains why Burke rejected the 1792 petition of the Unitarians. He now believed that these dissenters were a proselytising faction whose ultimate aim was to overturn the established Church.[5] In other words, once it became apparent that the extension of the right of private judgement had detrimental implications for the established Church, those arguments had to be rejected for the ultimate security of Church and State.

The establishment and its enemies

In the 1790s Southey was critical of all religious establishments. But he was far from indifferent to religion: first and foremost he remained a Protestant opposed to both atheism and, especially, Roman Catholicism. Fear of the latter, as is well known, was widespread throughout Britain, but it was not confined to the politically conservative. Dissenters could be among the firmest opponents of Catholicism, because they believed that it was a genuine threat to the achievement of complete Protestant reformation. Many of them fervently believed that the French Revolution heralded the downfall of Rome and the end of superstition. Many also believed, however, that

3 Cited in B. W. Young, *Religion and Enlightenment in eighteenth-century England: theological debate from Locke to Burke*, Oxford 1998, 70–1.
4 E. Burke, 6 Feb. 1773, in *The parliamentary history of England*, London 1806–20, xvii. 285.
5 Idem, 11 May 1792, ibid. xxix. 1393–5.

oppression was the cause of rather than the cure for Catholicism. Hence it was argued that once Catholicism was tolerated and accepted it would gradually wither away, because freedom of the conscience would allow the truth to emerge. This belief enabled some dissenters to co-operate with Catholics in trying to extract concessions from the state, for example in Ireland in the 1780s and 1790s. The government, also, took a more open attitude towards Catholicism. The Catholic Relief Acts of 1778 and 1791 removed a number of disabilities, enabling Catholics to worship openly, and to build their own churches and chapels. The second of these acts provoked little opposition at the time, but hostility to further liberalisation was to increase markedly after 1800.

Southey remained hostile to Catholicism throughout his life. He insisted that his first-hand experience of Portugal and Spain between 1795 and 1796 and 1800 and 1801 confirmed his worst fears, asserting that 'superstition is presented in all its splendours and all its terrors', and blamed both the despotic state and the Catholic Church for the backwardness of the two countries. The ignorance and depravity of the people was plain to see. The controls on the press made freedom of discussion very difficult, and without free inquiry it was virtually impossible for truth to emerge, and thence for society to develop. Although he conceded that there were signs of improvement in the cities, on the whole all ranks were ignorant and progress was stagnating.[6] Southey restated these thoughts in his letters and journal from the second visit to Portugal, where he also elaborated on the reasons why Catholicism had such a powerful hold on the minds of the people. After discussing some examples of 'idolatry', he told his brother that 'Religion is kept alive by these images, &c., like a fire perpetually supplied with fuel. They have a saint for every thing ... It is a fine religion for an enthusiast – for one who can let his feelings remain awake, and opiate his reason. Never was goddess so calculated to win upon the human heart as the Virgin Mary.'[7] Images and idols appealed to the feelings of the people rather than to their reason, and in doing so deepened their religious attachment. This reveals an interesting scepticism towards religion solely based on reason, and provides one explanation of why Southey feared Catholicism: as a proselytising religion it was effective in making converts. It also followed that there were lessons to be learned from the attachment of ordinary people to a religion that aroused the feelings and stimulated the imagination.

It was this first point that made Southey uneasy about how far Catholicism should be tolerated in Protestant countries. This became a more pressing issue after Pitt's failure to implement Catholic emancipation for Ireland in 1801. There was also growing disquiet about the continued presence of the *émigrés*

---

6 See Southey, *A short residence*, 43, 59, 72, 234, 308–9, 363–4.
7 Southey to T. Southey, 23 May 1800, *LC* ii. 72; R. Southey, *Journals of a residence in Portugal, 1800–1801 and a visit to France, 1838*, ed. A. Cabral, Oxford 1960, 13.

in England, and the rapid growth of a visible Catholic population.[8] While in Portugal, Southey gave the issue some consideration, concluding that although he was a defender of toleration, he thought that proselytism had gone too far in England. He told Wynn that 'You might as well let a fire burn or a pestilence spread, as suffer the propagation of popery. I hate and abhor it from the bottom of my soul, and the only antidote is poison.'[9] He hoped that monastic establishments in England would be dissolved and that the French priests would return home. More broadly, he continued to believe that Catholics were a threat to the security of Church and State and to the Reformation project more generally. A Catholic's allegiance to the pope would always come before his loyalty to any particular state, and so any further toleration was extremely dangerous especially since the weak minds of the populace meant that they were easy prey.[10] Southey therefore recommended a list of reforms that the Catholic Church should implement before further liberalisation could be considered. These consisted of no less than removing all canons that sanctioned persecution, expunging persecuting saints from the calendar, condemning council proceedings, abolishing the inquisition, establishing full toleration and an admission of Church fallibility. In other words, it was not the mass, 'polytheism' or celibacy which was the problem, but the existence of persecution and the claims to absolute authority. Until such reforms were enacted Catholicism remained a danger to all reformed Churches, and could not expect further concessions from them.[11] It followed that when the ministry of 'All the Talents' resigned in 1807 because of George III's refusal to allow a small measure of Catholic relief, Southey could not help but agree with the king, and claimed that only he and Coleridge, amongst their friends, thought alike in opposing it.[12]

Something had to be done about Ireland however. Like many English people, Southey held a low view of the Irish, and a short visit in 1801 convinced him that it would be hard to 'civilize' such a lazy people.[13] Initially he thought that the best hope was a Catholic establishment, and speculated that Jesuits and Benedictines would help improve the country by humanising the populace and cultivating the land.[14] A few years later, however, he had retreated from this view, believing it would do more harm than good by increasing the bigotry of the populace.[15] The real solution was the promotion and circulation of knowledge. But, he continued, 'is it to be produced

---

8 D. Bellenger, 'The émigré clergy and the English Church, 1789–1815', *JEH* xxxiv (1983), 407–9.
9 Southey to Wynn, 21 Feb. 1801, *LC* ii. 132.
10 Southey to Wynn, Apr. 1807, ibid. iii. 75–7.
11 [Southey], 'Europe, 1811', 137–9.
12 Southey to Wynn, 27 Mar. 1807, *NL* i. 443.
13 Southey to E. Southey, 16 Oct. 1801, *LC* ii. 169–70.
14 Southey to Rickman, 22 Mar 1805, and Southey to Wynn, 6 Apr. 1805, ibid. ii. 320, 323–4.
15 [Southey], 'Europe, 1808', 131.

by upholding and encouraging a church, of which the main principle is ever to keep its subjects in ignorance?' He opposed the idea that nations should enjoy their 'superstitions', however 'monstrous', because it was a 'heartless and hopeless Pyrrhonism' which approached politics solely in expedient terms, and took no account of the difference between truth and falsehood.[16] Some attempt should be made to shake the faith of the Catholic population and to implant Protestantism, because it was a better religion and because it advanced civilisation. As for political reform, Southey contended that Irish Catholics possessed full liberty of conscience and the use of the press. Emancipation, he thought, was the aim of few men; it really served as a pretext for those who wished for repeal of the union, for independence or for a Catholic establishment. The emancipationists had little concern for the real welfare of Ireland.[17] It was hard, he argued, to see how the ability of a few men to hold office would improve the condition of four million peasants.[18] The state of the tenant population was a disgrace to the respectable class of Ireland, and Southey advised that as soon as possible the government should abolish the tithes, begin the education of the people and admit Catholics to every office of 'emolument, trust, or honour' except parliament.[19] These reforms were hardly sufficient to the problem, but they do show his firm belief that unjust social arrangements, rather than exclusion from parliament, were the cause of discontent.

Southey should therefore be understood as a committed Protestant who believed that the Reformation project was by no means complete.[20] This is evident from his opinions about the Reformation itself, where he strongly disagreed with his Unitarian friend William Taylor. Between 1807 and 1808 Taylor was involved in a debate in the *Monthly Magazine* about the nature and consequences of the English Reformation. He attacked Martin Bucer, whom he blamed for perverting the doctrine, liturgy and discipline of the Church, and for encouraging the extermination of both Catholics and Unitarians. Taylor's purpose was to undermine Anglicanism by showing that it was a foreign import, and founded on a bloody and unnecessary persecution. This provoked a heated debate,[21] which prompted Taylor to consider the question 'Was the Reformation beneficial to Europe?' He referred to the recent *Essay on the spirit and influence of the Reformation of Luther* by Charles Villers, which had argued that the Reformation 'was not merely a step in the progress, but in the amelioration, of social order'. Taylor doubted this conclusion, suggesting

---

16 Ibid. 10, 130.
17 [Idem], 'Europe, 1811', 135–7.
18 [Idem], 'Europe, 1808', 128.
19 [Idem], 'Europe, 1811', 136.
20 See N. Tyacke (ed.), *England's long Reformation, 1500–1800*, London 1998.
21 [W. Taylor], 'Concerning a war-whoop', *Monthly Magazine* xxiii (1807), 327; J. Watkins, 'Defence of Bucer and the English Reformation', ibid. 418–21; [W. Taylor], 'No Bucerism in reply to Dr Watkins's Defence of Bucer', ibid. xxiv (1807), 24–5; J. Watkins, 'To the editor', ibid. 225–7.

that the growth of civilisation over the last three hundred years had much more to do with material factors than with the Reformation. 'This progress', he claimed, 'both of populousness and of refinement, resulted chiefly from the increase of wealth; and the increase of wealth resulted chiefly from that extension of commerce which grew out of the conquest of Hindostan, and the colonization of America; events independent of the reformation.'[22] The actual Reformation originated in a backward part of Europe, and much of the good associated with it was inevitable anyway. Its doctrinal conflicts had hindered progress and decreased civil liberty, while toleration was the product more of the sceptical mind of Bayle than the principles of Reformation leaders. For Taylor, the ideal Reformation would have arisen from the followers of Socinus, who 'would have shapen, into a severely beautiful consistency, the articles of a narrower, simpler, purer and sublimer creed'.[23] As he explained to Southey, 'Praising the Reformation I hold to be religious toryism, and to operate, like praising the constitution, as a ground for not reforming further.'[24]

Southey took a very different approach, and was much closer to the argument of Villers's *Essay*, which he had praised in the *Annual Review*.[25] The point Southey took from the *Essay* ran completely opposite to Taylor's argument. The Reformation ended the persecution against learning associated with Catholicism and opened the floodgates of free inquiry. Despite the persecution of Muncer and Servetus by Luther and Calvin respectively, it was nevertheless true that moral and political progress were due to the Reformation. Even the wars of religion that followed this great event ultimately aided the liberty, virtue and happiness of humanity, because they were necessary to destroy Catholicism. The continued existence of Austria, Spain and Italy showed that much needed still to be done. Imagining the alternative to Protestant Reformation, Southey raged that 'Fanaticism would every where have continued to make bonfires of reformers and philosophers, and pederasty to walk abroad in purple.'[26] However, despite the centrality of the Reformation to Southey's beliefs, he was not uncritical. He thought that Villers had too easily dismissed Muncer, whose radicalism he likened to the spirit of Lycurgus: it displayed 'justice, virtue, and happiness'.[27] He also thought that the Reformation had hindered the global spread of Christianity, evidenced by the sustained lull in missionary activity.[28] Another disadvantage was

---

22 [W. Taylor], 'Was the Reformation beneficial to Europe?', ibid. xxvi (1808), 205.
23 Ibid. 207.
24 Taylor to Southey, 31 Oct. 1808, in Taylor, *Memoir*, ii. 224.
25 [R. Southey], 'Villers' essay on the spirit and influence of the Reformation and Luther', AR iv (1806), 178–87. See L. O. Frappell, 'The Reformation as negative revolution or obscurantist reaction: the liberal debate on the Reformation in nineteenth-century Britain', *JRH* xi (1980), 293.
26 [Southey], 'Villers' essay', 179.
27 Ibid. 181.
28 Ibid. 187.

later to play a major role in his thinking. The dissolution of the monasteries destroyed endowed institutions of learning, and made authorship a pure trade. 'We laugh at the ignorance of these orders', he told Rickman, 'but the most worthless and most ignorant of them produced more works of erudition than all the English and all the Scotch universities since the Reformation.'[29]

One central effect of the Reformation in Britain was the proliferation of sects, and Southey was particularly interested in whether these were a help or a hindrance to continued reformation. Although he noted that rational dissent had been deeply feared by Churchmen and anti-Jacobins, he did not think, in the 1800s at least, that it was a great threat to the Church or the people. These dissenters lauded reason and loved 'unbounded freedom of opinion', but they were in fact, as Southey's Espriella noted in Letters from England, the establishment's allies. They were 'an advanced guard who have pitched their camp upon the very frontiers of infidelity, and exert themselves in combating the unbelievers on one hand, and the Calvinists on the other'.[30] They helped resist both atheism and enthusiasm. Southey even commented in 1809 that if France had allied itself to Socinianism rather than to infidelity during the revolution it would now be a free country.[31] However, despite these favour-able comments, he also believed that rational dissent was destroying itself from within because of its obsession with materialism. After reading some papers of Taylor's in the Monthly Magazine which defended a materialist view of the origin of ideas, Southey told him that his theology did mischief and thinned the ranks of Unitarianism. 'That Monthly Magazine is read by all the Dissenters, – I call it the Dissenters' Obituary, – and here you are eternally mining, mining, under the shallow faith of their half-learned, half-witted, half-paid, half-starved pastors.'[32] More generally, Southey worried about the psychological effects of absorption in metaphysics, materialism and science. A humorous swipe at the Royal Institution in Letters from England suggested that an excess of these ideas could actually lead to atheism.[33] As he told Walter Savage Landor in 1809, such activities 'seem to deaden the imagina-tion, and harden the heart [of the scientist] ... they frequently become mere materialists, account for every thing by mechanism and motion, and would put out of the world all that makes the world endurable'.[34]

The real threat to progressive religion, however, was Methodism. Southey's belief that enthusiasm was reviving drove him towards defending the estab-lished Church. He and Coleridge were worried because they doubted that theirs was an age of reason. One of the chief purposes of Letters from England, for instance, was to show that the population was not much more rational

29 Southey to Rickman, 22 Mar. 1805, LC ii. 320.
30 LE ii. 37, 38. See also [R. Southey], 'On the evangelical sects', QR iv (Nov. 1810), 485–6.
31 Southey to Taylor, 15 Jan. 1809, in Taylor, Memoir, ii. 265.
32 Southey to Taylor, 23 June 1803, ibid. i. 459–60.
33 LE iii. 315–16.
34 Southey to Landor, 23 Apr. 1809, LC iii. 231.

or educated than it had been at the time of the Reformation. The popularity of millennialists such Richard Brothers and Joanna Southcott seemed to show that the 'masses' remained ignorant. The rise of Methodism was only further proof, and it generated increasing concern among political writers from the late 1790s.[35] As early as 1802 Southey said that he would 'roar aloud if the Mother Church be in danger'.[36] And roar he did, publicly and privately, because he thought Methodism was a grave danger to the Church and to liberty. Wesley and Whitfield, he argued, promulgated ideas such as predestination, the new birth and the worthlessness of good works, and created a morbid obsession with personal sin which deprived religion of its grace and joy. Their skill as preachers, however, produced a kind of intoxication among their auditors, who often believed themselves immediately saved: it was a religion that encouraged 'fanaticism and madness'.[37] Furthermore, Wesley had erected an authoritarian system of church government and exercised the minutest control over his followers. This 'sectarian spirit' was 'nourished at the expense of national spirit' and the growth of Methodism 'is like that of an incysted tumour in the body politic'.[38] Southey even claimed that it might soon be strong enough to reclaim the depleted established Church.[39] Meanwhile, Whitfield's evangelicals were no less dangerous because their teachings tended to 'narrow the judgment, debase the intellect, and harden the heart'.[40] They seemed obsessed by particular acts of providence, superstitiously asserting that individual and natural occurrences were the result of divine intervention.[41] They undermined the Church from within by proclaiming that unlike their fellow Anglicans they followed the Thirty-Nine Articles. Their aim, as Southey interpreted it, was to shift the Church in a more Calvinistic direction. From either brand of Methodism much was to be feared. They would introduce strong penal laws and a reign of saints would end the civil and religious freedom that had been so hard won. It would be a revolution of 'ignorance, craft and fanaticism' which would renew intolerance and persecution, and inaugurate 'another twilight of human reason'.[42]

While Southey feared the rise of Methodism, he also believed that its popularity revealed something about the nature of religion and the inadequacies of Anglicanism. Infidelity and atheism were not genuine threats because it was human nature to be religious. Methodism had been able to capitalise on this during the eighteenth century – at the risk of excessive emotion-

---

35 See W. R. Ward, *Religion and society in England, 1790–1850*, London 1972, 39–53. For Coleridge's views see J. D. Boulger, *Coleridge as religious thinker*, New Haven 1961, 18–19, 46–9.
36 Southey to Rickman, Jan. 1802, *NL* i. 267.
37 [Southey], 'Evangelical sects', 496–503 at p. 502.
38 Ibid. 510.
39 [Idem], 'Myles's history of the Methodists', *AR* ii (1804), 208, 210.
40 [Idem], 'Evangelical sects', 508.
41 Southey to Wynn, 14 Mar. 1806, *SL* i. 367.
42 [Southey], 'Myles's history', 210. See also [idem], 'Society for the suppression of vice', *AR* iii (1805), 230.

alism – because Anglicanism was weak. Its clergymen were either complacent gentlemen steeped in secular pleasures, or curates too poor to be respected. As Espriella, Southey argued that the Church had been divested of its spirit and substance, leaving only a spectral form behind. 'There is nothing here for the senses', he proclaimed, 'nothing for the imagination, – no visible object of adoration, at which piety shall drink.'[43] The Methodists were successful because they appealed 'to the conscience, and the imagination, and all the mainsprings of the human mind'.[44] Southey's worry, however, was that the mysticism of Methodism replicated the worst features of Catholicism, and he was critical of writers like Thomas à Kempis, William Law and Jacob Behmen for the same reason.[45] Nevertheless there was a need for a middle way between reason and mysticism, a form of 'affectionate religion' which was neither overly rational nor excessively enthusiastic. In the early eighteenth century this position had been advanced by Isaac Watts and Philip Doddridge, who defended the use of reason but thought stirring of passions was an essential motive to religious action. As Isabel Rivers has noted, however, they found it difficult to maintain this position against those who attacked them for enthusiasm and the abandonment of reason. Such a position would help to explain Southey's defence of passionate religion while rejecting the seeming fanaticism of Methodism.[46]

Unless the Church mended its ways, it would find survival difficult. One solution was doctrinal reform from within. Southey repeatedly stated that while the Thirty-Nine Articles were generally Calvinistic, the majority of the clergy were Arminian. Either the Articles should be properly enforced, or preferably they should be abolished. This would make the Church more open to those who loved the Gospel, and would enable those with knowledge and virtue to oppose the ignorance of Methodism. He also often suggested that once the Test Act was removed the dissenters would cease to exist as a separate body.[47] Southey's position in the mid-1800s was therefore close to the latitudinarians of the Feather's Tavern Association: the established Church should be maintained, but on a more comprehensive setting to heal the breach with dissent. It is therefore interesting to note that at this time Southey was in contact with Richard Watson, bishop of Llandaff. Watson, who had been a noted reformer in the 1770s, followed Benjamin Hoadly in arguing that the Church was a voluntary institution that had been created for public order. He had opposed the French Revolution for its irreligion, but he

---

43 *LE* iii. 16.
44 [Southey], 'Evangelical sects', 488.
45 Ibid. 502.
46 I. Rivers, *Reason, grace and sentiment: a study of the language of religion and ethics in England, 1660–1780*, Cambridge 1991–2000, i. 185–204. Southey showed his support for Watts's position in *Horae lyricae by Isaac Watts, with a memoir of the author by Robert Southey*, London 1834, pp. xxvi-xxxi.
47 [Southey], 'Myles's history', 213; 'Villers' essay', 187; Southey to Wynn, 6 Apr. 1805, *LC* ii. 323; *LE* iii. 11–13.

continued to support clerical reform at home, including some liberalisation of the Articles. Although he was a supporter of further relief for Catholics, he and Southey were in agreement in other areas. In June 1806 Southey dined with Watson and was pleased to note that his companion did not adhere to all Thirty-Nine Articles. '[H]e is a staunch Whig, & would willingly see the Athanasian Creed & half a dozen other absurdities struck out of the liturgy as I should.'[48] Both men agreed that a reform of Church doctrine would help unite its members against its enemies. Other reforms, such as dismantling pluralities and raising the living standard of curates, were, Southey noted, already taking place silently and effectively.[49]

As he became more fearful of the threat to the establishment, however, he became less willing to countenance doctrinal reform. He did not, however, support those who wished to curtail toleration. In 1811 Lord Sidmouth put forward a bill to amend the Toleration Act in order to deal with the menace of Methodist itinerancy. This proposed that licences to preach would only be granted if applicants presented testimonials of their character from six reputable and substantial householders, who would be approved by a magistrate. The outcry against this bill was substantial, with Methodists proclaiming their loyalty, and others arguing that it infringed religious liberty. Lord Liverpool tried to persuade Sidmouth to withdraw the measure because it would provoke Protestant dissent, and force it into the arms of Irish Catholic activists.[50] Southey and Coleridge also opposed the bill, partly because it was too great an attack on religious liberty, and partly because it would be ineffective anyway. Coleridge did, however, think a more specific measure was necessary to prevent people from teaching whatever they pleased and appealing to toleration as a justification.[51] For Southey the only way to repress disagreeable religious opinions was complete intolerance, as practised in Italy, Spain and Austria. While effective, this approach was 'the foulest spot upon human nature' and it was to be hoped that the British government was 'too wise, too enlightened, too humane' to follow such a course of action.[52]

Southey's chief concern in defending the establishment was not rational dissent but the twin threats of superstition and enthusiasm. His anti-Catholicism may seem like simple prejudice, but it was based on the belief that Catholicism was antithetical to liberty and progress, and that its priests were highly effective in making converts. Emancipation was therefore a grave threat to the blessings that Britain had secured since the Reformation. The evils of enthusiasm, as embodied in all forms of Methodism, would undermine reason and learning, encourage prejudice and end toleration. Southey's

---

[48] Southey to T. Southey, 28 July 1806, BL, MS Add. 30927, fo. 118. See also Southey to May, 18 June 1806, SL i. 390–1.

[49] [Southey], 'Europe, 1808', 177–9; [idem], 'Europe, 1810', 242.

[50] See M. R. Watts, The dissenters: expansion of evangelical nonconformity, Oxford 1995, 367–77.

[51] EOT ii. 144–6, 158–60.

[52] [Southey], 'Europe, 1809', 361. See also 'Europe, 1811', 173–82.

position was the latitudinarian and enlightened defence of the established Church as the best bulwark of reason, liberty, tolerance and progress. He retained these ideals even as he became more paranoid about the threats to the establishment. In 1812, in the aftermath to the assassination of Spencer Perceval, he believed that there was an alliance between Irish Catholics and Protestant dissenters to introduce emancipation, repeal the Test Act and ultimately destroy the establishment. At the same time, he feared that rural antipathy to tithes would force the clergy to be salaried by the state. It would not be long before the Methodists came forward and offered a national Church at a cheaper rate, with consequences even worse than in the seventeenth century: 'the reign of the saints led to the reign of the sinners in days when there was more virtue and more wisdom in England than can be found now among us'.[53]

The inner light

Southey's own religious beliefs were not as orthodox as his defence of the establishment might suggest. Indeed, as Shelley understood, they had not changed much since the 1790s. Generally, however, he kept them to himself. In part, he had come to the conclusion that controversial matters of faith simply could not be conclusively resolved by appealing to Scripture. He agreed with the Quakers that some tenets were 'unnecessary provocations to disputes and doubts' and that it was best not to be dogmatic.[54] His reticence was also a prudent response to the editorial conservatism of Gifford at the *Quarterly Review*, who disliked any whiff of heterodoxy. Moreover, as he became convinced of the utility of the establishment, and hostile to its critics, it would have been counter-productive to his prime intentions to parade his own rather unusual religious views.

The clearest statement of his beliefs was made in two letters to James Grahame in 1808. Grahame was a Scottish poet and advocate who entered the ministry in 1809, and had written to Southey for advice after reading the religious sections of *Letters from England*. In offering Grahame his opinions, Southey told him that 'I proceed to speak of things which I regard with too sacred and deep a feeling ever to be exposed to those who treat it lightly.' While many sects, he went on, had a clear conception of part of the Christian system, none of them understood the whole, 'perfectly pure and simple as that system is'.[55] Southey claimed to set aside all creeds, catechisms and commentators, and to base his own faith solely on the words of Christ. The interpretation he gave was extremely radical:

[53] Southey to T. Southey, 12 May 1812, *SL* ii. 275. See also *LE* iii. 13–15.
[54] Southey to Wynn, 3 Dec. 1807, *SL* ii. 31.
[55] Southey to J. Grahame, Apr. 1808, *NL* i. 472. For an earlier discussion see Southey to May, [19 Apr., 1 May 1803], in *Letters to May*, 73–4, 76.

To me nothing can be clearer than that Christ Jesus has expressly forbidden his disciples either riches or authority; that his words are to be received in their plain and incontrovertible meaning, instead of being explained away into nothing; and that they lead to nothing short of a total revolution in the whole constitution of human governments, and the establishment of a new order of things, in which no man is to exercise authority over another; none are to be rich and none poor, but all do their part in the general labour, and receive their portion of the produce.[56]

The Christian ideal, then, was the eradication of distinctions of wealth and authority, the ideals Southey had held during the heyday of pantisocracy. He continued by arguing that the institutions of society were in conflict with the will of the maker, but 'Were that will to be obeyed moral evil would be anni-hilated, and by far the greatest part of physical evil with it.'[57] If all humanity adhered to Christian precepts there would be no need for government or distinctions of property, but until such a state was reached political institu-tions were essential.

Southey hesitated to set his beliefs down with great conviction, because he found no conclusive evidence for many of them. Nevertheless, he disagreed with the plenary inspiration of Scriptures and firmly rejected original sin, 'as it is commonly understood', because it was inconsistent with divine justice and with the language of Christ. It followed that traditional ideas, in which the suffering and death of a god was necessary to redeem man from a state of sin, were rejected. As he told Grahame, 'I prefer Pelagius to St. Augus-tine.' The Trinity, similarly, was abandoned because there was no evidence for it, either in Christ's words, or anywhere in the New Testament. His heresy inclined 'rather to Arius than to Socinus', for he believed that Christ formed a greater portion of 'the Divine Mind' than any other man. He claimed to find his views consistent with Scripture, but told Grahame 'Many of them you may perhaps think erroneous, but you will see with how little justice I have been reviled as an unbeliever, and an atheist.'[58] They were certainly highly heterodox and help explain Shelley's belief that his hero was still a deist. Southey was stating that individuals could be saved on the basis of their moral life (working in conjunction with grace) rather than of their religious beliefs. Salvation was open not only to those outside the Church, but also those outside Protestantism. This meant that neither the Church of England nor any other Church was an apostolic Church; rather they were purely human inventions that could be defended or opposed on those terms. However, before we turn further to explore the implications of this, it would be valuable to inspect more closely Southey's suggestion to Grahame that he inclined most closely to Quakerism in these years. Why was this?

Southey was intensely interested in Quakerism, and even began a life of

---

56 Southey to Grahame, Apr. 1808, *NL* i. 472–3.
57 Ibid. i. 473.
58 Ibid. i. 473–4. See also Southey to T. Southey, 23 Jan. 1811, *NL* ii. 6.

George Fox in the early 1820s. But his closest point of sympathy was in the later 1800s, perhaps provoked by reviewing Thomas Clarkson's *Portraiture of Quakerism*, and meeting the author. He declared that the Quaker system was nearly the 'true system of the Gospel', that its morality was perfect, and that if it were more widespread it would produce the 'greatest possible good'.[59] In *Letters from England*, Southey wrote that despite being widely persecuted in the seventeenth century, the Quakers were never provoked to anger and seemed to have extinguished selfishness: no one 'could lead more blameless lives, and display more heroical self-devotement'.[60] Fox had attained religious truth by following wholly 'the feelings of his own heart', and his followers believed that when man was reborn into the spirit he was restored to a pre-fallen state.[61] Quakers therefore stressed inspiration, and speaking what was internally directed rather than what was rationally thought. Although Southey admitted that this risked antinomianism, he thought it produced a better effect on Quaker feelings than, for example, Calvinism. It could, however, be taken to extremes: 'That the admonition of the spirit ... when it be wisely and earnestly cultivated is an infallible guide of conduct, may and must be admitted; but that which will make a good man act well, will not always make him talk wisely.'[62] The other striking point about Quakers was that although they began as an enthusiastic sect, they were now sober, patient, industrious and hence wealthy. They took a lead in charity and maintained their own poor. 'Were it not for their outrageous and insufferably heretical opinions', wrote Southey in his guise as the Catholic Espriella, 'it might be thought that any government would gladly encourage so peaceable, so moral, and so industrious a people.'[63]

Around the same time, Coleridge was also taking an interest in Quakerism. During the preparations for his weekly newspaper, *The Friend*, he had learned from Clarkson that the *Portraiture* had earned 'upwards of £1000' because of the number of Quakers who had subscribed to it. Eager that his venture might do well, Coleridge engaged Clarkson to procure a similar audience for it.[64] But the links between Coleridge and Quakers go deeper than the pecuniary. During the 1800s he was gradually moving away from what he thought of as the dominant mechanistic approach to Christianity, and began trying to fuse subjective emotionalism with objective rationalism into a coherent unified philosophy. He found some of this emotionalism in the writings of Fox, as well as in Behmen and Law.[65] '[I]n the essentials of

---

[59] Southey to Wynn, 3 Dec. 1807, *SL* ii. 31. See also [R. Southey], 'Clarkson's portraiture of Quakerism', *AR* v (1807), 594–607.
[60] *LE* iii. 80.
[61] Ibid. iii. 76–9.
[62] Ibid. iii. 92.
[63] Ibid. iii. 75–6.
[64] D. Coleman, *Coleridge and* The Friend *(1809–1810)*, Oxford 1988, 83.
[65] See Boulger, *Coleridge*, chs ii–iii, and D. Hedley, *Coleridge, philosophy, and religion: Aids to reflection and the mirror of the spirit*, Cambridge 2000, chs iii–iv.

their faith', he stated, 'I believe as the Quakers do', and in response to a query asking whether he believed in an 'internal Monitor' he affirmed that he did. 'Would, O would! that my whole Being were as clear in listening to, & obeying that Voice within, as my Convictions are clear in its existence & divine Nature.'[66] There were important similarities between Quakerism and the Platonic and Kantian approach to ethics and religion that Coleridge was developing. Essentially, he argued against enlightened self-interest, and criticised systems of morality that reduced virtue to consequential calculations.[67] He favoured instead an 'intellectualist' approach in which morality was seen as conformity to the good and the rational, in other words, to the divine. This was achieved, as Douglas Hedley puts it, by 'obedience to the divine will as it is revealed to the moral agent through the indwelling spirit'.[68] Also, and perhaps in contrast to the later Kant, Coleridge did not denigrate the role of the affections in the moral life. True Christian morality required the harmonisation of love and duty, and actions that arose from both were a fulfilment of the potential for 'God*like*-ness' in everyone.

Although his Quaker subscribers found much of this impressive, Coleridge was ambivalent about expressing his ideas purely in their terms.[69] He tried not to conflate reason with the conscience, because while reason was absolute and universal, the will was always prone to imperfection.[70] This distinction was evident in his treatment of Rousseau. He was certainly impressed by the Genevan's account of morality, and even wrote a homage to reason which is strikingly similar to the hymn to conscience in 'The profession of faith of the Savoyard vicar'. He could not, however, accept a simple application of reason to politics, and instead adopted a measured defence of 'expediency'.[71] This did not suit Quaker tastes, and as the months went by subscriptions fell. Nevertheless, it is important to stress that for Coleridge the inner light of the Quakers had affinities both with Rousseau's thinking about the conscience, and with his own Platonism and Kantianism.[72] Southey's appreciation of Quakerism can be viewed in the same terms. Although he had little knowledge of Kant, his position was similar because of his early interest in both Rousseau and stoicism. In Letters from England, Southey likened the Quaker's faith in spirit to 'the faculty of conscience' which 'when it be wisely and earnestly cultivated is an infallible guide of conduct'.[73] He distinguished this from pure reliance on the spirit, which could be perverted into enthusiasm, and so preferred a conscience that was harmonised with reason. The

---

66 Coleridge to P. Nevis, [c. 31 Dec. 1808], CL iii. 157, 158.
67 TF ii. 281.
68 Hedley, Coleridge, 191.
69 Coleman, Coleridge, 75–9, 98–101; Boulger, Coleridge, 92.
70 TF ii. 8.
71 Ibid. ii. 125–6.
72 For Rousseau's influence on Kant see Taylor, Sources, ch. xx, and J. B. Schneewind, The invention of autonomy, Cambridge 1998, 487–92, 502–7.
73 LE iii. 92. See also [Southey], 'Quakerism', 603.

echoes of Rousseau should be clear. At the same time he likened the Quakers to stoics, telling Landor that 'I wish you were as much a Quaker as I am. Christian stoicism is wholesome for all minds.'[74] This helps to explain why Southey thought that if everyone were a Quaker the consequences would be enormously beneficial. Ideally, as morality progressed, people would be able to control their unwholesome passions, would apprehend the good and act accordingly, and in doing so they would realise their potential.

Southey also admired the political ideals of Quakerism. This was evident in his praise of William Penn, and the American colony he founded. Pennsylvania had been established on 'sound morals and sound policy', and, unlike most other American colonies, its people had maintained their upright sense of morality.[75] Moreover, Southey thought that the internal government of the Quakers, from the local, monthly parish meeting to the national, annual meeting, was a 'pure' system of democracy. Whereas most collective bodies were governed according to majority will,

> The Quakers admit no such principle: among them nothing is determined upon unless it is the sense of the whole; and as the good of the whole is their only possible motive, (for no member of the society receives any emolument for discharging any office in it,) they never fail, whatever differences of opinion may at first have existed, to become unanimous.[76]

Southey liked this emphasis on participation and deliberation until genuine consensus was achieved. An enlightened politics could only be based on a disinterested desire for the common good, and a general acceptance of what that good was. This pure democracy, however, was only possible once individuals were directed by conscience and benevolence. In the present state of the world, unfortunately, politics could not be grounded on such high ideals. Hence, although pacifism was desirable, it was not practicable until all humanity had become more like the Quakers. In the meantime war could be justified, not least because of the residual and stubborn instinct for self-defence.[77] Unsurprisingly the biggest point of difference between Southey and Quakerism was over the establishment. Quakers believed that earthly government had no right to interfere in religious matters and they passively bore the penalties which their refusal to maintain the established Church entailed. In the case of tithes, Southey, as Espriella, rather lamely hoped that they would obey the law by paying them, 'and salve their consciences by protesting against it'.[78] Although he thought it right that dissenters should pay for the upkeep of the national Church, he did not think this amounted to an infringement of their freedom of mind. Indeed, 'except Catholics, and

---

[74] Southey to Landor, 22 May 1808, LC iii. 144.
[75] [R. Southey], 'Accounts of two attempts towards the civilization of some Indian natives', AR v (1807), 589.
[76] LE iii. 91.
[77] [Southey], 'Quakerism', 604; Southey to Wynn, 3 Dec. 1807, SL ii. 31.
[78] LE iii. 93–4.

perhaps Calvinists', most people agreed that government should not interfere in the consciences of their subjects.[79] Ultimately Southey's admiration for Quakerism indicates the resilience of his earlier moral and political ideals, even if the time was not yet right for their implementation.

The utility of the establishment

Those who wished to defend the establishment were faced with a choice. Either they could follow an orthodox ecclesiology or they could formulate a more inclusive theory. While High Church writers adopted the former position, other thinkers worried that this approach merely exacerbated ideological conflict. After all, to defend the Church in terms of its 'truth' merely invited its opponents to assert that their vision was the real 'truth'. Rather, it was better to offer a defence that critics would find hard to oppose. The most famous attempt to do this was William Warburton's *Alliance between Church and State*. Although recent historians have downplayed the influence of this work, it was widely known in the eighteenth century and beyond.[80] Warburton's arguments were deemed powerful even by those who opposed him, and there is evidence to suggest that Southey found them useful in his own writings.

The *Alliance* went some way towards keeping religion and politics separate, but also wanted to show that there were good civic reasons why the state should support an establishment. Following Locke, Warburton argued that man entered civil society in order to protect his liberty and property, and that, because salvation was possible in a pre-social state, religion was not directly concerned with its foundation. However, because questions about the existence of God, the role of providence and the nature of morality were essential to the peace and order of society, it was necessary that the state took a stance on them.[81] It was therefore useful to enter into an 'alliance' with the largest religious group because of the separate benefits it conferred on both Church and State. First, an establishment preserved the 'Essence and Purity' of religion. A Church that lacked civil protection would either wither away over time, or would become so powerful and corrupt that it could overwhelm the state. The alliance prevented both extremes. Second, an establishment made religion more useful to the state by increasing reverence for the civil magistrate, by empowering religion to promote morality and by ensuring that the Church supported the State.[82] Finally, the state avoided the civil disorder that necessarily resulted from contending religious sects. For its part, the

---

[79] [Southey], 'Quakerism', 604.

[80] S. Taylor, 'William Warburton and the alliance between Church and State', *JEH* xliii (1992), 271–86; Clark, *English society*, 102–5, 273–4, 305–6, 356–7.

[81] W. Warburton, *The alliance between Church and State*, London 1736, in *The reception of Locke's politics*, ed. M. Goldie, London 1999, v. 195–6.

[82] Ibid. v. 216–19.

Church accepted the alliance because it was protected from other religious groups and given security by the state. It was also endowed with property and entitled to representation in parliament.[83] The final part of the *Alliance* defended a test law because it was thought essential to admit only those who adhered to the national religion into public administration. All other sects, driven by 'Envy at the Advantages the Established Church enjoys, act in consort, and proceed with joint Forces to disturb its Peace'. For the purposes of security, then, a test law was imperative to prevent the subversion of the establishment.[84] In sum, Warburton tried to present a fool-proof argument for the utility of the establishment, which he hoped even critics would have to concede. His conclusion was 'THAT THE TRUE END FOR WHICH RELIGION IS ESTABLISHED, IS NOT TO PROVIDE FOR THE TRUE FAITH, BUT FOR CIVIL UTILITY'.[85]

It should be clear how far Southey's aims coincided with those of Warburton. In his early preparations for the *Book of the Church*, he read the *Alliance*, commenting to Wynn that 'It is the fashion to ridicule the alliance between Church and State; but if the one falls, the nature of the alliance will speedily be seen in the fate of the other.'[86] He repeatedly told friends that although the creed of the Church could not stand 'sound criticism', the existence of the establishment was 'an infinite blessing' to the country. At times he privately suggested that a better one could be constructed by taking the best elements from the various branches of Christianity and blending them into an 'Eclectic Church' which would become a universal faith once wisdom and morality had progressed across the globe.[87] However by 1812 his chief concern was to defend the existing establishment from its opponents, no matter that in private he could not agree to many of its doctrines. The agitation over the tithes, as we have seen, bothered him enormously, and he followed Harrington in arguing that an endowed clergy was essential for a national Church to survive.[88] His aim was therefore to stress the usefulness of the establishment, and (whether intentionally or not) he proposed ideas similar to those in the *Alliance*.

While Warburton's defence proceeded from general principles, Southey used historical narrative to demonstrate the Church's utility. His aim was to 'make the rising generation feel and understand the blessing of their inheritance'.[89] In an article on the 'History of the dissenters', he took the story back to the Reformation, in order to show the reader how the establishment

---

83 Ibid. v. 221–2, 225–9.
84 Ibid. v. 252.
85 Ibid. v. 278.
86 Southey to Wynn, 4 Feb. 1812, *SL* ii. 251. Warburton was cited in R. Southey, *The origin, nature, and object of the new system of education*, London 1812, 204–6.
87 Southey to T. Southey, 23 Jan. 1811, *NL* ii. 6.
88 See *CPB* i. 103–4. These quotations can be found in *The political works of James Harrington*, ed. J. G. A. Pocock, Cambridge 1977, 766–7, 844–6.
89 Southey to Hill, 31 Dec. 1811, *LC* iii. 321.

had prevented England from being dragged into either popery or enthusiasm, and how it had been essential for peace and happiness. He insisted, like Warburton, that during the sixteenth century it was impossible to form a national Church which would have satisfied everyone and that 'that therefore was best, which, without making any improper concession, should include the greatest number'.[90] By the seventeenth century the country was riven by competing sects who claimed to speak the 'truth' and intolerantly damned all those who disagreed. The granting of toleration was therefore a major victory for reason and liberty. However, even though dissenters were the beneficiaries of toleration, Southey believed that they placed so much stress on the right of private judgement that they frequently despised everyone else's opinions, and were accordingly prone to schism.[91] He concluded his article by praising the national Church for its ability to bind the populace together with a common culture, insisting that 'Happy are they who grow up in the institutions of their country, and share like brethren in the feelings of the great body of their countrymen!'[92] Dissenters, by contrast, remained resentful towards the establishment and continued to harbour ambitions against it. These must be resisted, for dire consequences would result 'if the principles and feelings of men should again be loosened; if the cables of faith should be cut, and they should be left to drive about at the mercy of the winds and tides!'[93] An age of 'moral and religious anarchy' would ensue which would only end when an establishment similar to the one already in existence was re-formed. This echoed Warburton's endorsement of Wollaston: 'Were it not for that Sense of Virtue which is principally preserved, so far as it is preserved, by NATIONAL FORMS AND HABITS of Religion Men would *soon lose it all*, run wild, prey upon one another, and do what else the worst of Savages do.'[94] Those who opposed the establishment had to be resisted, not because their theology was wrong, but because they would destroy an institution of great utility. If salvation was possible outside the Church, the establishment was justified because of its civil benefits.

Foremost among these was education, about which all three lake poets were passionate. Since the 1780s the education of the poor had become a central issue for social reformers, and by the 1800s the role of the Church in its provision was proving controversial. In part this was because of the Bell–Lancaster controversy. Although originally formulated by Andrew Bell, the 'Madras' system of education was popularised by Joseph Lancaster. It used pupils themselves as tutors or 'monitors' to other students, and thereby held out the hope that a basic education could be extended to the population rapidly and efficiently. Lancaster, however, was a Quaker, and while his schools did teach

---

[90] [R. Southey], 'History of dissenters', *QR* x (Oct. 1813), 93; cf. Warburton, *Alliance*, 251.
[91] [Southey], 'Dissenters', 102, 130.
[92] Ibid. 139.
[93] Ibid. 93.
[94] Cited in Warburton, *Alliance*, 216.

the Bible, they eschewed the Prayer Book. While some Anglicans were not unduly bothered by this, others were more critical. In 1811 Herbert Marsh published a sermon attacking Lancaster's system, and insisted that national education must be founded on the principles of the national religion, or else dreadful consequences would follow. He argued that this was the case even if one took a Warburtonian view of the Church, for 'its alliance with the *State* implies *utility* to the State'.[95] The National Society for the Education of the Poor was formed to this end, and directly to counter Lancaster's system, which had been given respectability when the Royal Lancastrian Institute was formed in 1810.

The lake poets became embroiled in this debate, and attacked Lancaster's system with vigour.[96] Even in the 1790s Southey had seen the educational advantages of the establishment, stating that 'I believe the best effect of a church establishment is that it places in every village of the kingdom one who has certainly had the education of a scholar & generally has the manners of a gentleman.'[97] This argument became more important once he concluded that social turbulence was partly caused by lack of education. He first encountered the 'Madras' system when he reviewed Lancaster's writings in the *Annual Review* in 1806 and 1807.[98] There he pointed out that the system of monitors had originally been formulated by Bell, but he praised Lancaster for establishing schools which could spread literacy and numeracy widely. As the success of these schools grew, Lancaster became more vocal in attacking Bell, who countered by publishing *The Madras system or elements of tuition* in 1808. In the same year, Coleridge and Southey became acquainted with Bell, and read his book. Coleridge thought the subject important enough to add a lecture to his series at the Royal Institution, despite having been verbally abused by Lancaster's supporters.[99] Wordsworth also learned of Bell's ideas from Coleridge and incorporated a discussion of national education into book nine of *The excursion*.[100] Southey, who had been present at Coleridge's lecture, had the opportunity in 1811 to contribute to the debate, which had intensified as a result of Marsh's sermon. Gifford, however, drastically edited his article, prompting Southey to issue a longer version as the *Origin, nature, and object of the new system of education*.[101]

95 H. Marsh, *The national religion the foundation of national education: a sermon*, London 1811, 28.
96 See Connell, *Romanticism*, 133–41.
97 Southey to H. Bedford, 11 June 1797, Bodl. Lib., MS Eng. Lett. c. 22, fo. 194.
98 [R. Southey], 'Lancaster's improvements in education', AR iv (1806), 732–6; [idem], 'Lancaster's plan for education', ibid. v (1807), 278–82.
99 S. T. Coleridge, *Lectures, 1808–1819: on literature*, ed. R. A. Foakes, London–Princeton 1987, i. 96–109.
100 Wordsworth, *Poetical works*, 692–4. See R. A. Foakes, '"Thriving prisoners": Coleridge, Wordsworth and the child at school', *Studies in Romanticism* xxviii (1989), 202–3.
101 [R. Southey], 'Bell and Lancaster's systems of education', QR vi (Aug. 1811), 264–304; Southey to May, 2 Nov. 1811, LC iii. 319; R. Southey, *The life of the Rev. Andrew Bell*, London 1844, ii. 625–60.

A number of important themes emerge in these writings. Bell's claim to have 'discovered' the system of monitors was defended vigorously, but this point does not require elaboration. More important were the differences detected between the two systems. One of the main problems with Lancaster's approach was its regimented and mechanistic features, evident in its liberal use of rewards and punishments. Coleridge singled this out for attack in his 1808 lecture, and Southey followed in his *Origin*, where he also noted that it was odd that a Quaker would defend the use of rewards.[102] Moreover, holding out the prospect of gain as a stimulus for behaviour was inconsistent with good morality. All would agree, Southey claimed, 'that boys should be taught their duty because it is their duty – for its own sake, not for what they are to get by doing it'.[103] The real rewards were in the exertion, esteem and happiness that followed the performance of duty. The danger of Lancaster's approach was that it trained students to think in terms of self-interest. 'Mr. Lancaster's plan of rewards', Southey claimed, 'is founded upon the system of those base-minded sophists who make selfishness the spring of all our actions; it reduced that system to practice, it establishes it as a principle of education, goes to verify it by the deterioration of feeling which it must necessarily produce.'[104] These comments may stand as a further indicator of Southey's hostility to all moral systems grounded in self-interest. Likewise, he also opposed Lancaster's extensive use of punishments, because the fear of pain and shame did not stimulate good action. Rather, it led to resentment and to insensitivity to pain which would remove, as Coleridge had noted, all fear of Newgate in adult life.[105] Bell's system, by contrast, tried to avoid punishment. Transgressions were recorded in a black book, and at the end of the week the boys themselves tried and sentenced the offender. Southey claimed that this trained boys 'in the habitual use of that privilege which is the pride of the English nation; and the offender himself knows that his punishment is awarded by rule and reason, never by caprice or passion'.[106] He also followed Bell in recommending that the rod should be spared, and even in suggesting that corporal punishment should cease.[107] More broadly, Coleridge and Southey opposed cramming, stressed the need to appeal to the child's understanding and praised the autonomy given to their learning. Overall they believed that by educating children with love it was possible to bring forth the 'vital excellencies' which contributed to the proper development of their moral selves. Education was not simply about social control, but was absolutely essential to the progress of virtue.[108]

The other significant area where the lake poets supported Bell was in the

---

102 Coleridge, *Lectures, 1808–1819*, i. 106, 586–8; Southey, *Origin*, 60–4, 81.
103 Southey, *Origin*, 83.
104 Ibid. 84.
105 Ibid. 94–6.
106 Ibid. 53.
107 Ibid. 94; Coleridge, *Lectures, 1808–1819*, i. 106.
108 Southey, *Origin*, 7–11, 52; Coleridge, *Lectures, 1808–1819*, i. 106–7, 584–6, 589. See

Anglican basis of the schools. Dissenters were opposed to this, and argued that their own children were being excluded. Southey did not find this very convincing and suspected that they were motivated more by hostility to the establishment than by principle. He pointed out that the main purpose of the new schools was to educate the poor, and it was widely known that most religious sects had both the time and the wealth to educate their own children.[109] Anyway, among the orthodox dissenters, only the Baptists would be excluded by the use of the catechism. From a more principled point of view, Southey developed a point put forward by Warburton. Even Quakers admitted to some idea of a Church, and given that Lancaster excluded Jews and deists from his schools, he explicitly admitted that some religious principles should be taught.[110] Once this was conceded there was no intrinsic reason to oppose Anglican tenets. It was better to support what was 'known and approved' rather than an untried substitute.[111] Another reason for making schools Anglican was that a neutral education loosened attachment to the religious and political establishment:

> [T]he well-being of the State must be considered, as well as the moral improvement of the individual. A state is secure in proportion as the subjects are attached to the laws and institutions of their country; it ought, therefore, to be the first and paramount business of the state to provide that the subjects shall be educated conformable to these institutions ... the national government and national religion.[112]

The state had the right to exclude people on the grounds of its 'self-preservation'. In other words, a national religion charged with education was the most efficient way to bring about both individual salvation and moral improvement. However, it was also essential to use the national religion to foster a unified culture which promoted attachment to Church and State. This coincided with Warburton's point that an established religion had a duty to support the state and in turn the state must uphold the established religion. Overall, national education was the means whereby prosperity and happiness could be securely founded.[113]

Without an establishment the state would be attacked from every side by contending sects, and the ignorance of the populace would make them easy prey for fanatics. Southey genuinely believed that the establishment was the preservative against the return of superstition or enthusiasm, but he should not be seen as a High Church reactionary. His own theology was possibly

A. Richardson, *Literature, education and romanticism: reading as social practice, 1780–1832*, Cambridge 1994, 91–103.
109 Southey, *Origin*, 112–15.
110 Ibid. 204–6.
111 Southey to J. White, 28 Feb. 1812, *SL* ii. 255.
112 Southey, *Origin*, 106.
113 Southey to Hill, 1 Sept. 1812, *SL* ii. 291.

more unorthodox than that of most dissenters, and yet bore certain important similarities to Coleridge's use of Platonism and Kantianism. But the fact that he could not agree with particular tenets of Anglicanism did not matter from a civil perspective, because without them there could be no established Church. The Church was a body justified by its social utility rather than its absolute truth. As Southey's fears about the disestablishmentarian zeal of various sects grew, he became more implacable about any reform of the establishment. Unlike later liberal Anglicans he believed that the utility of the establishment could only be preserved by resisting reform rather than conceding it. Ultimately for Southey the bridge between private theological liberalism and public ecclesiastical conservatism was the idea of utility.

5

Nations, States and the People

'Since the stirring day of the French Revolution', Southey told John May in June 1808, 'I have never felt half so much excitement in political events as the present state of Spain has given me.'[1] He was referring to the popular uprising against Napoleon's occupation, which he thought marked the beginning of European 'deliverance'.[2] All three lake poets were intensely interested in the cause of the Spaniards, and Southey fervently hoped that they would rid themselves of the Bourbons and form a federal republic. Yet only four years later the poets feared that the assassination of Spencer Perceval marked the beginning of revolution in Britain. Southey thought the only solution was a suspension of both press liberty and *habeas corpus*. As for the Luddites, 'I would hang about a score in a county, and send off ship loads to Botany Bay'.[3] This chapter will examine the development of the lake poets' politics, explaining how they could enthuse about revolution abroad, and fear it at home. The first part considers their views about Spain, and critically looks at their 'nationalism'. The second part turns to British politics, arguing that their shift from a reforming to a conservative position between 1808 and 1812 was more subtle than historians have suggested. As they saw it their aim was to preserve an enlightened polity in the face of an unenlightened populace.

The national spirit

The idea that the lake poets were early nationalists goes back at least to Dicey's work in the 1910s, but it is not without problems.[4] The term 'nationalism' was rarely used in either the eighteenth or early nineteenth centuries, and when it did appear – as in the Abbé Barruel's *Memoirs illustrating the history of Jacobinism* – it was used as a synonym for excessive patriotism.[5] The term 'nation', however, had been in common usage for centuries, referring simply to peoples of a common ancestry or culture. Samuel Johnson offered nothing new when he defined it as 'A people distinguished from another

---

1   Southey to May, 28 June 1808, SL ii. 77.
2   Southey to Coleridge, 13 June 1808, LC iii. 148.
3   Southey to T. Southey, 12 May 1812, SL ii. 274.
4   Dicey, *Statesmanship of Wordsworth*.
5   Hont, *Jealousy*, 499–503.

people; generally by their language, original, or government.'[6] From this there emerged considerable interest in establishing the features of 'national character' and understanding what implications it had for politics.[7] The 'nation' only began its career as a political concept when it was defined as modern popular sovereignty in revolutionary France. By contrast, 'patriotism' had long been a political concept, and it was closer to ideas of nationalism than has usually been thought. It is well known that patriotism was the virtue which placed the good of one's country above other considerations, and in Britain it was used to defend the liberty which the constitution provided against sectional interests. Its liberal credentials, however, were qualified, first, because it could be exploited by virtually any political figures to elicit support for their aims, no matter what their actual politics were. And second, in the international arena patriotism could be used to justify the intensely aggressive and expansionist aims of eighteenth-century states. The xenophobic sentiments associated with modern nationalism were considered by cosmopolitans to be an essential part of traditional patriotism.[8]

In 'The history of Europe' which he contributed to the *Edinburgh Annual Register*, Southey discussed how best to defeat France and free Europe. He was adamant that Britain should support 'national' movements against Napoleon rather than relying on 'oppressive' and 'faithless' governments of pre-revolutionary Europe. This approach would have called forth 'nations, which are more to be confided in than governments, and principles that are more powerful than armies, – the remembrance of old glory, and the sense of present degradation; resentment at intolerable wrong, – hatred, and anguish, and indignation; heroic pride and religious self-devotement, and joy, and hope, which is the strength of man'.[9] Southey believed that such nations could and should form independent states. Corsica, for instance, had been subjugated to Italy, France and now Britain, yet it was 'a country large enough, and sufficiently distant from the nearest shores, to have subsisted as an independent state'.[10] This required, however, a strong feeling of common culture. The people of Bohemia might cherish the idea of freedom but they had little chance of real independence. '[T]heir literature is extinct, their national pride is gone', Southey lamented, 'no Bohemian, whatever be his talents or his fortune, can now reflect honour upon his country, – he has no longer a country, it is only his native soil; his country it cannot be called since it has

---

6   Cited in A. Hastings, *The construction of nationhood: ethnicity, religion and nationalism*, Cambridge 1997, 5. See C. Kidd, *British identities before nationalism: ethnicity and nationhood in the Atlantic world, 1600–1800*, Cambridge 1999.

7   See R. Romani, *National character and public spirit in Britain and France, 1750–1914*, Cambridge 2002.

8   Hont, *Jealousy*, 502. See M. Viroli, *For love of country: an essay on patriotism and nationalism*, Oxford 1995.

9   [Southey], 'Europe, 1809', 456.

10   Idem, *Nelson*, i. 92.

been blended with the other dominions of Austria.'[11] The Balkans, similarly, lacked a distinctive culture because of centuries of misrule, revolution and migration.[12] By contrast, while there was a German culture, only the people of Saxony demonstrated 'manly and honourable pride' in their country and had 'warm attachment' to their native land.[13] Perhaps the best known patriots, however, were the Tyrolese. As Wordsworth put it, the 'herdsmen of the Alps' defended 'The Land we from our fathers had in trust, | And to our children will transmit, or die'.[14] Taken together, these diverse observations highlight Southey's belief that patriotism required a shared cultural inheritance, and a strong attachment to that tradition. Without these liberation of the nation was impossible.

These thoughts were largely forged in response to the patriotic uprising in Spain. In 1807 Napoleon invaded Portugal, and in the following year turned his attention to Spain. He forced the ineffectual Charles IV, and his heir Ferdinand (around whom a popular opposition to Charles had formed), to give up the throne in favour of his brother Joseph. He was unprepared for the popular outcry that spread across the country from May 1808. Juntas supported by local nobles were formed in the towns and provinces, and they argued that until Ferdinand was acknowledged as king, the nation was the temporary holder of sovereignty.[15] These events provoked keen interest in Britain, and the government resolved to clear Napoleon first from Portugal. This was effected in August and the armistice between the British and the French was formalised in the Convention of Cintra. However, there was widespread public outcry when its terms became known the following month, for it allowed the French army of around 26,000 men to retreat, with all their baggage, property, arms, artillery and cavalry.[16] The lake poets were horrified. Wordsworth claimed that no public event had caused him such suffering for many years, while Southey was reminded of the disgust he had felt at the execution of the Girondins in 1793. The Convention was a blatant example of the inability to pursue the war with vigour, but Southey felt that at least 'the nation has redeemed itself' by its outcry.[17] Wordsworth began work on the *Convention of Cintra*, which was eventually published in May 1809,[18] and Coleridge contributed to the debate in his 'Letters on the Spaniards' in *The*

---

11 [Idem], 'Europe, 1809', 449.

12 Ibid. 449–51.

13 Ibid. 592.

14 Wordsworth, *Poetical works*, 250. See also [Southey], 'Europe, 1809', 640–6.

15 M. Broers, *Europe under Napoleon, 1799–1815*, London 1996, 148–64; C. Esdaile, 'War and politics in Spain, 1808–1814', *HJ* xxxi (1998), 295–317.

16 P. Spence, *The birth of romantic radicalism: war, popular politics and English radical reformism, 1800–1815*, Aldershot 1996, 73–92.

17 Southey to May, 12 Oct. 1808, *SL* ii. 100. See Wordsworth to R. Sharp, 27 Sept. [1808], in *Letters*, ii. 267.

18 J. E. Wells, 'The story of Wordsworth's *Cintra*', *SP* xviii (1921), 15–76; G. K. Thomas, *Wordsworth's dirge and promise: Napoleon, Wellington, and the Convention of Cintra*, Lincoln 1971.

Courier. Southey, meanwhile, used the *Edinburgh Annual Register* to publicise the patriotic cause.[19]

The lake poets were excessively optimistic in their conviction that the Spaniards were invincible. Southey thought it 'morally impossible' that they would be subdued, while Wordsworth was sure Napoleon could not win.[20] 'So it will ever fare with foreign Tyrants', he proclaimed, 'when (in spite of domestic abuses) a People, which has lived long, feels it has a Country to love; and where the heart of that People is sound.'[21] The central point was that the Spanish possessed a strong and distinct culture which was under-pinned by common history, common manners and a common language. Even the emergence of absolutism had not destroyed it, because the Spanish were 'the only people who have undergone no national degradation when their country was degraded'. Anyone, Southey suggested, who had met a Span-iard saw the 'passionate transfiguration' he underwent when he compared his proud history to his shameful present: 'his brave impatience, his generous sense of humiliation, and the feeling with which his soul seemed to shake off the yoke of these inglorious days, and take sanctuary among the tombs of his ancestors'.[22] This love of country expressed in terms of history and memory was central to Wordsworth. 'Perdition to the Tyrant', he raged, 'who would wantonly cut off an independent Nation from its inheritance in past ages; turning the tombs and burial-places of the Forefathers into dreaded objects of sorrow, or of shame and reproach, for the Children.'[23] This sense of nation ensured that the Spaniards rose 'from one common feeling, acting co-instan-taneously over the whole kingdom'. Napoleon was a fool to think that a people with a proud culture would submit to those utterly different in 'laws, actions, deportment, gait, manners, customs' as well as language.[24]

Spanish patriotism was fuelled by religion. In explaining this to Rickman, Southey referred to his introduction to the *Chronicle of the Cid*, where he had suggested that although it was a corrupted form of Christianity, Catholi-cism had still proven superior to Islam.[25] Indeed, 'even its corruptions' helped the cause, because the invocation of saints had rallied Cid and his followers and struck fear into the Moors.[26] The same was now true of the Spaniards who invoked 'Our Lady of Battles' against the French. 'The fire flamed the brighter for this holy oil of superstition', Southey suggested. Whatever the many 'baleful effects' of 'popery' on the Spaniards, 'it has kept alive their imagination, the noblest faculty of man'.[27] Images of the virgin and the child,

---

19 Southey reused his material from the *Register* as the basis of his *Peninsular war*.
20 Southey to T. Southey, 12 Oct. 1808, *LC* iii. 172.
21 CC, 319.
22 [Southey], 'Europe, 1808', 229, 277–8.
23 CC, 328.
24 [Southey], 'Europe, 1808', 278; CC, 319.
25 Southey to Rickman, 13 Sept. 1808, *LC* iii. 169.
26 R. Southey (ed.), *The chronicle of the Cid*, London 1808, p. xxxii.
27 [Southey], 'Europe, 1808', 280.

of Christ on the cross, of saints and martyrs made a deep impact on the imagination, and were felt to be as real as lost loved ones.[28] By kindling passion and
devotion, Catholicism thereby contributed to the ardent patriotism of the
Spaniards. Wordsworth argued that although superstition was a 'stain' it had
been transmuted by 'intense moral suffering' and the 'fervent hope' of success
into something which was true religious feeling:

> The chains of bigotry, which enthralled the mind, must have been turned
> into armour to defend and weapons to annoy. Wherever the heaving and
> effort of freedom was spread, purification must have followed it. And the
> types and ancient instruments of error, where emancipated men shewed
> their foreheads to the day, must have become a language and a ceremony
> of imagination; expressing, consecrating, and invigorating, the most pure
> deductions of Reason and the holiest feelings of universal Nature.[29]

Because he did not want to offer an overly positive view of Catholicism,
Wordsworth was arguing that the cause of freedom had, as it were, burned
through the superstition of the Spaniards. As Coleridge put it, the struggle
was powered by 'insulted FREE WILL, steadied by the approving CONSCIENCE',
and expressed as the love of country, 'a filial instinct'.[30] The very morality of
the cause enabled Southey to luxuriate in a language of valour and heroism
that fused religion and patriotism: the 'whole greatness of our nature was
called forth', he recounted, as men fell with the 'feeling, the motive, and the
merit of martyrdom'.[31]

The lake poets distinguished the nation from the polity, because the former
could survive even when the latter had been destroyed.[32] Coleridge argued
that a people could struggle for political stability, but 'if it does *not* find it, and
yet the Nation subsists nevertheless, and proceeds in its career of power and
glory, *then*, I affirm, that People must have a high *national* sense and unusual
virtues, the firmness of which must have compensated for the unsteadiness
of their political Constitution'. It was not the constitution of ancient Rome
which prevented the growth of tyranny 'but an invisible feeling of the civic
virtue and dignity of their Countrymen. The life of the Republic ... was in
the *Roman character* of the Romans themselves'.[33] However, not all characters and cultures were conducive to patriotism. While the sixteenth-century
Dutch had possessed a national sense strong enough to expel the Spanish,
their character was subsequently so poisoned by colonial tyranny and
commerce that Louis XIV had overrun their country in a matter of months.[34]

[28] Ibid. 281, 320–1.
[29] CC, 293.
[30] EOT ii. 52, 53.
[31] [Southey], 'Europe, 1808', 321. See the exchange between Rickman and Southey, 20,
30 Nov. 1813, in Williams, *Lamb's friend*, 169–72.
[32] LE iii. 140–1.
[33] EOT ii. 95–6, 97.
[34] Ibid. ii. 95.

'The hearts and understandings of the higher order of the Dutch', Southey believed, 'had too long been exclusively directed to the mere object of gain; the rule of Profit and Loss was to them law, gospel, and constitution: calculation supplied the place of patriotism and principle.'[35] In other words, the character of a nation could be warped to the point where the national spirit was lost. This had not happened to the Spanish. They possessed national pride and national honour and so were 'a people worthy of being free, and virtuous enough to preserve their freedom'.[36] This led on to a broader point about the relationship between national spirit and political independence. 'A nation', Wordsworth argued, 'without the virtues necessary for the attainment of independence, have failed to attain it.' It was absurd to believe that a nation might lack 'the qualities needful to fight out their independence' and yet possess 'the excellencies which render man susceptible of true liberty'.[37] Only people with a sufficient national spirit to defend their territory would be capable of erecting a free constitution. Even then some countries – such as France – might lack the moral core required for 'true liberty'. But Spain, Wordsworth optimistically proclaimed, possessed the morality 'for as much liberty as their habits and knowledge enabled them to receive'.[38]

It has often been suggested that Burke was the source of these ideas. It is true that he viewed society as a complex web of manners and attachments, but allusions to him in the writings of all three lake poets are inconclusive at this time.[39] Many of Burke's ideas were in fact part of the mental furniture of the eighteenth century. Roberto Romani has shown that the concept of 'national character' was widely accepted, but that there was considerable disagreement about how fixed or malleable it was, and about its political importance.[40] Rousseau, for instance, thought a distinctive culture was necessary to encourage a love of the fatherland. Moses, he argued, had preserved his nation by giving it morals and practices which 'could not be blended with those of the other nations'. He had made sure that 'all the bonds of fraternity he introduced among the members of his republic were as many barriers which kept it separate from its neighbours and prevented it from mingling with them'.[41] The Neapolitan revolution of 1799 is also instructive. Some patriots argued that it had failed because it copied the manners and ideas of the French, and that the patriots did not connect with the culture of the people. A true patriot

---

[35] [Southey], 'Europe, 1810', 331.

[36] [Idem], 'Europe, 1808', 293. See also idem, *Peninsular war*, i. 2–3.

[37] CC, 237.

[38] Ibid. 229. For the French character see p. 332; [R. Southey], 'Depons' travels in South America', AR vi (1808), 75; [idem], 'Europe, 1811', 362.

[39] Southey to M. Betham, 2 July 1808, in *A house of letters*, ed. E. Betham, London 1905, 112; TF ii. 22, 123–4, 141; J. K. Chandler, *Wordsworth's second nature: a study of the poetry and the politics*, Chicago 1984.

[40] Romani, *National character*, 22–37, 39–46.

[41] J. J. Rousseau, 'Considerations on the government of Poland and its projected reformation', in J. J. Rousseau, *The Social contract and other later political writings*, ed. V. Gurevitch, Cambridge 1997, 180.

must value his own national culture for one can 'never love the country if one does not value the nation'. If the Italians wanted a *patria* they must first possess a *nazione*, or a 'national spirit'.[42] The freedom of the former required the strength of the latter. Just as traditional love of country was sustained by the common feeling of the city-state, so freedom in larger states required a relatively cohesive culture to bind the people together.[43]

The thinking of the lake poets should be understood in similar terms. They believed that nations had distinct cultures, and that the love of these cultures sustained patriotism. In this respect they differed from the patriotism advocated by Price in his *Discourse on the love of country*. He had defined country as the political community of which citizens were members, and seemed uninterested in the cultural features of a nation. He had gone on to argue that duty to one's own country should not clash with the justice due to all peoples.[44] The lake poets, however, stressed that it was natural for people to feel most for objects close to them: as Southey put it, 'patriotism grows out of local attachments'. This did not mean, however, that they were xenophobic or aggressive patriots.[45] Wordsworth was clear on this point when he argued that 'the man, who in this age feels no regret for the ruined honour of other Nations, must be in poor sympathy for the honour of his own Country'. It followed that if he was indifferent to the sufferings of other peoples, he probably lacked due regard for smaller communities. 'Contract the circle, and bring him to his family; such a man cannot protect *that* with dignified love. Reduce his thoughts to his own person; he may defend himself, – what *he* deems his honour; but it is the *action* of a brave man from the impulse of a brute, or the motive of a coward.'[46] Wordsworth's ultimate hope was a Europe made up of large independent states, which he was convinced would help preserve an effective balance of power, but it was also desirable on 'national' grounds.[47]

Meanwhile, the Spanish were trying to understand the political implications of their revolt against Napoleon. Initially the juntas exercised authority in the name of an absent king, but the idea soon emerged that after Ferdinand's usurpation sovereignty had reverted to the people and had then been invested in the juntas. The pivotal question was whether the Central Junta was the legitimate representative of the people's will, and its reluctance to give up power prevented the *cortes* from being convoked before 1810. The other major issue of controversy was what form the *cortes* would take. Moderates such as Gaspar de Jovellanos, who admired British bicameralism, preferred that it be established on the traditional basis of separate representation of

---

42 Cited in Viroli, *For love*, 109–10; cf. Southey, *Peninsular war*, iii. 927.
43 See G. Varouxakis, *Mill on nationality*, London 2002.
44 Viroli, *For love*, 96–9; Hont, *Jealousy*, 498 n. 91, 503 n. 98.
45 [Southey], 'Inquiry', 338. For a later restatement see idem, *The doctor*, ed. J. W. Warter, London 1848, 80–2.
46 CC, 329. See also p. 340.
47 Wordsworth to Pasley, 28 Mar. 1811, in *Letters*, ii. 480.

estates, while liberals such as Blanco-White and Quintana, who were more attracted to French unicameralism, argued that it should be remodelled. Spain required a 'constitution adapted to our circumstances ... that will make all of the Provinces that compose this vast Monarchy a Nation truly one; where all are equal in rights, equal in duties, equal in burdens. With it there should vanish from sight the differences among Valencians, Aragonese, Castilians, Basques: all should be Spaniards'.[48] The liberals eventually gained the upper hand, and the *cortes* met in a single chamber which declared itself sovereign. They immediately set about creating the constitution of 1812 which, as well as expanding the franchise, amalgamated all the realms of Spain into a single state.

The lake poets followed these events closely. None of them had any desire for the immediate restoration of Ferdinand, and they believed that Spain now had the perfect opportunity to rid itself of a government 'imbecile even to dotage'. 'The interests of the people', Wordsworth wrote, 'were taken from a government whose sole aim it had been to prop up the last remains of its own decrepitude by betraying those whom it was its duty to protect; – withdrawn from such hands, to be committed to those of the people.'[49] Southey agreed that the right of the Spaniards to appoint their government was inherent in the people.[50] Wordsworth believed, however, that the provincial juntas had parted with their power too quickly by establishing the Central Junta. If power had been kept close to the people it would have prevented corruption and soon disclosed talented men to take their places in a new *cortes*. Instead, a 'pernicious Oligarchy crept into the place of this comprehensive – this constitutional – this saving and majestic Assembly'.[51] Southey believed that while some kind of supreme government was necessary for the purposes of military organisation, national confidence and financial efficacy, it should have been chosen by the people and not from among the juntas. He thought that 'the people were qualified to elect a cortes by the same right in virtue of which they had chosen the juntas, – the right of self-preservation; the right of appointing a government when they were without one; the right of recovering, maintaining, and establishing their freedom'.[52] A junta composed of only eighty men could not, as Wordsworth put it, be 'an image of a Nation like that of Spain, or an adequate instrument of their power for their ends'.[53] It failed adequately to represent the interests of the country, and as it would soon be dominated by the higher ranks, it would lose the confidence of the people. Southey and Wordsworth were in agreement, then, that Spain had

---

[48] Cited in R. Herr, 'The constitution of 1812 and the Spanish road to parliamentary monarchy', in I. Woloch (ed.), *Revolution and the meanings of freedom in the nineteenth century*, Stanford 1996, 79–80.
[49] CC, 298.
[50] [Southey], 'Europe, 1808', 283
[51] CC, 318.
[52] [Southey], 'Europe, 1808', 390.
[53] CC, 318.

the perfect opportunity to dispense with absolutism and model a new government.

Southey initially hoped that Spain and Portugal would unite to form a federal republic. Both countries should rid themselves of their monarchies which were 'equally weak and unworthy in their remotest branches'.[54] He did not think that their absolute monarchs could ever be successfully limited, but he also suspected that popular enthusiasm for Ferdinand would ensure that any kind of republic was anathema. As for federalism, he hoped that each province would have its own *cortes*, and that a general congress would meet at Madrid. Ideally the national government should be built upwards from the people and the regions because this would ensure that the peninsular was united while maintaining its various provincial differences.[55] The problem Southey did not examine was whether such a state would possess the necessary common culture to hold it together. Coleridge seemed to be aware of this problem when he discussed the spirit of patriotism in the ancient world. He argued that there was a distinct Greek identity: 'Greece resembled a collection of Mirrors set in a single frame, each having its own focus of patriotism, yet all capable, as at Marathon and Platea, of converging to one point and of consuming the common Foe.'[56] In other words, distinct identities were possible within a wider common patriotism, and it is possible that Southey had something similar in mind when he recommended federalism.

At this point it would be useful to examine the links between moderates in Spain and Whigs in Britain. Although he was torchbearer of the Foxite tradition, Lord Holland differed from his colleagues in being convinced that Spain would defeat France. He believed that a *cortes* should be established as soon as possible and that the people should have a 'legitimate share in the management of affairs which, it should never be forgotten, are theirs'.[57] As a good Whig, he also hoped that Spain would reject the French-inspired ideas of the liberals in favour of mixed constitutionalism on the British model. During his travels there in 1808 and 1809 he explained that bicameralism prevented rash legislation, and made one convert in Blanco-White, who by 1810 was 'well cured of my *bona fide* Jacobinism to agree upon the great use of this separation of the representatives of the people, in order to avoid the evils of precipitation and surprise'.[58] Holland was also friendly with Jovellanos, and in May 1809 sent him a copy of the *Annual Register* for 1806, much of which had been written by the librarian of Holland House, John Allen: 'I think you

54 [Southey], 'Europe, 1808', 390.
55 Southey to Coleridge, 13 June 1808, LC iii. 151; Southey to May, 29 June 1808, SL ii. 77. See also CC, 323.
56 TF ii. 324.
57 Cited in L. G. Mitchell, *Holland House*, London 1980, 229.
58 Cited in B. R. Hammett, 'Spanish constitutionalism and the impact of the French Revolution, 1808–1814', in H. T. Mason and W. Doyle (eds), *The impact of the French Revolution on European consciousness*, Gloucester 1989, 74. See M. Murphy, *Blanco-White: self-banished Spaniard*, New Haven 1989, 53, 56–7, 65–76.

will understand the state of our parties and even the principles of our consti-tution, as much as, if not more than from any other book.'[59] Revealing his sympathy for traditional Whig thinking, Jovellanos replied that

> No one is more inclined to restore, strengthen, and improve, and no one more loathe to change or start over again. ... I distrust political theories intensely, and abstract ones even more. I believe that every nation has its own character, and that this comes from its past institutions. By some it is changed, and by others it is mended. Different times do not necessarily require different institutions, rather a modification of the old ones.

Jovellanos thought it better to modify the existing constitutional structure rather than embrace anything new. He defended old institutions not out of any dogmatic adherence to the idea of estates but because they had deep roots in national character. In any event, the improvement of education was more important than abstract constitutions. 'In a word, all that a nation needs is the right to assemble and talk. If it is educated, its liberty will always win and never lose.'[60] The following month Jovellanos read Allen's *Suggestions on the cortes*, and told Holland that the points raised in it 'are a delicacy no less sweet and agreeable than healthy and useful. Not only will I eat it, but I will chew it over to digest it better'.[61] Allen's outline therefore reveals how Whigs thought that the British constitutional model could be applied to Spain.

Allen's Whiggery was evident from the outset in his argument that while the people possessed an inalienable right to change their government, they were not qualified to form opinions about its particular shape. He wanted to retain the traditional structure of the *cortes* but thought that certain innova-tions were also necessary. The first point was that all classes ought to have a feeling for and interest in the assembly, and to that end every district ought to be small enough to enable voters to have a good idea about who their representative was. The voting system should also be direct. As in England there would be varied franchise qualifications to ensure that every interest was represented but that none – especially the poor – dominated. Turning to the division of the districts, Allen stressed that it was important to respect the customs and privileges of the system because 'no free government can subsist without a religious veneration for established rights'.[62] Therefore, the clergy and nobility should be represented, and the cities which had formerly sent representatives should continue to do so. He thought, however, that three separate chambers was too many, while

---

[59] Lord Holland to G. de Jovellanos, 21 May 1809, in G. de Jovellanos, *Obras completas*, ed. J. M. Caso Gonzalez, Oviedo 1984–99, i. 860. I thank Dr Glyn Redworth for trans-lating these references.

[60] Jovellanos to Holland, 22 [May] 1809, ibid. i.861.

[61] Cited in Mitchell, *Holland House*, 231.

[62] J. Allen, *Suggestions on the cortes*, London 1809, 10.

Reason and experience declare equally against a single legislative assembly: wherever the experiment has been tried, such an assembly has been found inattentive to forms in its proceedings, and regardless of justice in its decisions, precipitate and changeable in its determinations, and governed entirely by the popular clamour, and temporary interests of the day.[63]

An upper house was a good bulwark against ministerial artifice and popular clamour and provided a suitable home for men of gravity and experience. A place in the lower house could be occupied by any man as long as he was a natural-born subject of a certain age, sound mind and independent means. A *cortes* so constructed, Allen argued, would contain a 'fair proportion of the property and talents of the state' and would become 'the best security which wisdom has been able to devise against the excesses of power, the corruptions of justice, or the mal-administration of public affairs'.[64] Allen did not say so, but this was an attempt to export Whig constitutionalism virtually wholesale.

The lake poets held a similar view. Southey told Taylor that 'Spain has only to recur to its old constitution, long suspended but never repealed or destroyed, to be a free nation.'[65] But innovation should not be rejected. Wordsworth warned the Spaniards that veneration of antiquity should not blind them to change: 'It is their duty to restore the good which has fallen into disuse; and also to create, and to adopt. Young scions of polity must be engrafted on the time-worn trunk: a new fortress must be reared upon the ancient and living rock of justice.'[66] As long as the country possessed a popular assembly which could represent the people, the conditions were in place for civil liberty, guaranteed by law and agreed by public debate. For this reason Southey disparaged the constitution which Napoleon had tried to introduce in Spain. It was to be a *cortes* of three estates but its sittings would not be public and the printing of its proceedings was to be an offence: it embraced all the forms of a free assembly with none of its essential practices.[67] Coleridge also believed that large and open public assemblies were desirable because they were difficult to corrupt. 'The history of all free States confirms this observation', he wrote. 'It furnishes not a single instance of an individual establishing a tyranny by his influence over a representative Senate.' A large assembly was also able to retain the confidence of the people, because 'the public body elected by the public will, and the representative of the public cause, remaining distinct from the particular measures, remains aloof from the influence of their results'.[68] More broadly, assemblies provided for the emergence of talent, guided public opinion and helped diffuse public spirit.

63 Ibid. 12.
64 Ibid. 18–19.
65 Southey to Taylor, 15 Jan. 1809, in Taylor, *Memoir*, ii. 263.
66 CC, 342.
67 [Southey], 'Europe, 1808', 328–30.
68 *EOT* ii. 66, 67.

In making these recommendations, it would appear that the lake poets saw moderate Whiggery as the best way forward for Spain.

By the early 1810s Southey was becoming more depressed about the prospects for Spain. He was pleased that when the *cortes* was established in 1810 it blended 'established forms' with 'present circumstances'.[69] While the Whigs and Blanco-White (whom Southey had met in 1811) were unhappy that the indirect mode of election severed the relationship between elector and representative, Southey thought that such a system made 'undue influence or interference impossible'.[70] Of greater concern were the deputies themselves. On the one hand were the majority who were so conservative that they were unwilling to accept even a reasonable measure of press freedom.[71] On the other hand were the liberals. While Southey admired their assaults on feudalism, the slave trade, torture and the inquisition, they seemed to manifest a 'revolutionary delirium'.[72] They were prone to 'metaphysical discussions' about the new constitution: 'the doctrine of the sovereignty of the people was supported with a temper which sufficiently indicated how soon that sovereignty would become unendurably tyrannical'.[73] By 1813 he thought with Blanco-White that 'the Cortes, by their folly, will afford too plausible a pretext, and too tempting an opportunity for undoing the good which they have done'.[74] He was right: when Ferdinand was released he announced that Spain would return to absolute monarchy.[75] When in 1815 Southey met some of the liberals at a dinner in London, he commented that while he respected them as individuals (despite their atheism), they 'certainly justify Ferdinand, not in his capricious freaks of favour and disfavour, but in the general and decided character of their measures'.[76] Spain's problem was that while the small educated class of reformers who might have done good were dazzled by French philosophy, the minds of the mass of patriots were crushed by Church tyranny and state absolutism. Squeezed between these two, there was little ground for optimism: 'Alas, that the despotism of the old country, and the republicanism (how is the name polluted!) of the new, should be equally blind, equally bloody, and almost equally detestable!'[77] Southey's hopes for Spain had always rested on the belief that patriotism would lead to a desire for political and religious freedom, and that wise leaders would introduce a reformed polity to which the people were attached. His hopes failed when it

[69] [Southey], 'Europe, 1810', 484.
[70] Ibid. See Mitchell, *Holland House*, 233–4, and Hammett, 'Spanish constitutionalism', 68.
[71] [Southey], 'Europe, 1810', 505.
[72] Ibid. 492.
[73] [Idem], 'Europe, 1811', 365.
[74] Southey to Wynn, 17 Jan. 1813, *LC* iv. 12.
[75] See Southey, *Peninsular war*, iii. 906–17.
[76] Southey to Wynn, 15 Dec. 1815, *NL* ii. 127.
[77] Southey to White, 7 Sept. 1814, *SL* ii. 376.

became apparent that these thoughts bore little relation to the political realities of Spain.

Politics of the 'people'

The demand for constitutional reform resurfaced during the second half of the Napoleonic War, and was primarily spearheaded by two men. William Cobbett's immensely popular and deftly populist *Political Register* began to push the issue from 1806, while Francis Burdett became the champion of the radicals after his successful independent candidacy for Middlesex in 1807. Their reasons for supporting reform were largely the same. While some people blamed high taxation on the war, Cobbett and Burdett pointed to the prevalence of parliamentary corruption. They believed that the artificial prosperity of wartime enriched fundholders and impoverished the people. These men of new wealth lacked 'birth, character, or talents' but they were encouraged into parliament by the offers of places, pensions and sinecures.[78] In other words government patronage was not an essential component of wartime bureaucracy, but an insidious system which enabled greedy ministers to pursue their ambitions irrespective of the people's wishes or the country's welfare. A number of events seemed to be proof of this. The impeachment of Melville for misusing government money in 1806 was followed by the outcry over the Convention of Cintra in 1808. Most spectacularly, early 1809 saw the duke of York, the commander-in-chief of the army, accused of profiting from his former mistress's talent for trafficking army commissions.[79] The attempt by the government to absolve the duke seemed to be clinching proof of its corruption and arrogance towards the people. These events were followed in 1810 by the imprisonment of Burdett in the Tower for a breach of parliamentary privilege. For a brief while interest in reform was at fever pitch, and Burdett was viewed as a martyr for liberty. Many opponents of reform feared that the public disorder surrounding these events was potentially revolutionary, but after Burdett's release the furore died down.

The reforms proposed by Cobbett and Burdett were couched in terms of a restoration of the 'real constitution' established in the aftermath of the Glorious Revolution. The three issues to which they were committed were reform of representation, frequent parliaments and the removal of placemen and pensioners from parliament. The first of these was intended to combat the nomination of members by wealthy families and the purchasing of seats. It would enfranchise the propertied part of the country and therefore make the Commons a more democratic representative assembly. Frequent parlia-

[78] Cited in P. Harling, *The waning of 'old corruption': the politics of economical reform in Britain, 1779–1846*, Oxford 1996, 93.
[79] Idem, 'The duke of York affair (1809) and the complexities of war-time patriotism', *HJ* xxxix (1996), 963–84.

ments would ensure that members could be removed easily if they became corrupt. Finally, and perhaps most important, the removal of all placemen and pensioners from both houses had radical implications for the constitutional structure. The king would now be free to choose and dismiss his servants at will, and parliament would have little to do with the executive branch of government. These reforms, it was believed, would dramatically reduce the expense of patronage and enable the Commons to become a representative and independent body of the people. The pure balance of the constitution would be ensured by separating its elements and confining them to their proper functions. This, of course, had been the argument of many 'country' critics in the early eighteenth century, but Cobbett and Burdett differed in desiring greater extension of the franchise and in viewing the monarch favourably. They reserved their wrath for his ministers.[80]

The lake poets were also perturbed by the state of politics in the late 1800s. Wordsworth thought that the government's attempt to silence critics of the Convention of Cintra was illiberal, especially given that the right to petition was established in 'the grave and authentic charters' of Englishmen. The problem, as he saw it, was the amorality of statesmen, which arose 'by the very circumstance of their contending ambitiously for the rewards and honours of government, [and because they] are separated from the mass of the society to which they belong'.[81] That statesmen acted prudentially was a virtual inevitability of power. Southey felt that politics was all 'delay, blunder, jobs, and rascality' and that there was '[n]o strength of mind, no rectitude of heart, no feeling of honour, no sense of shame, among our trading politicians'.[82] The government's behaviour during the duke of York affair exemplified this, and when in March 1809 he was acquitted, Southey thought that the Commons had knowingly given a false verdict.[83] Both he and Wordsworth believed that politics required purification, but neither had any desire for revolution (although Southey did once remark that he was for a 'thorough reform, – for Forsyth-ing the rotten tree of the constitution, and, if that did not do, for planting a new one in its place'). Wordsworth thought parliament was full of 'pitiful drivellers' and believed that 'temperate reform' would be sufficient to prevent the country losing its liberties. The problem, as they understood it, was that there was too little independence and talent among parliamentary members. Whether supporters or opponents of the government, too many MPs lacked 'common honesty and common talent'.[84]

In *Letters from England* Southey offered some critical thoughts on the

---

[80] For example *Cobbett's Political Register*, 9 May 1807, 836–7; 13 May 1809, 721–3. See R. J. Smith, *The gothic bequest: medieval institutions in British thought, 1688–1863*, Cambridge 1987, 137–40, and Spence, *Romantic radicalism*, passim.
[81] CC, 285, 305.
[82] Southey to T. Southey, 30 Oct. 1808, SL ii. 118.
[83] Southey to Danvers, 20 Mar. 1809, NL i. 505–6.
[84] Southey to Taylor, 24 May 1809, in Taylor, *Memoir*, ii. 276; Wordsworth to D. Stuart, [26 Mar. 1809], and 25 May [1809], in *Letters*, ii. 296, 345.

English electoral system.[85] Many elections were shameful and violent affairs during which candidates distorted the truth and made extravagant promises in order to be elected, thereby ensuring that decent and talented men were marginalised. The control of smaller boroughs by government or wealthy individuals was so well known that vacancies were advertised in the papers. For Espriella this was necessary because 'the house of commons must necessarily be a manageable body. This is as it should be; the people have all the forms of freedom, and the crown governs them while they believe they govern themselves'. Southey was putting the usual defence of patronage into the mouth of an absolutist Spaniard, thereby giving the impression that defenders of the electoral system were equally illiberal. To reinforce the point a footnote alerted the reader: 'Spaniard! But is he wishing to recommend a Cortes by insinuating that it would strengthen the power of the crown?'[86] Clearly Southey was suggesting that government control of boroughs dangerously increased the power of the crown. But corruption of a different sort was evident in larger constituencies. Here the candidate dealt directly with the voters, who sold themselves to the highest bidder. Only in large cities was 'any trial of public opinion' made, and even there candidates used bribery and booze in order to ensure victory.[87] It seemed that nearly all borough MPs were the product of either direct control or undue influence, and so it was hardly surprising that they lacked real ability.

Here Southey diverged from the reformers. While Cobbett wanted to remove patronage to ensure that MPs were genuinely chosen by the people, Southey's primary concern was about the lack of talent in representatives. Members were chosen from among the wealthy, and such a narrow group was bound to be deficient in ability. Poorly educated, and lacking the knowledge essential for public life, they had little feeling or understanding for the 'great body' on whose behalf they legislated.[88] Sometimes poorer men were supported by patrons, but this only constrained their actions. As for lawyers, Southey believed that they were generally partisan. Therefore the two routes by which talent was thought to enter parliament were ineffective. Politics had become an established trade 'to which a certain cast are regularly born and bred' but in which 'no predisposing aptitude of talents has been consulted, and no study of the profession is required'.[89] Therefore while both Cobbett and Southey wanted MPs to be more independent, the substance of their political thinking differed. Cobbett desired that parliamentary members be tied closely to the people, and recommended large franchises and short parliaments to that end. By contrast, Southey thought that members should be the most talented persons in society, and that they should represent the people but not be controlled by them.

[85] See *LE* ii. 309–26.
[86] Ibid. ii. 316.
[87] Ibid. ii. 319.
[88] Ibid. ii. 323.
[89] Ibid. ii. 325.

An opportunity for weeding out electoral corruption occurred in May 1809, when J. C. Curwen introduced a bill to prevent the sale of seats by insisting that members took an oath swearing that no money had been exchanged. Curwen hoped that this would reduce both treasury and opposition control of seats, but his bill was resisted at every stage. Perceval knew that it would obstruct government patronage, and so amendments were introduced to remove the oath and to exclude the offer of places from the provisions of the bill. Reformers thought that these changes made it worthless, because although cash transactions were outlawed, the control of offices would remain in the hands of government.[90] Southey took the same view, arguing that while the preamble established that seats should not be purchased, the bill as a whole 'leaves the power in the Treasury, and destroys it everywhere else'. This meant that a man who used to buy an opposition borough was no longer able to 'but Government can still manage theirs, and pay for them in half a thousand ways'.[91] It appeared that the act consolidated government's power of patronage by denying it to anyone else.

Before examining Southey's turn against parliamentary reform, it would be useful to consider Coleridge's political thought at this time. Although he too was concerned about the state of politics, he was more equivocal about reform than either Southey or Wordsworth. He tried to separate off the radicalism of men like John Cartwright and John Horne Tooke from the concerns of the more respectable body of the country. As he told T. G. Street,

> I can despise as heartily as you & every man of sense the disgusting Trash of Westminster Meetings; but yet it were blindness not to perceive, that in the *People* of England, not the *Populace* – apud *populum* non *plebem* – there is heaving and a fermentation, as different from the vulgar seditions of corresponding Societies and Manchester clubs, as A. Sidney from Horne Took[e].[92]

Coleridge was strongly opposed to radicals such as Burdett and Cobbett. While he accepted that their actual ideas were not necessarily extreme, the danger arose from the way they wrote and spoke, which was certainly inflammatory. They used oratory in order to inflame the passions rather than to enlighten the intellect of the populace, leading Coleridge to consider how they could be controlled without curtailing the freedom of the press.[93] While he therefore thought that a radical overhaul of the constitution was not desirable, he recognised that something needed to be done about corruption at the top. He believed that ministers were the 'absolute Menials of the Royal *Person*' and were under 'no responsibility' and that what was needed was 'an actual dependence of the Officers & Servants of the Government on Parliament,

---

90 J. Cannon, *Parliamentary reform, 1660–1832*, Cambridge 1973, 155–6.
91 Southey to T. Southey, 6 July 1809, *SL* ii. 149.
92 Coleridge to T. G. Street, [7] Dec. 1808, *CL* iii. 137.
93 See *TF* ii. 38–87.

and of the Parliament on the People', by which he meant the respectable 'people' and not the mere 'populace'.[94] This 'venal state' of parliament might be cured by '20 additional honest Senators' who could increase, steady and direct the convictions of the people.[95] Being independent of both the crown and the people these senators would be in a position to pursue the common good and to influence public opinion. The important point was that politics could be reinvigorated without conceding ground to the radicals.

These issues were explored further in *The Friend*, which appeared between June 1809 and March 1810, and was intended to be a work of principles which would counteract the errors of contemporary morality and politics.[96] In an essay on political philosophy, Coleridge suggested that there were essentially three arguments about the rightful origin of government. The ideas of Hobbes were quickly rejected on the grounds that the legitimacy of the sovereign was based only on its ability to compel obedience and that therefore political obligation was emptied of moral content.[97] More attention was given to the ideas of Rousseau, whom Coleridge characterised as arguing that every individual had the ability to judge right and wrong and so could not be compelled to do anything contrary to reason:

> If therefore Society is to be under a *rightful* constitution of Government, and one that can impose on rational Beings a true and moral obligation to obey it, it must be framed on such Principles that every Individual follows his own Reason while he obeys the Laws of the Constitution, and performs the Will of the State while he follows the Dictate of his own Reason.[98]

For this to work, Coleridge argued, Rousseau had to have an optimistic idea of the general will. Accordingly, when the people were assembled – either in person or through their representatives – 'the actions and re-actions of individual Self-love balance each other; errors are neutralized by opposite errors; and the Winds rushing from all quarters at once with equal force, produce for the time a deep Calm, during which the general Will arising from the general Reason displays itself'.[99] As his tone indicates, Coleridge was sceptical about this. It was more probable that the popular assembly would degenerate into faction and enthusiasm. After all, the result of trying to implement inalienable sovereignty in the 1790s had been had been 'wild excesses and wilder expectations'.[100] There was no likelihood that the will of all was any more consistent with pure reason than the will of one. It was not the masses that

---

[94] Coleridge to Street, [7] Dec. 1808, and Coleridge to Stuart, [c. 4 Apr. 1809], CL iii. 137, 189.
[95] Coleridge to Southey, c. 4 Dec. 1808, ibid. iii. 130.
[96] See Colmer, *Coleridge*, 87–121; Coleman, *Coleridge*, passim; and Morrow, *Coleridge's political thought*, ch iii.
[97] *TF* ii. 98–103.
[98] Ibid. ii. 126.
[99] Ibid. ii. 127.
[100] Ibid. ii. 128.

had the right of universal legislation but reason itself which existed in no man perfectly.

Coleridge's preference was for a political theory based on prudence. 'According to this Theory, every Institution of national origin needs no other justification than a proof, that under the particular circumstances it is EXPEDIENT.'[101] Whereas morality was concerned with inner motives, politics was concerned with outward circumstances, which fell beyond the scope of universal reason. The politics of expediency meant trying to apply the moral law to practical situations rather than defining it in purely prudential terms.[102] It also followed that there could not be a single constitution for all men at all times and that the form of government ought to be related to existing forms of social organisation. From this Coleridge inferred that the shape of the constitution and the political rights it conferred depended upon the possession of property, though he was careful not to imply that it should only serve the interests of large landowners.[103] He also felt it necessary to defend the idea of a contract – that legitimate government rested on the consent of the people – even if actual contracts had never existed. Ultimately 'if there be any difference between a Government and a band of Robbers, an act of consent must be supposed on the part of the People governed'. There was, therefore, a 'perpetual' contract which was visible in the reciprocity between government and people: the 'sense of Duty acting in a specific direction and determining our moral relations, as members of a body politic'.[104] In other words the people consented to the forms of government, which were based on property and prudence, by the trust they showed for them.

In contrast to radicals, Coleridge did not believe that an individual needed to participate in politics to possess civil liberty. In this he followed long-standing arguments about the distinction between participatory freedom and civil liberty. In the *Edinburgh Review*, Jeffrey developed these ideas in response to the views of reformers. He argued that the best way to represent the opinions of the people was to ensure that representatives were those who by birth, wealth, talent or popularity had proven themselves worthy to lead the nation. Parliament should contain a sufficient number and variety of persons to express the views of every interest, it should meet often and its deliberations should be public. The effect of this would be to develop the people's awareness of their rights and interests, sharpen their intelligence and exercise their spirit. More important, if these conditions were met 'it does not appear to us, that freedom can ever be extinguished, or the rights of the people very materially invaded'.[105] Although the *Edinburgh* thought an extension of the franchise was necessary, this had nothing to do with extending political participation. Rather, it was desirable because it would reinvigorate trust in

---

101 Ibid. ii. 103–4.
102 Ibid. ii. 124.
103 Ibid. ii. 131–2.
104 Ibid. ii. 103, 102.
105 [F. Jeffrey], 'Cobbett's political register', *ER* x (July 1807), 408.

government by removing the political monopoly of the established classes and introducing a wider range of persons into parliament.[106] The essential point, however, is that whatever other differences there might be between Coleridge and Jeffrey, they both held to Whiggish views about representation: civil liberty did not require universal suffrage.

By the end of 1810 Southey had moved closer to Coleridge's position. The events surrounding Burdett's arrest and imprisonment in the Tower were an important catalyst in this shift. When Burdett insisted in Cobbett's *Political Register* that the Commons had no right to imprison the people of England, Southey thought that he should not have forced parliament to make a judgement about a matter 'better left in obscurity'.[107] Burdett's attempt to resist arrest, and the excitement this produced among the lower classes, were disturbing to Southey. He began to fear revolution, and blamed the lack of talent and principle in parliament for deepening distrust of it. A year later he explained to his brother that he had wavered in his 'good opinion' of Burdett because he disliked his description of the Commons as '*this room*' and thought that various comments on army reform were designed to 'inflame the soldiery'.[108] This echoes Coleridge's anxieties. Most suggestively, Southey disliked the way in which Burdett flattered the crown while vilifying parliament. This reflects the fact that Southey and Coleridge did not think (as Cobbett and Burdett did) that the servants of the crown should not sit in parliament.[109] Jeffrey also thought that the reforms of Burdett and Cobbett were impracticable, and argued that MPs would still seek places even if the executive and the legislative were separated. Instead, he offered a new account of the constitution which legitimated both influence and opposition. The original balance between the three estates had now moved into the Commons alone, where the influence of the king and his ministers was matched by the relatives of peers and by other members. Such a balance was preferable because it ensured that decisions emerged gradually without the violent clashes engendered by three separate bodies.[110] Southey, however, did not adopt this argument, and merely insisted that without patronage 'no ministry could last three months' and the 'government of England would be virtually dissolved'.[111]

By 1811 Southey had concluded that parliamentary reform was not only impracticable but dangerous. In the second volume of the *Edinburgh Annual Register*, aided by Rickman, he began to make 'vigorous war' upon

[106] [Idem], 'Parliamentary reform', ibid. xiv (July 1809), 290–300.

[107] Southey to Taylor, 1 Apr. 1810, in Taylor, *Memoir*, ii. 291.

[108] Southey to T. Southey, 6 Mar. 1811, *SL* ii. 214. See also [Southey], 'Europe, 1809', 242.

[109] See Southey to T. Southey, 26 Apr. 1811, BL, MS Add. 30927, fo. 184.

[110] [Jeffrey], 'Cobbett', 411–15. See J. A. W. Gunn, 'Influence, parties and the constitution: changing attitudes, 1783–1832', *HJ* xvii (1974), 301–28.

[111] [Southey], 'Europe, 1809', 289.

the reformers.[112] A key problem was the notion of the ancient constitution. The reformers who asked for 'nothing but the constitution' did not seem to realise that it had evolved gradually over a thousand years, and that, more-over, its earlier incarnations were less liberal than its present form.[113] No perfect constitution existed in the past, and Southey followed many Whigs by arguing in a common law vein that 'A system has grown up among us unlike that of our ancestors, or of any other people; and that system, such as it is, has made us the prosperous, the powerful, the free, the happy people that we are.' But at the same time he had not abandoned his earlier political ideals:

> Better systems, no doubt, are conceivable – for better men. The theory of a pure republic is far more delightful to the imagination: it is to our constitution as a sun-dial to a time-piece, simpler, surer, and liable to no derangement – if the sun did but always shine. When society shall be so far advanced that all men live in the light of reason, then we may have the dial.[114]

Once humanity was more educated a republic might be possible, but in the meantime a constitution which provided civil liberty required defending. The reformers who demanded that 'public opinion' should have more influence did not appreciate that it was fleeting and populist rather than rational and moral. The public was an 'unruly pack' who regarded politics in terms of 'immediate interests' rather than with regard to 'principles' of 'eternal application'.[115] If all elections were made popular it would do nothing to prevent corruption, for the successful candidate would still be the one who 'flattered the mob most effectually'.[116] Those elected would not be the wealthy, the talented or the respectable, but the foolish, the disappointed and the desperate. Southey also believed that reformers wanted constituents to instruct MPs rather than allowing them freedom of judgement. If placing direct power in the hands of the people had failed in Athens, then it certainly would not work among the unenlightened populace of Britain. The ultimate consequence of democracy would be anarchy, which as France had shown, was soon followed by military despotism.[117]

Did he have any solutions to correct parliamentary incompetence? He suggested that a process of filtered elections – as in Spain – might be desir-able because it was more likely to avoid corruption and produce talented members. He also proposed that the value of the 40s. freeholder franchise be increased to 'what it originally was' which would remove voting rights from those 'who cannot possibly know how to use them' and so would create

---

112 Southey to Hill, 5 Feb. 1811, *SL* ii. 213. See also Southey to Rickman, 25 Jan. 1811, *LC* iii. 295–6.
113 [Southey], 'Europe, 1809', 285.
114 Ibid. 288.
115 Ibid. 53–4.
116 Ibid. 289.
117 Ibid. 290–1.

a more educated electorate. However, he also believed that there should be no property qualification for MPs because it narrowed 'the competition of merit'. A high threshold for voters, and none for members, would ensure that elections were conducted by educated men and that they chose able men.[118] The wider problem, however, was the 'overgrown aristocracy'.[119] As he told Rickman in early 1811,

> The evil I wish to see remedied is the aggregation of landed property, which gives to such a man as [our Lord Leviathan] the command of whole counties, and enables such men as [the Duke of Northumberland] to sing 'we are seven', like Wordsworth's little girl, into the ear of a minister and demand for himself situations which he is unfit for.[120]

This trend meant that the gentry and the yeomanry were dwindling away, thereby reducing the independent propertied electorate, and leaving behind men who were heavily influenced by the large landowners. Southey hoped that in time the aristocracy would find it profitable to sell parts of their estates in smaller lots. This had, he claimed, increased the number of freeholders from 8,000 to 28,000 in Lancashire, and a similar process was occurring in Yorkshire and Norfolk. This enfranchisement of small propertied men would counteract landed dominance without extending the franchise to those who lacked property or education.[121] Finally, he also thought that the indecision of government was compounded by the lack of an 'efficient head', and suggested that there needed to be a 'responsible prime minister, to whom all departments of state should be subordinate'.[122] While these proposals were not especially thorough, they do show that his chief concern was the promotion of integrity, intelligence and efficiency in politics.

The agitated condition of the populace in the early 1810s had a profound effect on Southey. It was during the peak of machine-breaking in the midlands and the north that he connected his critique of manufacturing with his views about political reform, thereby marking the beginning of his mature 'conservatism'. The most important catalyst, however, was the assassination of Perceval on 12 May 1812. Although the perpetrator, John Bellingham, was a madman whose actions had no political significance, Southey thought that this event marked the end of the 'happiest days of England'.[123] Coleridge wrote to tell him that the tap rooms were 'shocking – Nothing but exultation – Burdett's Health drank with a Clatter of Pots – & a Sentiment given to at least 50 men & women – May Burdett soon be the man to have Sway over

---

[118] Ibid. 291.
[119] Southey to Senhouse, 26 Apr. 1809, BL, MS RP 719, fo. 7.
[120] Southey to Rickman, 25 Jan. 1811, LC iii. 296; K. Curry, 'The text of Robert Southey's published correspondence: misdated letters and missing names', *Papers of the Bibliographical Society of America* lxxv (1981), 137.
[121] [Southey], 'Europe, 1809', 292.
[122] Ibid.
[123] Southey to T. Southey, [27] May 1812, SL ii. 272.

us!' Coleridge implored Southey to write something 'on that theme which no one, I meet, seem[s] to feel as they ought to do – and of which I [find] scarcely any, but ourselves, that estimate according to its true gigantic multitude'.[124] In 'Inquiry into the poor laws', Southey analysed radicalism, and stressed two important points. First, he introduced the idea of 'sunken Jacobinism'. This enabled him to argue that whereas the reformers of the 1790s were an enlightened minority who preached 'fine fabrics of society, the diffusion of general knowledge, and the millennium of wisdom and philosophy', those of the 1810s were mere children of Mammon in that they appealed only to the greed of the poor.[125] Second, he stressed the dangerous effects of the 'epistles of the apostles of sedition' in the manufacturing districts. 'It is upon men whom that system has depraved', he argued 'that the *diatribes* of the *anarchists* operate with full effect.'[126] It was for these reasons that he genuinely feared for the future of Britain.

'We are on the brink of the most dreadful of all imaginable evils', Southey wrote, 'a war of the poor against the rich, of brute ignorance against every thing above its own degraded level.'[127] The great danger of a *bellum servile* was that it would provide the pretext for the emergence of despotism. The nation was caught between a rock and a hard place. On the one hand, in order to prevent disorder, it would be necessary to introduce illiberal measures which undermined civil liberty, but on the other hand, if nothing was done, the polity would ultimately be destroyed by the radicals. To make matters worse, while an able and responsible prime minister, such as Perceval, might have been able temporarily to suspend liberty effectively, 'he has left no successor. … [M. Wellesley] is a vicious man, and a tyrant at heart. My fears are, that what will happen, the liberties of England are in greater peril than they have ever been before; and that the alternative is, whether we shall have a despotism before a civil war, or after it'.[128] Nevertheless, he advised that the government must act firmly and immediately against the licentious press: radical journalists should be confined or transported, and *habeas corpus* should be suspended. He accepted that such measures were destructive of 'everything which is valuable in society' but they were also necessary to preserve that freedom.[129] As he had explained in the first volume of the *Edinburgh Annual Register*, when he had still supported Burdett

It would be absurd to maintain that the Habeas Corpus Act may not, on just occasions, be suspended. It is the duty of Government to omit no precautions for its own safety, but it is equally its duty, wherever circumstances

[124] Coleridge to Southey, [12 May 1812], *CL* iii. 410.
[125] [Southey], 'Inquiry', 346. See also the deleted passages reinserted into idem, *Essays*, i. 128–9.
[126] [Idem], 'Inquiry', 342.
[127] Southey to T. Southey, [27] May 1812, *SL* ii. 272.
[128] Ibid. ii. 274; Curry, 'The text', 142.
[129] Southey to T. Southey, 18 Nov. 1812, *SL* ii. 304–5. He recommended these ideas in 'Inquiry', but they were edited out. See Southey, *Essays*, i. 140.

occur which render extraordinary precaution necessary, to be especially careful that no other rigour than what is indispensable be permitted.[130]

In the summer of 1812 he believed that such a situation had arisen, and so exceptional measures were required.

What emerges from Southey's writings about Spain and Britain is moderate Whiggery. The fact that all three lake poets disliked the Whigs for their stance on the war, on the Catholic question and other issues besides should not obscure this important point. They defended the benefits of constitutionalism in the same terms as Whigs, and they realised that political structures needed to be embedded into existing national characters. Their greatest concern lay in trying to find a way to ensure that more talent and independence was admitted into parliament. Once it became apparent to Southey that the real aim of reformers was not this, but in fact the wholesale reconstruction of the constitution, he became bitterly opposed to any notion of reform. While the Whigs came to believe that some measure of reform was necessary to ensure that the interests of the nation were fully represented, Southey increasingly believed that even moderate reforms were too dangerous. He refused to define himself in party terms because he saw the issue as a stark choice between preserving government and unleashing anarchy. To his enemies this made him a Tory, but in his own mind he took a rather different view. As he explained to Wynn in 1814, 'I was a republican; I should be still so, if I thought we were advanced enough in civilization for such a form of society.'[131]

---

130 [Southey], 'Europe, 1808', 106.
131 Southey to Wynn, 14 Jan. 1814, LC iv. 57.

PART III

CONSERVATISM

6

The Future of Peace

On 21 August 1815 Southey was joined by family, friends and neighbours on the slopes of Skiddaw to celebrate the victory against France at Waterloo. They ate roast beef and plum pudding, rolled blazing balls of tow and turpentine down the hillside, and sang 'God save the king' around burning barrels of tar. 'The effect was grand beyond imagination', Southey told his brother. 'We formed a huge circle round the most intense light, and behind us was an immeasurable arch of the most intense darkness, for our bonfire fairly put out the moon.'[1] This image may serve as a metaphor for the position he found himself in by 1815. Although he was celebrating the end of war with France, he remained fearful of the threat of social and political darkness. He thought that a 'spirit' of revolution had been unleashed at home and abroad, and felt that doing nothing would be a heavy 'sin of omission'. He could see further 'than most of my contemporaries' and could 'produce such an estimate of the wants as might possibly avert great danger, or lead to great benefits'.[2] He attempted to do just that in his *Quarterly Review* essays, and his thoughts came together in the *Colloquies* of 1829. Coleridge also became a public moralist: his two *Lay sermons* of 1816 and 1817 were aimed at the upper and middle classes while *On the constitution of Church and State* in 1830 was his lasting contribution to political theory. It may, however, be doubted how influential he was in these decades. Southey complained that Coleridge undermined his usefulness by muddying his writing with obscure metaphysics 'which scarcely half a dozen men in England can understand (I certainly am not one of the number)'.[3] Whatever Southey's failings as a thinker, he believed his role as a public moralist was aided by the clarity and concision of his writing.

'An age of revolutions'

A few months after the passing of Catholic emancipation in 1829, Southey told Amelia Opie that 'You and I have lived in an age of revolutions, and the greatest, as affecting this country, and ultimately the whole of Europe and of the Christian world, is yet to come.'[4] He was convinced that there was a

---

1   Southey to H. Southey, 23 Aug. 1815, *LC* iv. 122.
2   Southey to unknown, 12 Nov. 1816, in *The manuscripts of Lord Kenyon*, London 1894, 564.
3   Southey to Senhouse, 22 Mar. 1817, *LC* iv. 258.
4   Southey to A. Opie, 30 Aug. 1829, ibid. vi. 68.

'spirit of insubordination' at work in the world, and that it had its origins in the middle of the eighteenth century. The writings of Junius and the speeches of Wilkes (whom even Benjamin Franklin had thought a 'bad' character) had made 'liberal opinions' fashionable, and had provided the intellectual impetus for revolution in America, and, much worse, in Europe.[5] This trend was fuelled by a seditious and blasphemous press which, Southey argued, had emerged in the early eighteenth century as a result of the traditional professions becoming overstocked and educated men being forced to make a living by the pen. In earlier times learning had been confined to monasteries and colleges, and had been pursued for the love of understanding, but now this new class of 'literary adventurers' had turned letters into a trade. These writers appealed to the vices and passions of the populace by peddling 'scandal, sedition, obscenity, or blasphemy', and in doing so they debased their own moral feelings.[6] The frustration of their literary ambitions also led to discontent. 'Thus it is that of mere men of letters', Southey insisted, 'wherever they exist as a separate class, a large proportion are always enlisted in hostility, open or secret, against the established order of things.'[7]

The 'age of revolution' had spread from America back to Europe. Whatever the suitability of republicanism in the new world, Southey now believed that it was devastating when introduced into the complex and hierarchical world of the old.[8] Yet, he stated in 1812, there had been a need for reforms in France: 'the people were prepared for it; and by strong government and an able minister it might safely have been effected'.[9] Had men like Jean-Joseph Mounier and Antoine Barnave won the day in 1789 this might have been possible, for they had stressed the need to reform abuses while adopting a constitutionalism that stressed historical continuity. In Keith Michael Baker's words, they were 'Burkean before the letter'.[10] While this would have been preferable, Southey accepted that it was also unlikely. The government was weak, its finances parlous, and the royal family – except the king – deeply unpopular. The lower classes were ignorant, while the higher classes were irreligious: 'the character of the nation vain, fickle, and presumptuous beyond that of any other people'.[11] Worst of all, supposedly enlightened men and women were allowed to insult and attack the government with impunity. It was no surprise, then, that the revolution quickly escalated out of control and passed into the hands of men of 'monstrous vices' and 'frantic cruelty'.[12] The people became mere pawns in the ambitious and factious games of revolu-

5 [R. Southey], 'Rise and progress of popular disaffection', QR xvi (Jan. 1817), 530, 531.
6 Ibid. 538, 539.
7 Ibid. 540–1.
8 Ibid. 534.
9 [Idem], 'Lives of the French revolutionists', QR vii (June 1812), 412.
10 K. M. Baker, Inventing the French Revolution: essays on French political culture in the eighteenth century, Cambridge 1990, 260.
11 [Southey], 'French revolutionists', 413.
12 Ibid. 428.

tionaries until by the end of the 1790s all they wanted was peace and security. The familiar pattern was thereby confirmed: revolutions created anarchy and ultimately led to military despotism.[13]

By 1814 the war with France seemed finally to be drawing to a close. The abdication of Napoleon was followed by the restoration of the Bourbons, the prospect of which did not particularly enthuse Southey. 'I never can forget', he wrote, 'whatever have been the crimes of the French Revolution in its course, and the incalculable evils of its consequences, that the feelings which occasioned their expulsion were far nobler than those which would bring about their restoration.'[14] The terms of the first treaty of Paris were generous, for France was required neither to disarm nor to pay an indemnity, and she was restored to her borders of 1792. Southey and Landor (writing as 'Calvus' in *The Courier*) were outraged, believing that while France might keep colonies that would 'never be English', her territory should have been reduced to what it was before the time of Louis XIV, and a significant amount of compensation ought also to have been paid.[15] After Napoleon's hundred days and final defeat at Waterloo, the second treaty of Paris did just that, ordering France to pay 700 million francs indemnity, to support allied troops on her frontiers for five years and to reduce her borders to those of 1789. Even harsher terms had been rejected for fear of undermining the restoration. Ultimately Southey felt that '*moderation* and *generosity*' were the order of the day, and too much 'candour' and 'liberality' had been shown in negotiations.[16] Even in 1815 he thought that France had got as much liberty as Lafayette had contended for in 1789, and, he worried, it was 'more, far more than she deserved – more, far more than she was capable of enjoying'.[17]

As for the future of Europe, Southey's opinions were mixed. He shared Wordsworth's belief that strong and independent states were essential to continental security, but he judged the Congress of Vienna only partially successful. The joining of Belgium and Holland was sensible, but ideally Germany and Italy should also have been united, while the dismemberment of Poland was despicable.[18] It also soon became apparent that the congress wanted, as far as possible, to restore the pre-revolutionary *status quo*. The Holy Alliance between Russia, Austria and Prussia was envisaged as a means to that end, and showed its teeth in response to a series of revolts in Spain, Naples and Sicily between 1820 and 1821. Southey, however, thought it was based neither on 'definite principles' nor the 'general good', and until states were more equally balanced or their policy grounded in better princi-

---

13 See [idem], 'Parliamentary reform', *QR* xvi (Oct. 1816), 230.
14 Southey to White, 12 Dec. 1813, *SL* ii. 340.
15 Southey to T. Southey, 26 Apr. 1814, ibid. ii. 351–2; *The Courier*, 30 Mar., 21 Apr. 1814.
16 Southey to May, 25 Apr. 1814, and Southey to Scott, 24 Dec. 1814, *LC* iv. 67, 96.
17 [Southey], 'Wellington', 524.
18 Southey to White, 25 Jan. 1813, and Southey to Scott, 24 Dec. 1814, *LC* iv. 14–15, 96.

ples a system of lasting peace was unlikely.[19] 'I know not what to wish for', he explained, 'when on one side the old Governments will not attempt to mend anything, and on the other the Revolutionists are for destroying every thing.'[20] In the case of Spain, his hatred of Ferdinand was undiminished, and he still fantasised about forming a republic there. He had no faith in the new *cortes*, however, because, like its earlier incarnation, it was 'unmethodical, precipitate, metaphysical, and mischievous'.[21] Moreover, he could not see any easy solutions in a country where habits of obedience and industry had been destroyed, and which needed, but could not afford, an army to restore order. Increasingly he hoped for a vigorous ministry which would introduce social reforms without creating political instability. He reluctantly concluded that 'old despotisms can better be modified by a single will than by a popular assembly; and that in countries such as Spain and Portugal, a despotic minister (like Pombal) acting in conformity with the spirit of the age, is the reformer to be wished for'.[22] Because of his desire to avoid tyranny and anarchy, he ended up suggesting that until the people were ready for reform, some states were only suited for a type of enlightened absolutism.

In the case of Britain, the optimism of the summer of Waterloo was short-lived. The social and economic dislocation caused by the return to peace was the pretext reformers and radicals needed to renew their activities. The late 1810s were punctuated by mass meetings which frightened the government into repression. While traditionally seen as years of harsh 'high Tory' rule, the government's attitude was not in fact clear cut. While some members of the cabinet, such as Sidmouth and Eldon, insisted that strong measures were necessary to destroy radicalism, others, including Lord Liverpool, thought this approach counter-productive, and hoped that radicalism would wither away with a return to prosperity. Southey knew where he stood on this issue, and tried to use the *Quarterly Review* to warn the country of the danger it faced. The government was sufficiently impressed for Liverpool to ask if he would edit a pro-government newspaper. He was flattered, but declined the offer, worrying that the government needed to do much more to resist radicalism than dabbling in journalism. As for himself, 'what *can* I do that I have not been doing?'[23] One of the reasons he tolerated the way his articles were edited was because 'the Review gives me (and shame it is that it should be so) more repute than anything else which I could do, and because there is no channel through which so much effect can be given to what I may wish to impress upon the opinion of the public'.[24] But Gifford and Murray at times pressed

---

[19] STM i. 233.
[20] Southey to Townshend, 6 May 1821, LC v. 80.
[21] Southey to Hill, 27 May 1821, SL iii. 253. See also Southey to Wynn, 26 Oct. 1822, ibid. iii. 338–9.
[22] Southey to Landor, 8 May 1823, SL iii. 389–90. See also Landor's reply, 31 May 1823, in J. Forster, *Walter Savage Landor: a biography*, London 1869, ii. 94.
[23] Southey to G. Bedford, 8 Sept. 1816, LC iv. 203.
[24] Southey to Hill, 1 Feb. 1813, ibid. iv. 18.

him to tone down his politics, leading him to insist that the *Quarterly* was 'a great power in this country ... and that power ought not to lie idle'.[25] He was, for instance, frustrated that his advice about suppressing seditious meetings and transporting radicals had been edited out of his essay on 'Parliamentary reform'. Instead, he sent a memorandum directly to Lord Liverpool arguing that radicalism would not disappear when prosperity returned. In the short term effective measures were needed to control the licentiousness of the press. The laws against sedition did not prevent an imprisoned man from continuing to write and publish, so transportation was an effective and humane solution. If such a law could not be introduced, or if juries were reluctant to convict, an alternative solution was to suspend *habeas corpus* and prevent those apprehended from publishing. 'I beseech you', he concluded, 'do not hesitate at using the vigour beyond the law which the exigence requires.'[26] After Peterloo he again warned that strong measures were needed.[27] The Six Acts were a start, but they did not go far enough, and by the early 1820s ministers seemed to have cooled on the radical threat. Southey chided them for thinking that 'all is well because the manufactures are in employ, and there is no seditious movement going on'.[28]

By this time he was working on a fuller analysis of the 'progress and prospects' of the age. The *Colloquies* was initially conceived in the aftermath of the death of Princess Charlotte in 1817 and took its inspiration from Boethius' *Consolation of philosophy*.[29] Two years later – after Peterloo – Southey was asked by Murray to write something to counter radicalism. He replied, somewhat indignantly, that he had been doing just that for a decade, and that he now needed to bring his opinions forward 'in a connected shape' and with the 'perfect freedom' that was only possible when publishing in his own name.[30] He began what would become a series of dialogues that winter. In them, Montesinos – a thinly disguised Southey – was visited by the ghost of Sir Thomas More, and they discussed the ages in which they lived and assessed how far society had progressed. The execution of this form was not a complete success, primarily because More sounded suspiciously like Southey, lending the volumes a tone, on occasions, more of diatribe than dialogue.[31] When Murray complained that the work contained too much politics to sell, Southey responded that his aim had not been to entertain, but to stand well with 'the wise and the good'. He was convinced that his opinions 'will

25 Southey to Murray, 3 Apr. 1818, *NL* ii. 181.
26 Southey to Lord Liverpool, 19 Mar. 1817, in C. D. Yonge, *The life and administration of Robert Banks Jenkinson, second earl of Liverpool*, London 1868, ii. 299.
27 See the draft 'Address to the King', reprinted in *NL* ii. 202 n. 2.
28 Southey to the bishop of Limerick, 22 Oct. 1823, *LC* v. 146.
29 Southey to Wynn, 20 Nov. 1817, *SL* iii. 79–80. See G. B. Dolson, 'Southey and Landor and the *Consolation of philosophy* of Boethius', *American Journal of Philology* xliii (1922), 356–8.
30 Southey to Murray, 10 Nov. 1819, *NL* ii. 204.
31 This was noted by reviewers. See Madden, *Southey*, 335–6.

have a growing influence, when events shall prove how well I understand the tendency, and foresaw the consequences of those errors which I have, to the best of my powers, withstood'.[32] He was, by the late 1820s, prone to see himself as a lone voice continually but unsuccessfully warning of danger while an oblivious nation plunged headlong into harm.

This pessimism was largely caused by the passing of Catholic emancipation. Throughout the 1820s Southey was greatly concerned about the future of Britain's religious institutions and gloomily predicted that sooner or later the Test Act would be repealed, allowing both Protestant and eventually Catholic enemies of the Church into the state.[33] His long-planned *Book of the Church*, intended as a 'sketch of our religious history', generated a whirlwind of controversy on publication in 1824.[34] While it garnered support from the defenders of orthodoxy, others were deeply critical because 'it struck the Catholics and Puritans with hard blows' and, as Southey predicted, neither emancipationist nor dissenter were pleased.[35] It inaugurated an extensive pamphlet war on the pros and cons of Catholicism which was played out against the background of the rise of the Catholic Association in Ireland, and Burdett's emancipation bill in England.[36] Southey itched to write a direct critique of the emancipationists, but the *Quarterly Review*, now edited by J. G. Lockhart, refused to discuss the issue until Daniel O'Connell's election for County Clare in July 1828 forced the hand of the government. Lockhart felt compelled to publish Southey's 'Roman Catholic question and Ireland' for fear of losing one of his best contributors, but he knew that it 'may not please some of our friends'. Scott was livid, and suspected that it would aggravate Catholic and Protestant animosities across the country. On this issue, he claimed, Southey was fanatical, and he advised Lockhart to 'Let him quit and be d[amne]d'. But it was too late, for the essay had already been published, albeit with 'painful apprehensions'.[37] Southey was pleased to note that George IV had wanted it to be issued as a pamphlet, and early in 1829 he was doing his best to help the Protestant cause. He sent petitions to parliament and to the king, wrote to the *Westmorland Gazette* and tried to stiffen the resolve of his friends. In return he was vigorously attacked from many quarters. In the preface to *Colloquies*, which was then going through the press, he explained to critics that since the Union he had believed that

---

[32] Southey to Murray, 19 June 1829, *NL* ii. 338.

[33] Southey to G. Bedford, 23 Feb. 1823, *LC* v. 137

[34] Southey to Wynn, 4 June 1822, *NL* ii. 237.

[35] Southey to unknown, 8 Feb. 1822, *LC* v. 112.

[36] See G. Best, 'The Protestant constitution and its supporters, 1800–29', *Transactions of the Royal Historical Society* 5th ser. viii (1958), 105–27; G. I. T. Machin, *The Catholic question in English politics, 1820–1830*, Oxford 1964; and Gilley, 'Nationality', 409–32.

[37] See the exchanges between Lockhart and Scott, 23, 26 Oct., 3 Nov. 1828, in A. Lang, *The life and letters of John Gibson Lockhart*, London 1897, ii. 32, 34, 35. See also S. Bennett, 'Catholic emancipation, the *Quarterly Review* and Britain's constitutional revolution', *Victorian Studies* xii (1969), 283–304.

what Ireland needed was social improvement not supposed emancipation.[38] He was convinced that the measure would further destabilise that country, undermining the Church of Ireland and ultimately having negative consequences for Anglicanism. He felt bitterly betrayed, especially since Catholic emancipation was passed by Wellington and Peel, men he thought he could rely on, and against, so he believed, the sound feelings of the clergy and the king, the House of Lords and the 'voice of the people'.[39]

These years were filled with foreboding for Southey. The economy dipped into depression and led to the wave of Swing riots that swept agricultural England. The general election made necessary by the death of the king in 1830 revealed the depth of feeling about the need for government to tackle the ills of the nation.[40] France, too, appeared to be engulfed by revolution. In July Charles X lost a trial of strength with the liberals and was replaced by Louis-Philippe, who promised to govern as a constitutional monarch. While Whigs and liberals in Britain observed this largely peaceful revolution excitedly, Southey feared that he was witnessing a second French Revolution. But he felt no great love for either side. If it had been in his power, he told Margaret Hodson, to 'turn the balance between the contending principles of France, – which were Liberalism and Jesuitism, – I should have laid my hand with great misgiving on either scale': he chose the cause of order but not with conviction.[41] To further compound these worries, the fall of Wellington's government in November led to a predominately Whig government committed to reform. Unlike some ultras, Southey saw no necessity for reform, and he greeted it with horror. For the next year he followed its progress with avid trepidation, continually hoping it would fail, and insisting it would do nothing to help the agricultural and manufacturing poor. He was particularly incensed by the way the government appeared to cave in to the political unions and the radical press, and by the manner in which it used the 'mob' to coerce the Lords into passing reform. By the summer of 1832 Southey had seen four exhausting years during which, to his mind, the entire fabric of Church and State had been completely unravelled.[42]

Whether in Britain, Europe or America, he detected movements which were deeply opposed to established religious and political forms. He referred to them by various names – faction, sedition, irreligion, anarchism, radicalism – depending on the context of discussion, but he increasingly used the word 'liberal' to designate this 'spirit'. By the 1820s he was making reference to 'Revolutionary *liberalism*' – the italicisation indicating he was dealing with a recent coinage.[43] He was 'thankful for the word, – it is well that we

---

38 *STM* i, pp. xiii–xv. See *LC* vi. 24–48 passim.
39 [R. Southey], 'Moral and political state of the British empire', *QR* xliv (Jan. 1831), 289.
40 J. Parry, *The rise and fall of liberal government in Victorian Britain*, London 1993, 58–65.
41 Southey to M. Hodson, 10 Sept. 1830, *LC* vi. 115.
42 *LC* vi. 40–182 passim.
43 [R. Southey], 'Grégoire: history of the religious sects', *QR* xxviii (Oct. 1822), 19.

should have one which will at once express whatever is detestable in principle, and flagitious in conduct'.[44] To resist this 'spirit' of liberalism a new approach to politics was needed, and a new term came into circulation. The idea of 'conservative' principles filtered into Britain from French debate, and Southey was one of the first persons to use the term. He made reference to a 'vis conservatrix in the state' in 1816 and two years later noted that Clarendon's History of the rebellion had strengthened 'my hope in the conservative principles of society'.[45] By the early 1830s the term 'conservatism' had come into wider usage. However, Southey did not think these new terms mapped easily onto party labels, and he thought it necessary to reconceptualise the political landscape. The struggle was not between Whigs and Tories, or 'ins' and 'outs', but, across Europe, between 'the old and new systems of government, – that is, government by authority, and government by popular impulse'.[46] He had hoped that during the reform crisis the Whigs would realise that the conflict was 'between the mob and the government, between the conservative and the subversive principles, between anarchy and order'. 'There were but two parties in the country', he believed, 'that which sought to overthrow the constitution, and that which was resolved to support it: in these broad distinctions, all minor ones must, sooner or later, be merged; and this truth could not be recognized too soon for the constitutional cause and the general good.'[47]

History and the public voice

While he espoused 'conservatism', Southey was no simple reactionary. This is evident from the Colloquies, where fulsome praise and lengthy quotation was accorded to Kant's manifesto for progress, the Idea for a universal history from a cosmopolitan point of view.[48] Southey's fears about revolution, however, meant that contemporaries often lost sight of his faith in the future. Indeed he even used the allegorical part of the Poet's pilgrimage to Waterloo of 1816 to rehearse the grounds for optimism. There an 'Old Man' taunted 'The Poet' that after twenty-five years of war, Europe was no more improved than at the outset, and that beliefs about 'Liberty and Truth' and 'Rights Omnipotent of Equal Man' had come to nothing. There was only one conclusion: 'The

---

44 [Idem], 'Progress of infidelity', ibid. xxviii (Jan. 1823), 510.

45 [Idem], 'Works on England', ibid. xv (July 1816), 573; Southey to Rickman, 1 Sept. 1818, SL iii. 95. See J. J. Sack, From Jacobite to conservative: reaction and orthodoxy in Britain c. 1760–1832, Cambridge 1993, 1–7.

46 [R. Southey], 'Doctrine de Saint Simon: new distribution of property', QR xlv (July 1831), 434.

47 [Idem], 'British empire', 315.

48 STM ii. 408–13. He was quoting De Quincey's translation from the London Magazine in 1824. See The works of Thomas De Quincey, ed. B. Symonds and others, London 2000–3, iv. 204–16.

present and the past one lesson teach! | Look where thou wilt, the history of man | Is but a thorny maze, without a plan!'[49] As he felt the weight of despair growing on him, however, 'The Poet' was told by 'The Monitress Divine' that his hopes for Europe would one day be fulfilled but that he should not trust to 'innovations premature'.[50] She explained that there was purpose in history. Though 'the ways | Of Providence mysterious we may call', they should still be a source of comfort:

> For through the lapse of ages may the course
> Of moral good progressive still be seen,
> Though mournful dynasties of Fraud and Force,
> Dark Vice and purblind Ignorance intervene;
> Empire and Nations rise, decay and fall,
> But still the Good survives and perseveres thro' all.[51]

Southey took solace in this view, and whenever calamities, whether personal or public, seemed to be raging all around, it was to this that he returned. 'And now, you will ask', he wrote to Hodson during the emancipation crisis, 'where do I look for comfort? Entirely to Providence. I should look to nothing but evil from the natural course of events, were they left to themselves; but Almighty Providence directs them, and my heart is at rest in that faith.'[52] He retained a conviction that the condition of the world could and would be improved and that 'of the moral and physical evils which afflict mankind, many, very many, are remediable'.[53] But he did not assume that the flow of time was necessarily heartening. Whereas the advocates of the 'march of intellect' sometimes implied that all change was progressive, Southey was more fearful of retrogression.

It was commonly thought in the early modern period that the rise and fall of nations was inevitable. Just as individuals experienced birth and death, so too did political communities. This Machiavellian view of the 'cycle of commonwealths' was still being expressed in the eighteenth century, even though its advocates thought that the day of final dissolution could be staved off for a long time. Even a supposed pessimist like Adam Ferguson opposed the idea of inevitable decline and argued that societies continually renewed themselves.[54] Southey's providential thinking provided him with an explanation and a solution to decline. He was hardly unusual, as Boyd Hilton has shown, in seeing the hand of God in the affairs of man, but he believed that God's special intervention was restricted to nations rather than to individuals.[55] While a person was judged for their deeds after death, the fact that

49 R. Southey, *The poet's pilgrimage to Waterloo*, London 1816, 126, 132.
50 Ibid. 146.
51 Ibid. 165.
52 Southey to Hodson, 10 Feb. 1829, *LC* vi. 24.
53 [R. Southey], 'The poor', *QR* xv (Apr. 1816), 189.
54 D. Spadafora, *The idea of progress in eighteenth-century Britain*, New Haven 1990, 274.
55 Hilton, *Age of atonement*, 10–17.

nations only existed temporally meant that they must be judged on earth. It hence followed that the rise and fall of nations could be explained by their deeds.[56] It was unsurprising, therefore, that at the height of the reform crisis, Southey feared that the arrival of cholera was divine punishment, though he hoped it was a product of God's mercy rather than his vengeance.[57] This line of thinking, however, also meant that a nation could save itself. Southey noted Tacitus' arguments about the difficulties of preserving a good constitution, but suggested this was not because there was 'any inherent principle of change and decay and dissolution in political institutions and empires, as there is in the microcosm of man'. This, he claimed, was a common error and in fact the analogy could be switched around. Man had been made immortal but his sinful disobedience had enabled death to enter the world. The same could be said of communities: 'perpetuity, which is physically impossible for us in our fallen state, is surely possible for social bodies'. If they lacked strength they could be overthrown, 'but if they perish by decay or corruption, or any other causes from within, want of wisdom and of virtue is the primary cause, and the destruction which comes upon them is at once the natural consequence and the rightful punishment'.[58] If communities obeyed the will of God they would endure and progress, but if they deviated they would face decline and eventually destruction.

From the 1810s Southey increasingly defined himself as an historian, professing to prefer the 'calmer pleasures' of history because it excited the passions less than poetry.[59] He produced two lengthy pieces of formal history. The *History of Brazil* was published between 1810 and 1819, while the *History of the peninsular war* appeared between 1823 and 1832. He was extremely proud of both works, and ventured to hope that 'I shall ultimately hold a higher place among historians (if I live to complete what is begun) than among poets'.[60] *Brazil*, however, scarcely paid for its own materials, and by 1818 Southey had received less for it than for a single article in the *Quarterly Review*.[61] Although it was financially impossible for him to devote his time to works of historical scholarship, he founds outlets for his historical enthusiasms in nearly all that he wrote. Broadly, he followed the precepts of the neoclassical approach to history, or as the *Monthly Review* put it, 'the authority of the antients'.[62] He favoured linear narratives which aimed to be a true

[56] See [R. Southey], 'On the means of improving the people', QR xix (Apr. 1818), 90–1; [idem], 'Chronological history of the West Indies', ibid. xxxviii (July 1828), 234; and [idem], 'Barante: Histoire des ducs de Bourgogne', Foreign Review i (1828), 44.

[57] For example Southey to May, 18 Feb. 1832, LC vi. 179.

[58] [Southey], 'British empire', 267, 268.

[59] Southey to Montgomery, 26 Mar. 1812, in J. Holland and J. Everett, Memoirs of the life and writings of James Montgomery, London 1854, ii. 335.

[60] Southey to White, 8 Jan. 1816, LC iv. 147.

[61] Southey to J. T. Coleridge, 8 Sept. 1818, in W. Braekman, 'Letters by Robert Southey to Sir John Taylor Coleridge', Studia Germania Gandensia vi (1964), 113.

[62] Cited in Madden, Southey, 151. See P. Hicks, Neoclassical history and English culture: from Clarendon to Hume, Basingstoke 1996; J. G. A. Pocock, Barbarism and religion, II:

record of the past, and he avoided authorial digressions in the text, prefer-ring to place such material in notes. He also opposed the fashion for dividing history into its constituent parts (political, military, religious, literary and so on) because he felt that in order to understand 'their mutual connexion, their influence and dependence' it was better to bring all elements together into a narrative 'which proceeds according to the course of time and events, and records things as they are intermingled in the multifold concerns of society'.[63] He spent considerable time and effort – too much for many reviewers – gath-ering printed and manuscript sources, and claimed to be careful in using evidence: checking the sincerity of a document, weighing probabilities when dealing with conflicting sources, and trying not to claim more than was prov-able.[64] In the conclusion to the final volume of the *History of Brazil* he made it clear that he estimated the value of a history according to 'the store of facts which it has first embodied, to the fidelity with which they are recorded, and to the addition which thereby is made to the stores of general knowledge'.[65] 'I may be deceived concerning my own power', he claimed, 'but knowing what the duties of a historian are, those duties I know I have performed.'[66]

Unsurprisingly, he was not generally impressed by what he called philo-sophical history, and for two main reasons. First, he detected a tendency to be deterministic among some historians, though he named Guizot as 'the ablest of the class'. They 'carry the influence of general causes too far, consid-ering men as entirely the creatures of the circumstances wherein they are placed, and regarding them rather as the puppets of a fatal necessity, than as accountable beings, to whom it has been free to choose between good and evil'.[67] Second, he thought it ironed out factual complexity in order to disguise bias. Henry Hallam's *Constitutional history*, for instance, was the work of a 'decided partisan' which should be treated with suspicion because 'it deals in deductions and not in details'. More generally, Southey was critical of the way political history had become suffused with party bias. 'The historian who suffers himself to be possessed by this evil spirit', he loftily claimed, 'contracts an obliquity of moral vision; his views are narrowed; his understanding is warped; his sense of right and wrong is perverted; he has ceased to be just, and, therefore, he can no longer be generous.'[68] It was, then, to be a supreme irony that these were all things that Southey's own writings were charged with.

Narratives of civil government, Cambridge 1999; and M. S. Phillips, *Society and sentiment: genres of historical writing in Britain, 1740–1820*, Princeton 2000.
[63] [R. Southey], 'Hallam's constitutional history of England', *QR* xxxvii (Jan. 1828), 194.
[64] Southey to T. Burgess, 12 Apr. 1830, in J. S. Harford, *The life of Thomas Burgess, bishop of Salisbury*, London 1840, 463.
[65] *HB* iii. 879.
[66] Southey to Montgomery, 26 Mar. 1812, in Holland and Everett, *Memoirs*, ii. 335.
[67] [Southey], 'West Indies', 196. See also 'Histoire', 1–3.
[68] [Idem], 'Hallam', 195, 198.

Widely perceived as a reactionary turn-coat, Southey was thought to use his writings to peddle his own propaganda. His *Life of Wesley* brought criticisms from Methodists, and a proposed life of George Fox led anxious Friends to hope that their founder would be presented in a true light.[69] But it was the *Book of the Church* which was to be the most controversial. Because he intended it to be a manual for youth and not a work of research, Southey did not supply the usual references. His friends who told him that this was a mistake were proved right. *The Examiner* thought it a work of 'dogmatical arrogance', a 'tissue of misrepresentation and falsehood' written with a 'bold contempt of historical truth'.[70] The Catholic author John Milner pointed out that the Greek word for poet could also be translated as 'maker' or 'inventor', and so was not surprised that Southey 'makes use of his poetical license or faculty in writing history, rather than weary himself in hunting and bringing forward dusty records for the many extraordinary things he describes and tells'.[71] Similarly, Charles Butler made much of the absence of references in his *Book of the Roman Catholic Church*. This gave Southey the perfect opportunity to initiate a defence using copious supporting material. Even at over 500 pages, *Vindiciae Ecclesiae Anglicanae* was only half his intended reply. He explained why he had not supplied notes, but conceded that their absence 'is a point of more consequence to my reputation than I seemed to esteem it'. But he insisted on the veracity of his work, noting how a sceptical Catholic reader of the *History of Brazil* had become so convinced of 'my perfect fidelity as an historian, that he wrote to tell me what he had done'.[72] In writing history, he explained, he tried to represent all people in 'the truest light', and when offering moral verdicts always to be fair. 'Judging of actions by the immutable standard of right and wrong, I have endeavoured to judge men according to the circumstances of their age, country, situation, and even time of life, glad to discover something which may extenuate the criminality of the agent, even when I pronounce the severest condemnation of the act.'[73] The controversy over the *Book of the Church* shows clearly that Southey took attacks on his integrity as an historian very seriously indeed.[74]

Although writing history added to the 'stores of general knowledge', its use extended beyond that. De Quincey made a perceptive point. He suggested that although Southey was an 'anti-philosophical historian' because he preferred facts to 'preconceived theories', his 'high moral feelings' meant that 'he gives to his narrative an interest of another and a universal kind, which in some degree supplies a more philosophical character: so that he is

---

[69] See the exchanges with Bernard Barton about the 'Life of Fox': *SL* iii. 210–11; *LC* v. 47–8; *Selections from the poems and letters of Bernard Barton*, London 1849, 115, 117–18; and 'On Southey's histories of religious sects', *London Magazine* iii (1821), 637–41.

[70] Cited in Madden, *Southey*, 311, 312.

[71] [J. Milner], *Strictures on the poet laureate's* Book of the Church, London 1824, 4.

[72] R. Southey, *Vindiciae Ecclesiae Anglicanae*, London 1826, 44.

[73] Ibid. 45–6.

[74] See [idem], 'Hallam', 217–20.

quite as far removed as the most transcendental of theorists from the mere annalist'.[75] Southey's beliefs about providential religion and national progress were embedded in his approach to history, and ensured that lessons could be learned from the past. He quoted with approval Raleigh's dictum that history could be used to form wise policy 'by the comparison and application of other men's fore-passed miseries with our own like errors and ill-deservings'.[76] To the statesman, Southey suggested, history was like compass and chart to the sailor, but unfortunately 'our politicians are continually striking upon rocks and shallows' because they lacked familiarity with it.[77] Machiavelli's *Discourses* had shown that the misgovernment of states had 'arisen more from the neglect of that experience, – that is, from historical ignorance, – than from any other cause'. But, in contrast to Machiavelli, Southey believed that there was no clash between what history taught was expedient and what morality taught was true, because God's governance of the world ensured that they amounted to the same thing. So the 'sum and substance' of history consisted of 'general principles', and he who understood them 'has always, in the darkest circumstances, a star in sight by which he may direct his course surely'.[78] Hence the 'upright minister' may trust to the guidance of the Gospel and providence: 'for as national sins bring after them in sure consequence their merited punishment, so national virtue, which is national wisdom, obtains in like manner its temporal and visible reward'.[79]

While his friends and family saw him as an honest and modest man, those who knew Southey less well assumed he was calculating and haughty. There were two central reasons why he was a relatively ineffective public moralist: his political 'apostasy' and his polemical style. The *Wat Tyler* controversy vividly underlined the former, and, as we have seen, was exploited to the full by Hazlitt. Take the *Universal Review*, for instance, which attacked Southey as a mere literary opportunist: 'Nelson dies – a midshipman's duodecimo! The quartos are anticipated. Portugal is at odds with Brazil – a *History of Brazil*, ready to go off with the first gun, two quartos.' The staccato style and military metaphors give the impression of a writer who was ruthlessly efficient at maximising gain. He was 'a laureate of all trades' who possessed 'a commercial keenness equally dexterous, practiced and profitable'.[80] This was far from the truth, but it stuck none the less. Southey's style did nothing to dislodge this image, although he was in fact rather proud of the way he wrote. He claimed to have three rules: to be as perspicuous as possible, as concise as possible and as impressive as possible. 'This is the best way to be understood, and felt, and remembered.'[81] In his political journalism this directness often

---

75 De Quincey, *Works*, v. 170.
76 Cited in [Southey], 'Hallam', 198.
77 STM ii. 353.
78 Ibid. ii. 354–5.
79 Ibid. ii. 360–1.
80 Cited in Madden, *Southey*, 309–10.
81 Southey to Elliot, 9 Feb. 1810, LC iii. 275.

involved savage condemnations of opponents which rested as much on vivid images and moralistic contrasts as on sustained argument.[82] Butler was particularly scathing about Southey's style. In an age of 'temper and philosophy', he wrote, scholarly debate should be conducted with 'decency and politeness' and *'polemic* abuse' banished from 'all the liberal parts of society'. Southey, he claimed, adopted a *'harsh style of controversy'*, while Catholic writers avoided 'intemperate language' and 'illiberal invective'.[83] In effect Butler the Catholic was presenting Southey the Protestant as an intolerant fanatic. In reply, Southey insinuated that while Butler used the 'smoothest language' to conceal falsehood, he would not himself 'affect a reputation for candour, (as that term is now abused,) by compromising principles of eternal importance' and nor was 'that current *liberality* to be expected from me' which refused to condemn vice and praise virtue. In essence he was claiming that a 'liberal' manner concealed a moral relativism which he opposed, and that his own style was not the result of 'want of temper' but of a need to convey what was 'distinctly perceived and strongly felt' in the most important subjects.[84]

It had little effect. Southey's opponents were invited by his changing political views and his vituperative style to undermine his claims to speak authoritatively, and thereby silence the effectiveness of his public voice. The *Colloquies* were attacked in this vein. The *Westminster Review* thought Southey an advocate of the 'statesmanship of Strafford, and church-government of Laud', and so presented his opinions as outside the pale of conventional political discourse. He was one of the most 'wrong-headed men in England – the most astounding churchman, the most indescribable politician, the weakest logician, the wildest theorist, and the poorest philosopher, in Christendom'.[85] The young Thomas Macaulay hammered the point home. For Southey, 'reason has no place at all. ... He does not seem to know what an argument is'. 'A chain of associations is to him what a chain of reasoning is to other men ... what he calls his opinions, are in fact merely his tastes.' In effect it was not really necessary to unpick Southey's arguments because they were not 'a matter of science' but 'a matter of taste and feeling'.[86] Southey, of course, had his defenders in the *Quarterly*, *Blackwood's* and *Fraser's*. William Maginn suggested that he had probably forgotten more than Macaulay knew, and that just because he did not write with 'philosophical knottinesses and metaphysical intertwistings' did not detract from the importance of what he wrote. 'General history ... has been Mr. Southey's favourite branch of study and "*History is Philosophy teaching by example*".' If *Fraser's* was unsuccessful in

---

[82] Wynn begged Southey to adopt a conciliatory tone. See Southey to Wynn, 26 Mar., 6 Apr. 1817, *SL* iii. 68–9.

[83] C. Butler, *The book of the Roman Catholic Church*, London 1825, 216, 346. See Gilley, 'Nationality', 424–5, 430–1.

[84] Southey, *Vindiciae*, pp. xii, 46, 274.

[85] [Anon], 'Dr. Southey's Sir Thomas More', *Westminster Review* xi (July 1829), 194, 211.

[86] [T. B. Macaulay], 'Southey's colloquies on society', *ER* l (Jan. 1830), 529, 528, 533.

defending Southey from Macaulay's attack, it did at least understand something of the method of Southey's moralism.[87]

Less than a month after celebrating Waterloo on Skiddaw, Southey set off with family and friends to visit the site of the battle. This was to be his first time on the continent since leaving Portugal in 1801, and he used his experiences as the basis for the *Poet's pilgrimage*. The key events were recounted in reflective moments as 'The Poet' traversed the fields that had so recently seen bloodshed. Overall the mood is more contemplative than exultant. Southey dwelled at some length on the traces that the carnage had left – hoof prints in the earth, the sudden stink of exposed flesh, a streak of blood on a wall.[88] He was struck by how quickly signs of battle had been covered up. 'Was it a soothing or a mournful thought', the poet asked, 'To mark how gentle Nature still pursued | Her quiet course, as if she took no care | For what her noblest work had suffer'd there.'[89] The first half of the poem concluded by considering the people who lived near Waterloo, and who feared that they would never enjoy peace. Instead, they looked back to the times of their fathers 'Ere the wild rule of Anarchy began, | As to some happier world, or golden age of man'.[90] In the final stanza one detects some of Southey's own hopes and fears:

> One general wish prevail'd, – if they might see
> The happy order of old times restored!
> Give them their former laws and liberty,
> This their desires and secret prayers implored; –
> Forgetful, as the stream of time flows on,
> That that which passes is for ever gone.[91]

87 [W. Maginn], 'The *Edinburgh Review*; Mr Thomas Babbington Macaulay and Mr Southey', *Fraser's Magazine* i (June 1830), 591. See also [J. J. Blunt], 'Southey's colloquies on the progress and prospects of society', *QR* xli (July 1829), 1–27, and [S. O'Sullivan], 'Colloquies on the progress and prospects of society, by Robert Southey', *Blackwood's Magazine* xxvi (Oct. 1829), 611–30.
88 Southey, *Poet's pilgrimage*, 67, 68, 73.
89 Ibid. 74.
90 Ibid. 96.
91 Ibid. 98.

7

Civilising Peoples

'"Be fruitful, and multiply, and replenish the earth and subdue it." This', wrote Southey in 1812, 'was the first great commandment given for collective security, and what country has ever been so richly empowered to act in obedience to it as England at this day?' He proclaimed that 'The seas are ours, and to every part of the uninhabited or uncivilized world our laws, our language, our institutions, and our Bible may be communicated.'[1] This militant imperialism was not simply a necessity created by the exigencies of war, but was central to Southey's thinking about empire. He was aware that he was living in a time of transition. Until the middle of the eighteenth century, it was relatively easy to view the 'empire of the seas' as maritime and commercial: the British empire was Carthage not Rome. By the time of the Napoleonic War, however, Britain found itself in possession of an empire that was territorially vast, religiously varied and ethnically diverse. This posed enormous challenges of authority. While it was recognised that central rule needed to be asserted more strongly, it was also accepted that diverse legal systems and religious attachments should be tolerated if the newly acquired empire were to be stable and secure. Southey was preoccupied with these issues: his interest in world history, travel accounts and missionary literature formed the basis not just of many essays in the *Annual* and *Quarterly Reviews*, but also of his series of mythological poems and the *History of Brazil*. While he was rarely engaged with the politics and economics of empire, he was passionately attached to the idea of a civilising mission to the uncivilised world.

The 'melancholy map' of the world

Savagery, barbarism, civilisation: these were the terms by which thinkers typically classified the states of society across the globe. The eighteenth century pioneered natural histories of society – sometimes known as the 'four stages theory' – which were themselves an outgrowth of natural law accounts of the origins of property. They were designed to explain how some parts of the world had attained civilisation while others languished in barbarism or even savagery. In explicating the nature of these different states, thinkers drew on an expanding range of ethnographic material. America, for instance, was especially important in constructing the typical features of savage life. It was shown how under the pressure of population growth and depletion of

---

[1] [Southey], 'Inquiry', 355–6.

natural resources, societies shifted their mode of subsistence: hunting and gathering was replaced by the pastoral or shepherding stage, which was in turn succeeded by agriculture.[2] While some thinkers preferred to keep natural history distinct from sacred history, others attempted to find ways in which these two accounts could coexist.[3] Another important element of 'conjectural history' was the way it stressed that the progress of opulence brought with it the softening and refinement of manners and therefore a 'civilised' society. It was dissatisfaction with the state of this civilisation among some thinkers, most notably Rousseau, but also to some extent Diderot, which helped fuel the idea of the 'noble savage'. Drawing on information from North America and the South Seas, they argued that the 'savage' presented a picture of humanity in its uncorrupted form. This argument could be used to highlight negative features of modern societies, but also to provide a critique of imperialism by making a case for the incommensurability of widely different cultures.[4]

Southey was greatly interested in the state of civilisation (or rather the lack of it) across the world. Borrowing a phrase from Edward Young's *Night thoughts*, he wrote of the 'melancholy map' of the world and lamented that a large part of it was possessed either by 'savages' or 'by nations whom inhuman despotisms and monstrous superstitions have degraded in some respects below the savage state'.[5] He firmly dismissed the idea that the savage state was preferable to the social, claiming in the *Colloquies* that the notion 'never for a moment deluded me: not even in the presumptuousness of youth, when first I perused Rousseau'.[6] Inevitably, the theme of the 'noble savage' was a frequent target. 'Anti-Christian Philosophists', and even men of 'healthier intellect and sounder principles', had been beguiled by erroneous accounts of Tahiti, and had concluded that its inhabitants were closer to nature than civilised men.[7] Southey believed that these islanders practised infanticide and cannibalism, and so anyone who presented them as exemplars of savage innocence was woefully mistaken. As he insisted in one letter, it was 'stark naked nonsense' to assume that the savage state was 'the state of nature' because savage man was 'a degenerated animal'.[8] Accounts of 'savage' life drawn from America and Polynesia did not offer a window on humanity before corruption but were themselves examples of a form of corruption. It followed that in the beginning all the world was not America.

---

[2] See R. L. Meek, *Social science and the ignoble savage*, Cambridge 1976; A. Pagden, 'The defence of "civilisation" in eighteenth-century social theory', *HHS* i (1988), 33–45; and B. Buchan, 'The empire of political thought: civilisation, savagery and perceptions of indigenous government', ibid. xviii (2005), 1–22.

[3] Pocock, *Barbarians*, passim.

[4] S. Muthu, *Enlightenment against empire*, Princeton 2003.

[5] *STM* i. 61, 62. See E. Young, *Night thoughts*, ed. S. Cornford, Cambridge 1989, 44.

[6] *STM* i. 45.

[7] [R. Southey], Transactions of the missionary society vol i', *AR* ii (1804), 199, and [idem], 'Transactions of the missionary society in the South Sea islands', *QR* ii (Aug. 1809), 45.

[8] Southey to Rickman, 15 Jan. 1806, *LC* iii. 16.

Southey accepted that there was a sliding scale of savagery to barbarism to civilisation, but he often slipped into a binary distinction between the civilised and the uncivilised. This is important because he was writing at a time when definitions of 'civilisation' were altering. The 'orientalists' who increased western knowledge about the language, history and culture of India were inclined to admire this civilisation, but by the early nineteenth century, radicals like James Mill were arguing that its respect for tradition impeded progress, while missionaries drew attention to customs and practices – notably sati – which appeared to undermine its claims to be civilised.[9] Southey was beginning to share the concerns of the missionaries against the orientalists. In 1804 his brother Henry asked for advice about an essay competition on how to civilise India. 'Your prize question seems oddly worded', Robert replied, 'for, in the common acceptance of civilization, Hindostan is a highly civilized country.' But, he went on, 'If it means, how are the Hindoos to be brought to the standard of European civilization? – that is, how are they to be converted? – I can furnish you with some valuable facts.'[10] This tension between civilisation meaning complex social organisation and civilisation meaning advanced moral practices was also central to *Madoc*. It dealt with the Aztecas, the fictional forerunners of the Mexicans, and their relations with the simple and peaceful Hoamen, whom they have displaced. The Aztecas were superior in the technical arts of civilisation, having built the mighty city of Aztlan, but they were also a polytheistic and idolatrous people who possessed a 'system of atrocious priestcraft' which championed cannibalism and infanticide.[11] In the narrative Prince Madoc functions as a civilising missionary who will restore the Hoamen and destroy the rites of the Aztecas. The poem concludes with a volcano and a flood, a providential judgement which forces the Aztecas to flee, and the reader is informed that the survivors would later go on to establish a 'mightier empire' in Tenochtitlán, 'till Heaven | Making blind Zeal and bloody Avarice | Its ministers of vengeance, sent among them | The heroic Spaniard's unrelenting sword'.[12] The 'message' of *Madoc* was that the Aztecas possessed technical civilisation but they lacked its moral features, while the Hoamen might be a simple people but they at least lived with an understanding of God's laws.

In his various writings about the 'melancholy map' Southey tried to show that the eulogists of the 'noble savage' were mistaken, and that he could offer an accurate account of the 'manners and superstitions of uncivilized tribes'.[13] He pointed out instances where tribes had acquired the basic elements of

---

9 See P. J. Marshall and G. Williams, *The great map of mankind: British perceptions of the world in the age of Enlightenment*, London 1982, chs iii–vi, and Majeed, *Ungoverned imaginings*, passim.

10 Southey to H. Southey, 21 Nov. 1804, *SL* i. 284, 285.

11 R. Southey, *The curse of Kehama*, London 1810, in *Poetical works*, iv. 4.

12 Idem, *Madoc*, London 1805, ibid. ii. 273.

13 *HB* i. 2. See R. A. Humphreys, *Robert Southey and his* History of Brazil, London 1978, and M. Wood, *Slavery, empathy and pornography*, Oxford 2002, 199–217.

civilisation, which he defined as 'stationary habitations ... habits of settled life, a regular government, a confederated priesthood, and a ceremonial religion', and also noted those uncivilised tribes which were neither violent nor cruel.[14] In general, however, his accounts dwelled on depraved practices. He almost seemed to luxuriate in gruesome descriptions, as when describing four men whose heads were sawn off with oyster shells during a civil war in the Tonga islands. 'Almost, it might be believed, that a people capable of such hellish barbarity, were actually under the dominion of an evil spirit.'[15] He thought cannibalism was common, and the *History of Brazil* supplied some very elaborate instances. In one rite, the victim's arms and legs were used as props during a dance, while intestines were given to the women and brains to the children. In another, prisoners were forced to impregnate women, and the child of the union would be eaten when it reached adulthood.[16] Southey also agreed with the accepted view that the treatment of women and children was an indicator of the level of civilisation. He believed infanticide was very common, claiming that perhaps two-thirds of all babies in Tahiti were destroyed, and that many South American tribes thought it an acceptable form of population control.[17] Such behaviour, he thought, was 'common among uncivilized and semi-barbarous nations, from motives of selfishness or superstition'.[18] Similarly, 'savage' peoples often seemed to lack all sexual restraint: Tahiti was notorious in this regard, but in South America most tribes were polygamous, though a few practised serial monogamy. In general the oppression of women was 'usually dreadful among savages', and for that reason Southey was inclined to see truth in the rumours of a tribe of Amazonians.[19] Finally, he also thought that the brutality of savages was evident in their indifference towards the elderly, the ill and the dead.[20] He underlined the idea that most savages were interested only in self-preservation. The fact that they possessed 'little *natural* affection' and their '*natural* charities' were starved and withered suggests again that this was a state of degeneration not nobility.[21]

What, then, was the cause of this 'melancholy map'? Montesquieu had helped popularise the view that the 'character of the spirit and the passions of the heart' varied with the climate. Europe's temperate climate had produced moderate and industrious characters suited to political liberty and economic development. Asia, however, was a place of climatic extremes. In its southern

---

14 *HB* i. 85. See also i. 65, 378–82, 495–6; iii. 208.

15 [R. Southey], 'Accounts of the Tonga islands', *QR* xvii (Apr. 1817), 19.

16 *HB* i. 218–23.

17 [Southey], 'Transactions vol. i', 199; 'South Sea islands', 58–9; *HB* i. 118; ii. 374; iii. 387, 394.

18 *HB* ii. 374.

19 Ibid. i. 609. See also i. 119, 333–4; iii. 165, 203; and [R. Southey], 'Burney's chronological history of the voyages and discoveries in the South Sea', *AR* v (1807), 26.

20 *HB* i. 247–8; iii. 203–4; [R. Southey], 'Missionaries' letters on the Nicobar islands', *QR* xxi (Apr. 1814), 61.

21 *HB* i. 44 (my emphasis); [Southey], 'The poor', 209 (my emphasis).

parts, heat produced stronger passions, but also inertia: there was 'no curiosity, no noble enterprise' and ultimately no progress.[22] These climates tended to produce domestic servitude and political despotism, an analysis which Montesquieu extended to Africa and Central America.[23] This line of thinking was to prove enormously influential in the eighteenth century, but it was not without critics. Hume dismissed Montesquieu's arguments by stressing the centrality of moral causes – government, religion, education – in shaping character, and pointing out that the 'contagion of manners' was more important than the influence of the climate. In China, for instance, there was a relatively uniform character despite its varied environment, and, conversely, the peoples of classical Thebes and Athens had very different characters despite living in precisely the same climate.[24] Diderot, who had some sympathy with this view, commented archly that 'No one attributes the difference of manners in WAPPING and ST JAMES to a difference of air or climate.'[25]

Southey was deeply opposed to the climatic explanation, seeing in it a form of moral determinism which implied that God had designed the world so that achieving virtue was harder for some peoples than for others. 'These geographical philosophists', he railed, 'these wretched reasoners who would make morality depend upon degrees of latitude, cannot be too severely reprobated. Were the physical fact true, it would overthrow the moral order of the universe.'[26] The closest he came to offering environmental explanations of behaviour was the suggestion that easy access to food caused indolence and prevented progress.[27] The Tongans, unlike the Tahitians, had been forced to develop agriculture and to establish property in order to feed themselves. 'When the Creator deemed that in the sweat of his brow man must eat bread', Southey stated, 'the punishment became a blessing; a divine ordinance necessary for the health of the soul as well as the body while man continues to be the imperfect being that we behold him.'[28] In general, however, he preferred 'moral' explanations. While working on *Thalaba* he conjectured that 'oriental' despotism arose from the morally brutalising effects of polygamy, and rejected Rickman's argument that Montesquieu had shown climate to be the ultimate cause.[29] It was central to his thinking that 'savage' and 'barbaric' practices were corruptions of a more benign human nature. Just as he criticised those

[22] C. L. Montesquieu, *The spirit of the laws*, ed. A. M. Cohler and others, Cambridge 1989, 231, 234.
[23] Ibid. 278–84. See also Romani, *National character*, 25–7, 31–7.
[24] D. Hume, 'Of national characters', in D. Hume, *Political essays*, ed. K. Haakonssen, Cambridge 1994, 78–92.
[25] Cited in A. Pagden, *European encounters with the new world: from renaissance to romanticism*, New Haven 1993, 147.
[26] [R. Southey], 'Fischer's travels in Spain', AR i (1803), 41.
[27] [Idem], 'Travels in Iceland', QR vii (Mar. 1812), 84–5; 'Nicobar islands', 65.
[28] [Idem], 'South Sea islands', 45.
[29] Southey to Rickman, 17 Jan. 1800, NL i. 216, and 3 Feb. 1800, SL i. 91. See CPB iv. 211.

thinkers who depicted 'savages' as peaceful and natural, he also opposed those 'erring philosophers' – meaning Hobbes – who had speculated that the state of nature was a state of war. Rather, 'false religions and barbarizing customs have rendered it so from the earliest times after the dispersion of mankind'.[30] In the *History of Brazil*, Southey suggested various reasons why the tendency of society might be backward. Some countries were cut off 'from the influence of the civilized world' and especially the 'civilizing influence of commerce' so that there was little momentum towards improvement. In other cases, however, degeneration was intimately linked to institutions such as polygamy, which corrupted the sexual and social affections, and slavery and caste, which stifled ambition and development.[31] Ultimately the nature of government and especially religion were integral factors in shaping the progressiveness of a nation.

The traditional Mosaic account of history remained predominant in the early modern period. The research of Bishop Ussher had pinpointed creation to 4004 BC, and it was widely accepted that at some point after the flood the sons of Noah – Shem, Ham and Japeth – had spread into Africa, Asia and eventually America. By the eighteenth century this thinking was being exposed to scepticism and even ridicule.[32] Hume, for example, argued in his *Natural history of religion* that because polytheism was the religion of all primitive peoples, it must be the earliest form of faith, and monotheism, accordingly, a later development. Southey, however, rejected this Enlightenment scepticism, believing that 'all rational history' showed that humanity had descended from an original pair of humans about six thousand years ago.[33] From the patriarchs to the prophets to the apostles, the truths of monotheism had been maintained only in Israel, and for this reason he disagreed with Gibbon: Christianity arose 'not in dark times, nor among a barbarous people; but in the most enlightened age of the ancient world, and among the only people who from the beginning had continued to profess, as a nation, the belief of one God, to be worshipped in spirit and in truth, when all the rest of mankind were idolaters'.[34] As he explained in the *Poet's pilgrimage*, 'Our first parents brought with them the light of natural religion and the moral law; as men departed from these, they tended towards barbarous and savage life.'[35] The migrating descendants of Noah

> had the Law; – God's natural law they scorned,
> And chusing error, thus they pay the cost!

[30] R. Southey, *Lives of the British admirals*, London 1833–40, i. 17.

[31] *HB* iii. 773, 831.

[32] Kidd, *British identities*, ch. ii; Pocock, *Barbarians*, passim.

[33] Southey to Rickman, 15 Jan. 1806, *LC* iii. 16.

[34] [R. Southey], 'Church of England missions', *QR* xxxii (June 1825), 6. See E. Gibbon, *The history of the decline and fall of the Roman empire*, ed. D. Womersley, London 1994, i. 520.

[35] Southey, *Poet's pilgrimage*, 'Argument' unpaginated.

> Wherever Falsehood and Oppression reign,
> There degradation follows in their train.[36]

As people lost the knowledge of monotheism, they were increasingly impressed by the power and beauty of heavenly bodies and environmental elements and began to think them gods. It was easy for 'savage' peoples to attach great importance to dreams and deliriums, superstitions and signs: 'every thing animate or inanimate, on which the imagination happens to dwell, becomes an object of worship'.[37] A degenerated people, as Southey wrote in *Madoc*, gave to 'stocks | And Stones' the attributes of the one, true God and so they descended into polytheism.[38]

All religions, Southey believed, were corruptions of the patriarchal faith. It followed that Indian, Chinese and American history had to have occurred within less than six thousand years, whatever their own historical records might claim. The account proposed by Hinduism, for instance, was 'worthless', because 'History has nothing to do with trillions and quadrillions of ages'. It was important, however, to try to trace exactly how global dispersion had occurred. On the debate about whether the Indians had taught the Egyptians, Southey suspected that Egypt had priority, commenting that 'it by no means follows that all which is found in the East has originated there'.[39] In the case of Polynesia, he opposed Martinez de Zuniga's view that it was settled from America: physical appearance, 'national character' and 'superstitions' differed too much. The presence of the Malay language suggested that the islands were first reached 'by some forgotten people in the East' who were civilised enough to colonise. 'The character of their priestcraft, the sacred language which exists in some of these islands, the Tooitonga of the Tonga islands, and the allegorical mythology, indicate much less than the unequivocal testimony of their dialects, a relationship to the East, – the land of allegory and of priestcraft.'[40] These myths and stories provided clues about the origins of peoples, and if Southey did not attempt a key to all mythologies, he surely would have admired Mr Casaubon's efforts. Until someone interpreted the hieroglyphics, he wrote in 1803, much could be done 'by comparison of languages'. If around a hundred commonly used words were collected from every existing tribe 'such languages as have been diffluent we should certainly be able to trace their source'.[41] In the language and institutions of the Polynesians, he thought, 'there are proofs of old civilization, far exceeding that of the state in which our navigators discovered them'.[42] The same was true in America. The Jesuits claimed to have found in tribal oral traditions a belief in

---

36 Ibid. 169.
37 [Idem], 'Asiatic researches (vol. viii)', *AR* vi (1808), 646.
38 Idem, *Madoc*, 62.
39 [Idem], 'Asiatic researches (vol. viii)', 646; cf. [idem], 'West Indies', 194.
40 [Idem], 'Tonga islands', 38.
41 Southey to Rickman, 23 Dec. 1803, *LC* ii. 244.
42 [R. Southey], 'Polynesian researches', *QR* xliii (May 1830), 28.

'times before the age of the sword', leading Southey to comment that 'wherever a tradition of a golden age is to be traced, it is at once an acknowledgement and proof of degradation in the race'.[43]

While he opposed the Enlightenment critique of priesthood when applied to Christianity, Southey employed it to explain how other religions caused social degeneration. Once a people had descended into idolatry, it was all too easy for tyrants to deify themselves, and for priests to set themselves up as a power over the people. Without any other kind of evidence, they used 'dreams and visions, and revelations, and impulses' to buttress their claims to authority.[44] The desire for faith was a natural appetite but it could easily degenerate into 'a noxious and degrading superstition'.[45] In *Madoc*, the priesthood was responsible for outrages such as sealing a child in a cave and killing the wives of those slain in battle. This poem exemplified Southey's belief that across the globe most religions bred moral degeneracy, subjugated the people and impeded improvement.[46] The one conspicuous exception was Zoroastrianism, the ancient religion of Persia, which Southey had at one time considered using as the basis for a mythological poem. Voltaire had seen this religion as a superior form of deism, and the terms in which Southey praised it – even as a professed Anglican – reveal lingering sympathies for rational religion. 'The mythology', he noted, 'was imaginative and coherent, less monstrous, less absurd, and, in all respects, less offensive than any other that has ever been promulgated by an imposter, or grown up from popular errors and tradition.' It presented visible objects of adoration which were designed to appeal to the 'vulgar' classes, but it did not lapse into idolatry. Most important of all were the moral principles of Zoroaster ('good thoughts, good words, good deeds') which 'deserve high – almost, it might be said, unqualified praise; purity of mind was enjoined by them as of word and deed'. This religion, Southey concluded, did not die because it lacked attachment from the people, but because it was extirpated by the sword of Islam.[47]

The more sophisticated a religion, the more 'rooted' it was: 'where men are savages, they are ferocious and brutal; where they are civilized and corrupted, the springs of moral action are poisoned'.[48] Southey's writings on Islam and Hinduism were correspondingly unambiguous. The religion of India was neither peaceful nor moderate, but was rather responsible for much evil – from infanticide to sati – as well as for fanaticism. It was a religion of 'false humanity' and 'hideous cruelty', the worst institution of which was the 'pernicious' system of caste.[49] The 'Pooleahs' of Malabar were said to be banished from all society and forced to live in ditches and trees, and yet even

---

43 *HB* i. 229.
44 [Southey], 'Church of England missions', 6. See *HB* i. 136, 227–8, 620–1.
45 [Southey], 'Asiatic researches (vol. viii)', 646.
46 Idem, *Madoc*, 184–5, 227.
47 [Idem], 'Church of England missions', 13.
48 [Idem], 'Forbes's oriental memoirs', *QR* xii (Oct. 1814), 195.
49 Ibid. 193, 220.

they felt defiled by the touch of the 'Pariars'. To all intents and purposes this was a system of slavery which degraded the character of the people and robbed men of 'every motive of honest ambition to excel'.[50] The country had enormous potential for economic development but the conservatism of its religion – for instance, the sanctity of the cow – impeded reforms which would make agriculture more productive.[51] As for Islam, Southey explained that in *Thalaba* he had brought out the best features of that system by highlighting what it retained of the patriarchal faith rather than dwelling on the spirit of 'Oriental despotism which accompanied Mahommedanism wherever it was established'.[52] His real feelings at the time of composition were that the Koran was a 'dull' book and that the former greatness of Islam had been replaced by 'brutal ignorance and ferocity'. 'It is now a system of degradation and depopulation, whose overthrow is to be desired as one great step to general amelioration.'[53] Nearly thirty years later he restated his belief that because its 'whole tendency' was 'barbarizing' it checked the growth of civilisation.[54] However, because of the Islamic contempt for Christianity it was likely that this religion would only ever be destroyed by the sword rather than converted by the word.[55]

'[W]here Light is not, Freedom cannot be; | "Where Freedom is not, there no Virtue is;" | Where Virtue is not, there no Happiness.'[56] This was not a cause for despair, however, because even a degraded people were not totally lost: 'still in the heart of man | A feeling and an instinct it exists | His very nature's stamp and privilege, | Yea, of his life the life'.[57] Those who lacked knowledge of revealed religion still had a 'direct communication' from God which enabled them to know something of right and wrong.[58] While the Tahitians were deeply corrupt, the Hottentots – like the fictional Hoamen – were gentle and docile and their 'moral sense' was less tainted than that of other 'savages'.[59] In *A tale of Paraguay*, these themes were explored more fully. It was inspired by a story in the memoirs of the Jesuit missionary, Martin Dobrizhoffer, which dealt with the discovery of the last three members of a tribe destroyed by smallpox, and their happy conversion to Christianity.[60] The poem begins with a providential visitation which destroys the Guarani,

[50] [Idem], 'Tennant's Indian recreations', *AR* iii (1805), 660.
[51] [Idem], 'Buchanan's journey from Madras', ibid. vi (1808), 50
[52] Idem, *Kehama*, 4.
[53] Southey to May, 29 July 1799, *SL* i. 77, 78.
[54] [R. Southey], 'History of the dominion of the Arabs and Moors in Spain', *Foreign Quarterly Review* i (July 1827), 16.
[55] [Idem], 'Church of England missions', 15.
[56] Idem, *Poet's pilgrimage*, 170.
[57] Idem, *Madoc*, 62
[58] [Idem], 'Dymond: on the principles of morality', *QR* xliv (Jan. 1831), 84.
[59] [Idem], 'Barrow's Africa', *AR* iii (1805), 27.
[60] See [idem], 'Dobrizhoffer: account of the Abipones', *QR* xxvi (Jan. 1822), 277–323, and T. Fulford, 'Blessed bane: Christianity and colonial disease in Southey's *Tale of Paraguay*', *RN* xxiv (2001), unpaginated.

a tribe which had indulged in the typical practices of savage life. Quiara and Monnema, the only two survivors, come to realise they have been saved by God.

> Tho' of his nature and his boundless love
> Erring, yet tutor'd by instinctive sense,
> They rightly deem'd the Power who rules above
> Had saved them from the wasting pestilence.
> That favouring power would still be their defence.[61]

They had been purged clean of their tribal degeneracy and were now able to appreciate 'unerring Nature's order' because 'impious custom' no longer strove 'Against her law'.[62] Later, after Quiara is killed by a wild animal, Monnema raises their two children alone in almost prelapsarian bliss. In Mooma, 'Something of what Eden in might have been | Was shadowed there imperfectly', and the whole family 'retain'd a trace | Of their celestial origin'.[63] The children did not like stories about the savage customs of their forebears, and preferred instead half-understood tales of 'Father' the 'Great Spirit' who rewarded men and women after life according to their deeds.[64] The rest of the poem dealt with their encounter with the Jesuits, but the importance of the first half of the *Tale* lies in the idea that even a corrupted people had within it the knowledge of its redemption.

Europeans, however, had no reason to be complacent. In discussing the 'melancholy map' it was important 'to observe how small a part of what is called the civilized world is truly civilized; and in the most civilized parts to how small a portion of the inhabitants the real blessings of civilization are confined'.[65] These 'blessings' had only been achieved recently (until a few centuries previously the inhumane treatment of women and children had been common) and civilised man easily degenerated under 'unfavourable circumstances'.[66] Since the fall of the Roman empire, Christianity had initially spread civilisation to the barbarian invaders, but had then degenerated into papal despotism, only to be rescued by the Reformation. But there remained differing levels of civilisation across the continent. While Scotland was now 'a peaceable, orderly, and moral nation', only two centuries ago it had been 'as turbulent, ferocious, and brutal as the wild Irish are now'.[67] Spain and Italy were retarded by the dominance of the Church over civil life, while in France, conversely, society was corrupted by infidelity. The embrace of atheistical and selfish philosophies was having deleterious consequences elsewhere too. In Iceland and the nearby Feroe Islands, for instance, the precarious state

---

[61] R. Southey, *A tale of Paraguay*, London 1825, 27.
[62] Ibid. 38.
[63] Ibid. 50, 52.
[64] Ibid. 59.
[65] STM i. 62.
[66] Southey to Rickman, 15 Jan. 1806, LC iii. 17.
[67] [R. Southey], 'Landt's description of the Feroe islands', QR iv (Nov. 1810), 342.

of civilisation was being threatened by the corrupt manners of the Danes who had in turn been influenced by French thinking.[68] Once the virtues of civilisation were lost, all too quickly savage passions and cruelty re-emerged, as they had done during the French Revolution.[69] Christian and Machiavellian moralism were fused in the belief that 'national corruption brings on … the decay and downfal of states'.[70]

Colonising, converting, civilising

Criticism of empire grew in the second half of the eighteenth century. After the Seven Years War both Hume and Smith began to think that Britain was acquiring a taste for empire in the expansionist Roman vein, and they warned of the instabilities produced by imperial overstretch. In his dying days Hume was cheered by the loss of the thirteen colonies, while Smith famously argued that free trade not rigid empire was the source of competitive advantage.[71] Another element of the critique of empire was incommensurability. There was a growing appreciation of the cultural and political diversity of the globe, and the concomitant argument was that empires could not govern such diversity without oppressing their subject peoples.[72] The most wide-ranging assault on empire was Guillaume-Thomas Raynal's *History of the settlement of Europeans in the East and West Indies*, which described how the early modern empires were driven by ideas of universal empire and lust for unlimited wealth. The result was nothing less than the enslavement of Americans and Africans. Those sections written by Diderot, however, did reserve some praise for the British empire, which he thought was founded on liberty rather than conquest. The Puritans of New England and the Quakers of Pennsylvania were 'more wise in their constitution, more simple in their customs, more limited in their ambitions' than any other imperial people.[73]

Southey was both a critic of past empire and a supporter of present empire. He was familiar with Raynal's *History* which, for all its 'inaccuracies and errors', he commended as an important work, and he praised its author for a 'humane and generous heart'.[74] He also agreed with critics about the Spanish empire's dreams of universal monarchy and all-too-real desire for gold. The greedy adventurers who crossed the Atlantic were either the worst kind of men, or soon became so. They treated the natives brutally – Pizarro was purported to have burned them alive or fed them to his dogs to extract

---

68 Ibid. 335; [idem], 'Iceland', 64.
69 [Idem], 'Tonga Islands', 11–12, 25–6.
70 [Idem], 'Barante', 44.
71 D. Armitage, *The ideological origins of the British empire*, Cambridge 2000, 189–91.
72 A. Pagden, *Lords of all the world: ideologies of empire in Spain, Britain and France* c. 1500–c. 1800, New Haven 1995, 160–6.
73 Cited ibid. 167.
74 [Southey], 'Dobrizhoffer', 285.

confessions about the location of Eldorado – and did their best to subvert laws prohibiting slavery.[75] Although the Spaniards might have been an avenging hand against the Mexicans, their crimes were enormous, and in some respects worse than those they destroyed because they 'sinned against knowledge'.[76] Even if one took into account the circumstances of the age and the idolatry of the natives, 'the early history of Spanish America must for ever stand prominent in the records of human wickedness'.[77] Nor was Spain alone: by the end of the seventeenth century the French, the Dutch, and even the English (the planters in the West Indies rather than the settlers in New England) were responsible for their share of crimes.[78] Taken as a whole, what emerges again and again is Southey's hatred of empire based on plunder. It had led to the enslavement of indigenous peoples and the brutalisation of imperial populations, while the influx of specie back to the metropole had grave social consequences at home.

Yet the quotations with which this chapter opened suggest that Southey also defended empire. These words were written within a year of the appearance of Pasley's *Essay on the military policy and institutions of the British empire*, a book which, as we have seen, Southey had described as a 'political Bible'.[79] This work was controversial not because it called for more vigorous pursuit of the war, but because it recommended a much firmer policy of conquest. In doing so, Pasley was trying to reverse entrenched blue-water thinking about empire, which in itself was a solution to the enduring Machiavellian dilemma of how to achieve empire without losing liberty.[80] He argued that Britain had only been able to pursue a mercantile policy in the eighteenth century because the many divisions among continental states had made Europe weak. But the result was that Britain had experienced martial decline and had become 'a nation of traders, like the modern Dutch, destitute of every sentiment, but the grovelling wish of acquiring wealth'.[81] Pasley was especially critical of writers like Hume and Smith who, he thought, placed too much faith in commerce as the basis of security. The important point was that the shape of Europe was changing and that within thirty years France would rival Britain. The solution was found in the Machiavellian axiom that security required greatness, and this was not to be sought in an empire of small islands but of large possessions fruitful enough to sustain themselves economically and militarily. Pasley was aware of the classic conundrum that states designed for expansion undermined domestic liberty, but he argued that Harrington and Sidney had shown that the problem was not irreconcilable: the mixed consti-

---

75 *HB* i. 80, 257–9, 268–9, 376–7.
76 [Southey], 'West Indies', 195.
77 *HB* iii. 52.
78 Ibid. ii. 57; [Southey], 'West Indies', 193, 212, 229.
79 Southey to Landor, 11 Jan. 1811, *LC* iii. 295.
80 See Armitage, *Origins*, 125–45.
81 C. W. Pasley, *An essay on the military policy and institutions of the British empire*, London 1810, 114.

tution could withstand an infusion of military spirit without undermining domestic liberty.[82] It was his firm conviction that reason of state required that the British become 'a warlike people by land as well as by sea'.[83]

Southey and Wordsworth were both impressed with Pasley's views about a renewed military spirit, but they were adamantly opposed to his ideas about expansion, at least as far as they pertained to Europe. Pasley had suggested that Britain should not be afraid to acquire countries such as Italy and Switzerland, and that while she might eventually set them up as independent states, the law of nations meant she was quite justified in adding them to her empire.[84] Wordsworth argued that conquest could not confer right. 'I am afraid', he told Pasley, 'that you look with too much complacency upon conquest by British arms, and upon British military influence upon the Continent, for *its own sake*.'[85] Southey agreed, telling Scott that Pasley 'talks sometimes of conquest when he should talk of emancipation'.[86] Besides, if Britain followed this doctrine she became no better than France, and lost all claim to be the deliverer of Europe because of her possession of 'liberty, and knowledge, and pure morals and true religion'.[87] Coleridge was also insistent that Britain should not adopt a policy of aggrandisement, agreeing with Wordsworth that the acquisition of territory during war could only be justified by considerations of security. 'Greatness and Safety are with us Words of one meaning', he wrote, 'Not by choice or our own Ambition, but by necessity and from the Ambition of France.'[88] The three lake poets were all too aware of the Machiavellian dilemma. 'A system of unlimited conquest', Southey noted, 'leads at last to the consequences which we have seen exemplified in the fate of the Roman empire.'[89]

Opposition to conquest, however, was more muted if it was linked to a 'civilising' imperative. Napoleon had claimed just such a mission for France, leading Coleridge to comment that for the purposes of civilisation Europe was 'already one people, beyond the most boastful dream of Roman pride. What would mankind gain, by turning this brotherhood in science and manners, into a political amalgamation?'[90] One clear exception, at least for Southey, was Ireland. He often lamented that there had never been a truly serious attempt to civilise the Irish, and occasionally suggested that what was needed was 'Roman conquest and colonization'.[91] This point was more especially true of the wider world. In the *Convention of Cintra*, Wordsworth pleaded for inde-

---

[82] See ibid. 65–6, 128–34, 464–75.
[83] Ibid. 114.
[84] Ibid. 349–412.
[85] Wordsworth to Pasley, 28 Mar. 1811, in *Letters*, ii. 480.
[86] Southey to Scott, 2 Apr. 1811, *LC* iii. 307.
[87] [Croker and Southey], 'Capt. Pasley', 436.
[88] *EOT* iii. 197.
[89] Southey to Scott, 2 Apr. 1811, *LC* iii. 307.
[90] *EOT* i. 325.
[91] Southey to Wynn, Apr. 1807, *LC* iii. 77.

pendent states in Europe, but he qualified this by stating that when there was 'an indisputable and immeasurable superiority of one nation over another; to be conquered may, in course of time, be a benefit to the inferior nation: and, upon this principle, some of the conquests of the Greeks and Romans may be justified'.[92] Southey also at times stated that conquest was a means of introducing civilisation, and during the war suggested that Britain should permanently retain any possessions that it could civilise. Egypt should be seized and colonised to prevent the French from taking it, while the 'Roman system' would civilise India within fifty years.[93] In the *History of Brazil* he argued that 'Force may sometimes be the only means of civilization', though he recognised that ancient Rome was more successful than modern Spain in this regard, and that armies were generally poor civilisers unless they were supporting a wider plan of colonisation.[94]

While Southey countenanced the right of conquest, he nevertheless expressed the common anxieties about it. Britain was more comfortable with the right of occupancy, which received its most famous formulation in Locke's *Second treatise of government*, where it was argued that vacant or unowned land – *terra nullius* – could be taken into possession by those who could cultivate and hence improve it. This 'agriculturalist' argument was deeply rooted in humanism, and had a particularly influential statement in Thomas More's *Utopia*.[95] In order to supply an expanding population, the Utopians were justified in taking and making use of 'unoccupied or uncultivated' land. If the native population refused to conform to the laws of the new colony they were driven out, forcibly if necessary. 'The Utopians say it's perfectly justifiable to make war on people who leave their land idle and waste yet forbid the use and possession of it to others who, by the law of nature, ought to be supported from it.'[96] Southey understood and endorsed this argument. In America and Polynesia many natives would join with the settlers, while the rest would wither away as a result of their vices and ferocity. 'It is the order of nature', he remarked, 'that beasts should give place to man, and among men the savage to the civilized.'[97] But right did not just derive from occupancy. The Utopians had also defended wars to liberate the oppressed, and even to destroy 'vicious and disgusting' peoples.[98] As Richard Tuck has shown, humanists could justify invading the territory of barbarians to extirpate abhorrent religions and

---

92 CC, 322.

93 [R. Southey], 'Lord Valentia's travels', QR ii (Aug. 1809), 101. See also Southey to Wynn, 6 Apr. 1805, LC ii. 324–5, and Southey to G. Bedford, 30 Oct. 1809, NL i. 522.

94 HB ii. 261. See [R. Southey], 'A non-military journal; or observations made in Egypt', AR ii (1804), 66.

95 Pagden, Lords, 76–9; Armitage, Origins, 49–50, 90–1, 97–8; R. Tuck, The rights of war and peace: political thought and the international order from Grotius to Kant, Oxford 1999, 49–50, 120–6.

96 T. More, Utopia, ed. G. M. Logan and R. M. Adams, Cambridge 1988, 56.

97 [R. Southey], 'History and present state of America', QR ii (Nov. 1809), 322.

98 More, Utopia, 92.

customs, and viewed colonisation as the prime means of civilising.[99] Southey expressed the same point when he commented that it 'would be insulting the reader to prove the right of conquest – the right of conquering cannibals and child-murderers! the right of preventing human sacrifices by force'.[100] Those who had forsaken the laws of nature would have the opportunity to be reformed or else they would be destroyed.

Madoc exemplified this point. The Hoamen recognised the travellers from Wales as representatives of a superior civilisation, the 'children of a race | Mightier than they, and wiser, and by heaven | Beloved and favoured more'.[101] Madoc himself had not come to conquer but he was willing to support the oppressed Hoamen. After their initial defeat in battle, however, the Aztecas defend their rightful claim to the land.

> When we won this land,
> Coanocotzin said, these fertile vales
> Were not, as now, with fruitful groves embowered,
> Nor rich with towns and populous villages,
> Abounding, as thou seest, with life and joy;
> Our fathers found bleak heath, and desert moor
> Wild woodland, and savannahs wide and waste,
> Rude country of rude dwellers.[102]

Coanocotzin's argument is essentially that of *Utopia*: the Aztecas took possession of land that was not being profitably used by the Hoamen and transformed it through their own skills and energies. Madoc's response was suggestive, for he seemed to accept the Aztecas right of occupancy. He had no wish 'To wage the war of conquest, to cast out | Your people from the land which time and toil | Have rightly made their own'. But he did demand that, first, the Hoamen be released from subjection, for there was enough room in the land for both peoples, and second, that the Aztecas abandon a religion which offended the laws of nature.[103] Only in the second half of the poem, when it became apparent that the Aztecas had retained their bloody priest-craft, did Madoc conquer and dispossess them, proclaiming himself an agent of providence.[104] Southey was suggesting that while the Aztecas did have a right to occupancy of the land, Madoc also had a right of conquest because they refused to abandon their offensive practices. It could then be argued that by using these humanist arguments, Southey was able to repackage Pasley's reason of state expansionism into a seemingly more benevolent reason of humanitarianism.

Colonisation was a central ingredient of humanist thought. It could be

99 Tuck, *Rights*, 40–7.
100 [Southey], 'Transactions vol. i', 200.
101 Idem, *Madoc*, 44.
102 Ibid. 59.
103 Ibid.
104 Ibid. 247.

a means not just of supporting a growing population, as in *Utopia*, but also of bolstering greatness and promoting civilisation. Southey was a consistent and firm advocate of emigration for all these reasons, but it was only from the 1820s that the public began to take a closer interest.[105] The select committee report of 1826 proposed that colonial demand for labour could be supplied if assistance were offered to emigrants, who would then pay back the loan in instalments once they were settled. Southey enthusiastically endorsed the report in the *Quarterly Review* and unusually disagreed with Sadler who had argued against emigration because the notion of a 'redundant population' was a vile piece of Malthusianism.[106] Southey believed that in the current state of society the nation was overstocked, and as early as 1800 he argued that emigration acted as 'an outlet for the superfluous activity of the country' and ensured that 'general goods, & the blessings of civilization might be extended'.[107] Canada and Australia were vast and supposedly empty lands which could happily support Britain's expanding population for centuries. It was important, however, that more attention was given to the type of person who emigrated: shovelling out criminals and paupers was undesirable, as was encouraging restless and rootless adventurers. Instead, colonies should be settled with men and women who intended to cultivate the land and secure independence for their families. This would ensure that civilisation put down roots. Southey optimistically believed that the lower orders would happily exchange poverty for independence, but he worried that it would be harder to encourage the overstocked middle classes to emigrate.[108]

In becoming a 'hive of nations' ready to 'cast her swarms', Britain had to consider not just who to plant but where and how. Southey was thinking not only of supposedly 'uninhabited' parts of the world such as Canada and Australia, but also 'uncivilized' areas as well.[109] To be sure, some regions, such as West Africa, were not suited for colonisation because they were environmentally uncongenial to Europeans.[110] A more important difficulty was whether the colonising population was culturally compatible with the existing population. In Brazil, for example, the differences between the Portuguese and the Dutch in language, religion and manners ensured that the latter failed to plant lasting settlements. New institutions were not easily adopted 'for these things have their root in the history and habits and feelings of those with whom they have grown up, and to whose growth they

---

105 See H. J. M. Johnston, *British emigration policy, 1815–30: 'shovelling out paupers'*, Oxford 1972.

106 [R. Southey], 'Emigration report', QR xxxvii (Mar. 1828), 539–78, and 'West Indies', 194–5, 240. K. Lawes, *Paternalism and politics: the revival of paternalism in early nineteenth-century Britain*, Basingstoke 2000, 114–27, mistakenly identifies Southey as the reviewer of Sadler's *Ireland: its evils and their remedies* in QR xxxviii (July 1828), 53–84.

107 Southey to May, [18 Feb. 1800], in *Letters to May*, 52.

108 [Southey], 'Emigration', 571–8; STM ii. 260–93.

109 [Southey], 'Inquiry', 355–6.

110 [Idem], 'Report of the committee of the African Institution', AR vii (1809), 152.

have fitted themselves'.[111] For the same reason Southey was unhappy about proposals to introduce labourers from East Asia into the West Indies:

> The more the uniformity of habits, feelings, and opinions, in any community, the happier will that community be, and the more secure from foreign and internal danger: to introduce therefore into these islands a race unamalgamable with the existing population, would be not merely an anomalous experiment in policy, but it would be in direct opposition to the lessons which history holds out.[112]

That said, he did think it was possible for more civilised colonisers to graft their institutions onto less civilised indigenous peoples. In the case of Polynesia it would be easy, for 'the better and more teachable natives would connect themselves with their civilized neighbours' and so eventually their children would be 'exalted into the higher race'.[113] Indeed, one of the problems with Ireland was that the first settlers had imbibed the native character 'when the more civilized one should have been superinduced'.[114] The exportation of British institutions, whenever possible, was absolutely essential to successful colonisation and 'if we have not learnt from the Romans the wisdom of this policy, we have gone to school to little purpose'.[115] Southey believed that this strategy should be applied to India, and here he diverged sharply from the East India Company which remained attached to the ideas of the orientalists. He counselled that it stop flattering indigenous beliefs and practices and instead worked towards a time when the inhabitants 'speak the language, profess the religion, and imitate the manners of their rulers'.[116] Eventually a united and cohesive population would emerge. For this reason he judged the Portuguese policy of miscegenation in Brazil more successful than the rigid system of ethnic castes that had prevailed in Spanish America.[117] Britain should follow the practice of Utopia because it would ensure the stability of the empire by attaching indigenous peoples to it, and would also thereby enable civilisation to be spread more effectively.

Unsurprisingly, Southey thought that civilisation could not be understood without reference to religion. While false religions led to degeneration, he also thought that the forms of organised religion were central to the emergence of any society from savagery. In the History of Brazil he argued that when America was discovered 'the civilization of its different nations was

---

111 HB ii. 57.
112 [Southey], 'Europe, 1811', 202.
113 [Idem], 'Transactions of the missionary society', AR iii (1805), 623.
114 STM i. 268.
115 [Southey], 'Europe, 1810', 300.
116 [Idem], 'Valentia', 101.
117 [Idem], 'Koster's travels in Brazil', QR xvi (Jan. 1817), 384–5. A passage in [idem], 'Account of the Baptist missionary society', ibid. i (May 1809), 211, which denounced miscegenation, was almost certainly an interpolation of Gifford's, because Southey rejected it in 'Valentia', 98–9.

precisely in proportion to the degree of power and respectability which their priests possessed'. All the while priests were no more than showmen their influence was limited, but at some point a 'commanding spirit' emerged who was able to establish a believable mythological system, and so 'the improvement of his tribe begins'. He explained:

> A ritual worship creates arts for its embellishment and support; habits of settled life take root as soon as a temple is founded, and the city grows round the altar. The men who are set apart for the service of the Gods, and who are exempted from all ordinary occupations, being considered as superior to other men, soon learn to consider themselves so, and in reality become so. They have leisure to acquire knowledge, and to think for the people: it is among them in all countries that the rudiments of science have sprung up, and no nation has ever yet emerged from a savage state till it had a regular priesthood.[118]

In contrast to many Enlightenment historians, Southey believed that the power of the priesthood was not a consequence of an 'improved state of society, but the cause of it'. In a footnote he took issue with William Robertson's *History of America*, which had argued that civil government and not religious institutions was the central factor in explaining civilisation. Even if this were true in Mexico and Peru, it was not true of the Mayan people in Yucatán. 'The extraordinary state of civilization in that country is passed over in silence by Dr Robertson', and Southey was inclined to explain it by reference to religion rather than government.[119] However loathsome some forms of priestcraft were, he believed that they had a useful role to play in the early development of civilisation.

Ideally, of course, false religions should be supplanted by Christianity. This was not because evangelisation was a prerequisite of salvation but because Christianity tended 'to produce the greatest possible quantity of virtue and of happiness'.[120] He was therefore one of the earliest supporters of the revival of missionary activity at the end of the eighteenth century. Indeed, he was puzzled that while missionary work had been central to Catholicism, it had, with the notable exception of the Moravians, been virtually sidelined by Protestantism.[121] Certainly this had been true in Britain. To many Enlightenment sceptics the whole history of conversion was disheartening and unnecessary, and even many avowed Christians, such as Robertson, thought that attempts to convert peoples with utterly different worldviews were not only pointless but cruel.[122] Such views were reinforced by latitudinarian divines who insisted

---

118 *HB* i. 251. Southey quoted himself to G. Bedford, 30 Oct. 1809, *NL* i. 522.
119 *HB* i. 644. See N. Phillipson, 'Providence and progress: an introduction to the historical thought of William Robertson', in S. J. Brown (ed.), *William Robertson and the expansion of empire*, Cambridge 1997, 67–73.
120 [Southey], 'Baptist missionary society', 216.
121 [Idem], 'Church of England missions', 20–2.
122 Phillipson, 'Providence and progress, 65–6.

that knowledge of revealed religion was not essential to salvation. Only in the 1790s did Britain enter its age of missions under the impact of evangelicalism. The Baptist Missionary Society was set up in 1792, and its earliest efforts were directed towards India, while the London Missionary Society, which focused on Polynesia, was founded in 1796. Anglicans followed with the Church Missionary Society in 1799. By the 1820s, after a shaky start, missionary groups were attracting public support and they began to grow rapidly. These efforts quickly generated debate about the best means to spread civilisation. Some writers, including clerics like Richard Watson, maintained the older view that missions were ineffective and that the 'extension of science and commerce' was the best means of spreading civilisation. Even among advocates of missions there were arguments about whether Christianity or civilisation had priority. As Andrew Porter has put it, 'while many evangelicals tended to argue that Christianity *could* perfectly well precede civilization, there was certainly no clear feeling that it should *necessarily* do so'.[123]

In the 1800s there was a considerable push for the East India Company to open the continent up to Christianity. These efforts provoked strong criticism from Sydney Smith in the *Edinburgh Review*. He did not deny that there was a general duty to convert heathens, but felt that such energy was best devoted to utterly ignorant peoples. The danger of attempting to convert Hindus was shown by the uprising of sepoys at Vellore in 1806, which, it was argued, was caused by Baptists suggesting that Britain was planning forcible conversions. In any event, Smith contended, the strong attachment of Hindus to their religion and culture meant that conversion was unlikely to be successful. More important, Britain would undermine stability by challenging Hinduism. 'Attention to the prejudices of the subject, is wise in all governments', he pointed out, 'but quite indispensable in a government constituted as our empire in India is constituted.'[124] It would be dangerous to challenge these 'prejudices' for 'who can foresee the immense and perilous difficulties of bending the laws, manners, and institutions of a country, to the dictates of a new religion?'[125] Smith conceded that some customs – such as sati – needed reform, but argued that this was best managed with the support and consent of the Brahmins. Overall, he supported the traditional view within the Company and aligned himself with those orientalists who saw India as a moral and civilised country in danger of being undermined by fanatical missionaries.[126]

Southey's first article for the *Quarterly* was a rebuttal of Smith's case. While he accepted that the missionaries were overly imbued with a spirit of enthusiasm, he blamed the Vellore uprising on the machinations of the Brahmins. He also argued that missionaries were not a threat to, but a saviour of, empire.

[123] A. N. Porter, '"Commerce and Christianity": the rise and fall of a nineteenth-century missionary slogan', *HJ* xxviii (1985), 600, 601.
[124] [S. Smith], 'Indian missions', *ER* xii (Apr. 1808), 172.
[125] Ibid. 178.
[126] Ibid. 178–9.

The main problem in India, he went on, was that there were few genuine adherents to Britain among the native population. The hot climate meant that extensive colonisation was unlikely to be successful, and so even more stress was placed on Christianity's power to draw the population into closer harmony with British institutions. He disagreed with Smith that Hindus were difficult to convert, pointing out that that the Portuguese had won over many converts in the sixteenth century, and suggesting that using recent converts as preachers would make the task of missionaries easier. The real obstacle to conversion, he claimed, was the caste system, but he believed that as Christian communities grew they would be able to provide employment and fellowship to those isolated by loss of caste.[127] Southey was convinced that Indians hated Hinduism and desired Christianity – 'liberty to the oppressed, emancipation to the enslaved, equality to the degraded' – but that only the domination of the Brahmins deterred them from conversion.[128] The introduction of Christianity, he contended, would breathe life into Indian society, and ensure its long-term attachment to Britain. 'Admit a converted Hindoo to the privilege of an Englishman', he told his brother, 'and the whole system will crumble like snow in sunshine.'[129]

The advocates of missions, however, could not draw complete sustenance from Southey's opinions, and he was in fact critical of the methods employed by both Catholics and Protestants. There were two ways to approach conversion. The first was to influence the feelings and the imagination of the potential convert, and the second was to try to work on his understanding.[130] This latter approach was adopted by evangelicals, but because of their 'irrational' religion it was largely unsuccessful.[131] Because 'savages are never very tenacious of their faith', converting Polynesia ought to have been easy, but instead the missionaries spent all their time insisting that the islanders understood evangelical theology before they could be converted.[132] Attempting to promulgate a gloomy religion obsessed with personal depravity and original sin was, Southey argued, a waste of time. In India also these missionaries demanded too much. 'It is not enough that a Hindoo is convinced of the falsehood of his own shasters, and the divine truths of Christianity, he must show he has had *grace*, that he has experienced the *call*, the *new birth*. Alas! they need not these thorns and brambles in the way to the strait gate!'[133] As for the first approach, this had been adopted by the Jesuits in the new world. Catholicism

---

127 [Southey], 'Baptist missionary society', 200, 211–12.
128 Ibid. 216.
129 Southey to H. Southey, 1804, SL i. 302. See B. Young, '"The lust of empire and religious hate": Christianity, history and India, 1790–1820', in S. Collini, R. Whatmore and B. Young (eds), *History, religion, culture: British intellectual history, 1750–1950*, Cambridge 2000, 91–111.
130 [Southey], 'South Sea islands', 54.
131 Ibid. 54–5. See also [idem], 'Baptist missionary society', 195, 222, 225.
132 [Idem], 'Transactions vol. i', 193.
133 [Idem], 'Periodical accounts relative to the Baptist missionary society', AR i (1803), 217.

presented 'tangible objects of adoration' and had the aid of 'imposing forms and ceremonies' which led to thousands of conversions to Christianity.[134] The problem was that these converts were not subsequently provided with Christian knowledge, and so when the Jesuits were expelled in the mid-eighteenth century there was nothing to sustain their faith, and they quickly slipped back into their old ways. Southey's favoured method of conversion blended the two approaches. It was necessary to begin by showing the potential convert, 'like the blind old man in Madoc, how little difference there is in the basis of our faith'.[135] Missionaries in India and Polynesia should try to underline the points of contact between indigenous faiths and Christianity. This was important because the 'way to reclaim idolaters is by changing their ceremonies: whatever they believe, so long as they are ignorant, they must believe superstitiously; while they are ignorant, therefore, too much stress cannot be laid upon the ritual of religion'.[136] By slowly changing the external forms of religion it was possible to make heathens nominal Christians, and the process of education would ensure that their children would become devout Christians.[137]

Southey also adhered to the 'civilisation first' perspective, that is the view that until 'savage' peoples had been subjected to civilising rationality and brought into settlements, it was premature to preach the Gospel.[138] He was influenced by Edmund Law's Considerations on the state of the world with regard to the theory of religion of 1745, which stressed that as humanity progressed so did its understanding of natural and revealed religion. Southey felt therefore that 'the true nature of revealed religion is gradually disclosed as men become capable of receiving it, generations as they advance in knowledge & civilization outgrowing the errors of their forefathers, so that in fulness of time there will neither remain doubts nor difficulties'.[139] Until people were civilised it was absurd to expect a rational faith from them, and so 'some degree of civilization must precede conversion, or at least accompany it'.[140] It was important for potential converts to be introduced to skills such as building and farming, and opened up to commerce, so that the practical advantages of the new religion were plain for all to see. In time they would be ready for the pure doctrines of faith. In 1829, however, Southey read William Ellis's

---

[134] [Idem], 'Church of England missions', 2.

[135] [Idem], 'Two attempts', 583. He was referring to a passage in which the similarities between the Christian God and the Aztecas' 'God of Gods' were drawn out: Madoc, 61–5, 293–5; CPB iv. 209.

[136] [Southey], 'Transactions vol. i', 198.

[137] HB ii. 378.

[138] Porter, 'Commerce', 597–621; B. Stanley, 'Christianity and civilisation in English evangelical mission thought, 1792–1857', in B. Stanley (ed.), Christian missions and the Enlightenment, Grand Rapids 2001, 169–97.

[139] Southey to J. T. Coleridge, [3 Feb. 1825], in Braekman, 'Letters', 23. For Law see Young, Religion, 42–3, 53–6, 76.

[140] HB ii. 378. For criticisms of Jesuit conversions in this regard see ii. 334–5, 344, 354, 360–1.

Polynesian researches and its account of the rapid transition to Christianity in Tahiti caused him to abandon the 'civilisation first' stance: 'The present volumes have convinced us, formerly we thought otherwise, that the missionaries judged rightly in taking an opposite course, and regarding our faith as a tree, which brings forth fruits of civilization as well as of good works.'[141] The evidence was clear all over Tahiti: schools, houses, clothing, farming. They had all developed after conversion had taken place. Perhaps, he had come to think, even if the natives were in an ignorant and depraved state, they could still perceive the truths that were being preached to them, and exposure to such faith could transform society.[142]

Compared to religion, Southey had little to say about the political shape of empire, although he did adopt the familiar parent–child analogy in thinking about metropole and colony. It was 'neither fitting nor possible' that large and distant countries could remain united under one government, but he also felt 'it is desirable on every account that the separation should be delayed till the colony is as advanced in civilization as the parent state'.[143] On this basis he believed that British America had separated too soon, and that Spanish America should hold on longer. In the latter case he accepted that major reforms were required in the imperial relationship, but his real worry was that the withdrawal of centralised rule would lead to 'a war of casts and colours'.[144] Venezuela, for instance, needed a more 'condensed' population: 'its knowledge must be increased, its casts amalgamated, and its morals totally changed before it can, with any benefit to itself, or to the world, become an independent state'.[145] For these reasons, he remained sceptical about the independence movement in the 1810s and 1820s, and agreed with his friend Blanco-White that Spanish America ought to wait until it was ready for full liberty.[146] Besides, there seemed to be some evidence that the demand for independence was not genuinely national but rather was engineered by a liberal elite influenced by the American Revolution and the French Enlightenment.[147]

Another reason why colonies had to be patient was that they were especially liable to retrogression. The history of colonies showed that the 'backsettlers of every new country, receding from civilization themselves while they prepare the way for it, live without law and without religion'.[148] The United States exemplified this problem. In isolated parts of the country the influence of religion was barely felt and so settlers observed nothing but their own self-

---

141 [Southey], 'Polynesian researches', 37. See *CPB* iii. 563.
142 Southey to Rickman, 17 Dec. 1829, *SL* iv. 161.
143 [Southey], 'Europe, 1811', 385.
144 Ibid. 368.
145 Ibid. 394.
146 [J. Blanco-White], 'Walton's present state of the Spanish colonies', *QR* vii (June 1812), 235–64.
147 [Southey], 'Europe, 1811', 392.
148 [Idem], 'New churches', *QR* xxiii (July 1820), 552. See also *HB* ii. 58.

interest. Only in established urban centres, and especially in New England, was the social function of religion understood, and so whenever a township was built a new church and a new school quickly followed.[149] Southey approvingly cited a Mr Beecher from Connecticut who warned of the dangerous political consequences of an ignorant and irreligious population. 'If knowledge and virtue be the basis of republican institutions', he had commented, 'our foundations will soon rest upon the sand, unless a more effectual and all-pervading system of religious and moral instruction can be provided.'[150] A related issue, Southey felt, was that popular republican government was fairly weak at the centre, and so it followed that virtual anarchy reigned at the periphery. The United States appeared to be an experiment to see 'with how little government, with how few institutions, and at how cheap a rate men may be kept together in society'.[151] Southey doubted that its citizens were yet morally and intellectually advanced enough for republicanism, and believed that either a reform of institutions or of manners would be necessary for the future stability of the country.

From the vantage point of the late 1820s, Southey speculated in the *Colloquies* about the future of the Americas. In the case of South America, he was puzzled about why republican institutions were desired when they had no roots in its history. Monarchy, surely, was more congenial to 'old customs, old opinions, and the condition of the people'.[152] The problem was that continuous direct rule from Spain had prevented any families from emerging as a respectable elite. If conquerors like Pizarro and Cortés had founded dynasties they could have become nation builders like Hengist or Clovis and eventually erased the divisions between 'casts and colours'. As it was, the Spanish Americans had learnt to hate hereditary monarchy because it oppressed them, but they had nothing to put in its place. They envied the republicanism of a prosperous United States, even though they lacked the 'habits and principles' that were necessary for it. There was no easy way out of this impasse and Southey suspected that eventually a successful military leader would establish a monarchy to which the people would submit.[153] He was not, however, particularly sanguine about the future even of the United States in this regard, and speculated that expansion would undermine republicanism. A popular victory for a military commander, such as the conquest of Mexico or Quebec, might enable the passage 'from Presidency to the Throne' to occur with little opposition: 'The change is easier from republicanism to monarchy in America, than from monarchy to republicanism in any of the European kingdoms.'[154] This point reflects a wider shift in Southey's thinking about

[149] [Southey], 'America', 331–3; [idem], 'Dwight: travels in New England', *QR* xxx (Oct. 1823), 36; *STM* ii. 178–9.
[150] Cited in [Southey], 'New churches', 551.
[151] [Idem], 'Dwight', 36.
[152] *STM* ii. 180.
[153] Ibid. ii. 180–2, 187–9.
[154] Ibid. ii. 200.

republics and monarchies by the 1820s. In one essay he quoted the passage he had written twenty years before where he praised republicanism as theoretically the best political system. But 'he who thus expressed himself would not now, in his maturer mind, prefer even in theory a commonwealth to a well-tempered monarchy'.[155] Contrary to progressive thinking, it was the new world which still had much to learn from the old, and not the other way round.

Consideration of the 'great map of mankind' might be cause for melancholy, but it was not cause for despair. However far peoples had migrated from the light, and however deep they had sunk into idolatry, they shared the same inner moral sense and were in fact one single people. Insofar as Southey hated empire, it was because all too often its history displayed the base lust for wealth and the brutal enslavement of natives. Admittedly, during the war years he accepted that the security of the homeland might require the conquest of foreign territories. He was also firmly convinced of the legitimacy of the right of occupancy. Ideally, this should extend to the native population the benefits of true religion, and bring them within the fold of real civilisation. While Southey did believe that commerce was also important in cementing civilisation, he agreed with other missionary enthusiasts that its role should not be overstated.[156] Of greater importance was the exportation of Britain's law, language and religion. Not only would this provide the institutional framework of liberty and progress across the 'melancholy map', but it would also create security by establishing feelings of attachment among diverse native populations. This was a duty indicated by providence. As the *Poet's pilgrimage* showed at some length, Britain's victory against France placed her in a prime position not just to better her own condition, but to lead the world in 'diffusing the blessings of civilization and Christianity'.[157]

---

155 [Southey], 'Dymond', 110. See also idem, *William Smith*, 24.
156 See Porter, 'Commerce', 602–6.
157 Southey, *Poet's pilgrimage*, 'Argument' unpaginated.

8

A Perilous Political Economy

In the early autumn of 1819 Southey joined Rickman and Thomas Telford on a tour around Scotland. Instigated by Rickman, who was, among his other official roles, secretary to the commission on the Caledonian Canal, the prime purpose of the trip was to examine the progress of Telford's works. In a journal Southey recorded his impressions, and was extremely impressed by the quality of roads and canals, and the extent of estate improvement.[1] In late September the party stopped off at New Lanark to visit Robert Owen's cotton-mills. Owen explained how his innovations in factory management had improved the lives of the workers, and was particularly keen to show off the recently completed Institute for the Formation of Character.[2] Southey's journal reveals that, though not uncritical, there was much that interested him at New Lanark. Three years before, in 1816, Owen was known to the public as a wealthy philanthropic manufacturer who was trying to excite interest in plans to relieve the poor from the distress brought on by the transition to peace. Knowing that Southey had written on such topics, Owen visited him in Keswick that August. They exchanged ideas, and Southey was sufficiently interested to promise to visit New Lanark and to read Owen's recent *Address delivered to the inhabitants of New Lanark*.[3] Though they disagreed vigorously over religion, in other respects they had much in common. This has been obscured because of the subsequent historiography which has cast Southey as the romantic reactionary and Owen as the rational socialist and thereby embedded each man within seemingly divergent intellectual traditions.

The 'science' of political economy

In the 1810s and 1820s the popularisation of political economy continued apace, seeping into the consciousness through periodicals, lectures, politics and eventually the universities. It is important to note that in England the tag 'political economy' was strongly associated with David Ricardo and the *Westminster Review*, and so it rapidly gained a reputation among critics for being disinterested in history and ethics, and, much worse, for being 'anti-

---

[1] See, for example, R. Southey, *Journal of a tour in Scotland in 1819*, ed. C. H. Herford, London 1929, 26, 67, 86–9, 139–40, 158, 203–7.
[2] Ibid. 259–65.
[3] Southey to Rickman, 25 Aug. 1816, *LC* iv. 195–7.

landlord, anti-clerical, and viciously secular'.[4] This was the period when the idea of political economy as a 'dismal science' was rapidly taking shape. Southey contributed to this process by expressing exasperation with this new subject. He thought its practitioners 'perplex weak minds, and pervert vain ones'. They were cranky Laputans infatuated with abstract but useless metaphysics, and although they confidently spoke of their discoveries as a science they could not even agree on the meaning of their terms let alone on their conclusions.[5] It followed that political economy was 'a science concerning which there is a great deal written and talked, and very little understood'.[6] This verdict was confidently asserted despite Southey's confession of his 'ignorance' and 'incapacity' for such 'metaphysical politics'.[7] His aim was to delegitimise political economy not by engaging in a debate with it, but by demonising and ridiculing it, and hoping that eventually its 'ponderous volumes' would sink 'into the dead sea of oblivion'.[8] Ricardo returned the compliment, observing in 1818 that 'the reveries of Southey on questions of Political Economy will I hope no longer be admitted in any respectable journal. He quite mistakes his talent when he writes on such subjects, and is really no more deserving of attention than Mr Owen or any other visionary'.[9] Macaulay repeated the point when he reviewed the *Colloquies*. Southey's discussion of political economy showed that he still had 'the very alphabet to learn', and in this respect he had much in common with Owen, a man 'more unreasonable and hopelessly wrong than any speculator of our time'.[10]

Southey had no wish to learn the ABC of political economy because it was a pseudo-science which repudiated morality and subordinated politics to the pursuit of wealth. Nassau Senior, for instance, had stated that as a political economist he was concerned 'not with happiness but with wealth' while John McCulloch thought it quite proper 'in all economical investigation' to approach man as a machine.[11] These were, for Southey, unambiguous statements which mistook 'wealth for welfare' in estimating the prosperity of a nation.[12] Coleridge made the same point in his *Lay sermon* when he argued that 'wealth' was concerned only with 'outward prosperity' while 'real welfare' also took 'happiness' into account.[13] He believed that political economy reasoned from abstract and reductive propositions about humans to generate erroneous laws of behaviour. It was a materialistic science concerned

4   Hilton, *Age of atonement*, 37. See also M. Berg, *The machinery question and the making of political economy, 1815–1848*, Cambridge 1980, ch. iii.
5   [Southey], 'British empire', 278.
6   *STM* i. 180.
7   Ibid. i. 178; Southey to Rickman, 22 Apr. 1818, in Williams, *Lamb's friend*, 203.
8   [Southey], 'The poor', 199. See also *The doctor*, 85.
9   D. Ricardo to H. Trower, 26 Jan. 1818, in *The works and correspondence of David Ricardo*, ed. P. Sraffa, Cambridge 1951–73, vii. 247.
10 [Macaulay], 'Southey's colloquies', 528, 533. See Stedman Jones, *An end*, 182–7.
11 [Southey], 'British empire', 278.
12 *STM* i. 158.
13 *LS*, 157.

only with the 'gratification of the wants and appetites' of the animal side of humanity.[14] Southey, similarly, believed that it was a 'gross and material' philosophy, 'of the earth, earthy'.[15] As we have seen, by endorsing the population principle and thereby rejecting harmonious natural theology, political economists seemed to accept that the world was, in Boyd Hilton's words, 'mad, bad, and dangerous'.[16] 'It is certain', Southey countered, 'that all the evils in society arise from want of faith in God, and of obedience to his laws.'[17] What was needed was a public philosophy quite different from political economy, one which 'must look farther and wider, rise higher and go deeper, have a better foundation to rest on, and a nobler end in view'.[18]

Yet for all this, Southey and Coleridge accepted the classic eighteenth-century defence of commercial society. In William Robertson's words, commerce 'tends to wear off those prejudices which maintain distinctions and animosity between nations. It softens and polishes the manners of men'.[19] In the *Life of Wesley*, Southey was critical of those Methodists who rejected all forms of luxury, because certain 'vanities' had their uses in spurring industry and in 'accelerating the progress of civilization'.[20] In the *Colloquies* he was more clear-cut, arguing that in its 'ordinary and natural consequences' commerce was 'humanizing, civilizing, liberalizing' and that it helped to bind 'nations to nations, and man to man'. To the criticism that it was driven by a 'desire for gain', Montesinos agreed, but argued that

> The pursuit of independence, – of that degree of wealth without which the comforts of life are not to be procured, – the ambition even of obtaining enough to command those luxuries which may innocently and commendably be enjoyed, must be allowed to be beneficial to the individuals who are thus stimulated to exertion, and to the community which is affected by their exertions. This is inseparable from commerce; in fact it is the main spring of that social order which is established among us.[21]

Here the 'desire for gain' was cast in terms of moderation and independence. This approach was common to those eighteenth-century writers who wished to stress the benefits of commercial society while opposing the excesses of luxury. Richard Price, for instance, idealised a middle way between 'the

[14] Ibid. 74. See Morrow, *Coleridge's political thought*, 102–5.
[15] *STM* ii. 262. See also *CPB* iv. 702.
[16] Hilton, *Age of atonement*, 50.
[17] *STM* i. 228.
[18] [Southey], 'British empire', 278.
[19] Cited in A. O. Hirschman, *The passions and the interests: political arguments for capitalism before its triumph*, Princeton 1977, 61.
[20] *LW* ii. 462.
[21] *STM* i. 197, 195. He suggested that a less 'equivocal' word than luxury was required for 'allowable' riches: R. Southey, 'Introduction' to J. Jones, *Attempts in verse*, London 1831, 14.

savage and the refined', 'between the wild and the luxurious state'.[22] Southey therefore accepted that many benefits arose from trade, but also believed that unrestrained selfishness was harmful. Similarly, while Coleridge complained of the 'over-balance' of the commercial spirit he did not attack its very existence. It was commerce which had led to 'our actual freedom' and a good share of 'our virtues', and the outward power and prosperity of the nation were owed to it also.[23] In attacking political economy, then, the lake poets believed that they were opposing a new 'science' which eulogised greed rather than the older and nobler tradition of *doux commerce*.

The causes of distress

After Waterloo, critics of the government argued that the depression was a consequence of the tax and debt created by an unjust and unpopular war. Southey and Coleridge, of course, defended the war and hence were keen to reject this analysis. In his *Lay sermon*, Coleridge reiterated his argument that the amount of tax raised from the nation was not really an issue because it was spent on the nation.[24] Southey adopted the same arguments, and, in a reversal of the Paineite view in *Wat Tyler*, stressed that high taxation and a large debt had been crucial to national survival during periods of war.[25] The real cause of distress was the swift transition to peace. 'That the depression began *with* the Peace', Coleridge commented, 'would have been of itself a sufficient proof with the Many, that it arose *from* the Peace.'[26] He and Southey argued that the demand generated by war boosted manufacturing, while agricultural expansion filled the gap left by unreliable grain imports. The end of war hit both parts of the economy hard. Even with the corn law of 1815, farmers found their means precarious, and their situation was worsened by rising poor rates, which were necessary to accommodate the demobilised and the unemployed. In manufacturing, foreign demand slumped just when the home population was in no position to soak up excess supply, and so unemployment was further worsened. If at this crucial time, it was argued, the state had also embarked on rapid retrenchment, it would have exacerbated the collapse in demand that was the root cause of the depression. Southey even opposed the repeal of the income tax in 1816, suggesting that the money might have better been used by government to fund public works, and so ease the transition to peace.[27]

---

[22] R. Price, *Observations on the importance of the American Revolution*, London 1784, in R. Price, *Political writings*, ed. D. O. Thomas, Cambridge 1991, 144–5. See Hirschman, *Passions*, 63–6, and Stedman Jones, *An end*, 48–9, 121–2, 128–9.
[23] LS, 169, 204–5.
[24] Ibid. 155–8.
[25] STM i. 182–3.
[26] LS, 162.
[27] [Southey], 'Works on England', 565–7; [idem], 'Parliamentary reform', 245, 276–8; LS, 158–63.

The causes of depression also generated considerable disagreement among political economists.[28] Ricardo saw distress as an inevitable but temporary response to major changes in the channels of trade. If capital and labour were allowed to adjust relatively freely, then the damage could be minimised. Accordingly, the reduction of the tax burden, the removal of the corn laws and the return to the gold standard were all essential reforms. Malthus, famously, did not agree, and earned the wrath of Ricardians for arguing in opposition to Say's Law. He believed that Britain was experiencing a general glut, and that the demand for goods would not fall into line behind the supply. At the end of the war corn prices had fallen while wages remained stable, thereby reducing the income of landlords and farmers and leading to agricultural unemployment and a drop in home demand for manufactured goods. In turn this led to the overstocking of export markets and the decline in mercantile fortunes. For Malthus the key problem was underconsumption. While he did not advocate increased public spending as a stimulus, he thought that it, and hence taxation, should only be reduced very gradually. He also argued that as long as they did not increase productive capacity, public works and luxury spending were desirable. The propertied classes were encouraged 'to build, to improve and beautify their grounds, and to employ workmen and menial servants'.[29] Finally Owen, though not acknowledged as a political economist, argued that the main problem was that machinery had enabled the expansion of manufacturing during the war, which could no longer be sustained during the peace. The result was severe overproduction coupled with declining wages. During the later 1810s he promoted various 'make work' schemes as a way of alleviating this problem, and argued for extensive education in order to create 'a permanent national, intelligent, wealthy, and superior popula-tion' which would help increase consumption.[30] These ideas came together in plans for new communities which he thought would counteract the selfish-ness of competitive society. Although they disagreed on much else, Malthus and Owen both stressed overproduction as a major post-war problem, and saw public works and relief schemes as a useful, albeit temporary, way to help the unemployed and to ride out depression.

It has recently been argued that Southey and Coleridge had more in common with Malthus' economic views than either was prepared to admit.[31] All three of them disliked manufacturing, accepted the importance of public works, and held similar opinions about the nature of tax and the debt. At core, however, Southey and Malthus had different conceptions of the role of self-interest in society. It would in fact be better to align Southey with Owen's overproductionism. He believed that the impetus given to manufacture by war, machinery and child labour had enabled this sector to expand so rapidly

[28] Winch, *Riches*, 358–63.
[29] Cited ibid. 363.
[30] Cited in Berg, *Machinery*, 97.
[31] Winch, *Riches*, 311–12, 318–19, 336–8, 363–4.

that by the mid-1810s new markets were flooded and filled almost as soon as they were opened.[32] By the late 1820s Southey was coming to the conclusion that speculation, overstocking and depression was a cyclical phenomenon. The process began with healthy trade and full employment and 'we congratulate ourselves upon the state of the country'. Then the returns on investments started to dry up, 'the goods are unpaid for – sold at a loss, damaged, wasted, spoiled, or, perhaps re-shipped for England'. Bankruptcy became common and 'fabrics of credit fall like a child's house of cards'. Finally, after much loss and waste, trade revived and a 'new race of merchant-adventurers ... comes forward to speculate, or, rather, to gamble with the capital of others; the same desperate game is again played with the same ruinous, but certain consequences, and thus the burning and the shivering fits alternate'.[33] An excessively competitive trade led to unstable employment, reduced wages and inferior goods, but speculators would do nothing to apportion supply to demand.[34] Although the problem of glut and crisis did eventually correct itself, in the meantime it produced suffering for ordinary men and women.[35] As Coleridge had famously put it, the matter was not so much that things found their level, but that 'all things are *finding* their level – as water does in a storm'.[36] The central point, however, is that Southey agreed with Owen that the problem was overproduction in manufacturing, and that this was created by greedy speculators obliviously overstocking markets.

Southey is well known for the long-term perspective he took on the growth of commerce and manufacturing. It is widely accepted that the *Colloquies* contrasted medieval social and economic relations favourably with those of the modern period, although this view needs some qualification. He believed that the experience of 'feudal slavery' was softened by the material security of the serfs, and by the influences of religion and chivalry over their masters. Indeed, in some parts of the country these bonds between landlord and peasant had endured long after feudalism had withered away.[37] Similarly, Coleridge noted that the 'ancient feeling of rank and ancestry' had been a counter-balance to the impetus of trade, but suspected that by the early nineteenth century it had ceased to exercise much influence.[38] But for all this, Southey did not defend feudalism. He was quite clear that any form of slavery was inconsistent with 'the principles of Christianity, – the principles of religious philosophy' and nor was he much impressed with the actual treatment of the labouring population at this time.[39] Magna Carta had 'not one stipulation' in

---

[32] [Southey], 'Works on England', 568; 'Parliamentary reform', 245; [idem], 'Popular disaffection', 544.

[33] [Idem], 'Emigration', 546–7.

[34] Ibid. 539.

[35] Southey to Rickman, 14 Sept. 1816, SL iii. 45.

[36] S. T. Coleridge, *Table talk*, ed. C. Woodring, London–Princeton 1990, i. 383.

[37] STM i. 67–72, 93; [Southey], 'On the means', 80.

[38] LS, 170.

[39] STM i. 71. In the early 1830s, however, he became more sceptical about ending slavery

favour of these classes, and in the aftermath of the Black Death their labour and wages were adversely regulated.[40] These early statutes, Southey argued, manifested 'one uniform spirit of injustice' towards the lower orders, 'to keep the poor labourer in the *caste* wherein he was born'. It would have been more just if wages had 'been allowed to find their course', for the shortage of labour would have ensured that they were high.[41] While the medieval period did manifest values which tempered the desire for gain, it was also clear that landlords wished to prevent the emergence of the free labourer, and to reduce his wages as far as possible.

The beginnings of a perceptible shift towards a market economy were evident in the sixteenth century. From the 1510s prices began to rise rapidly in response to a dramatic growth in population, and by the 1570s they had tripled. These developments had important consequences. Landlords began to search for ways to shorten leases and increase rents. The growing population also found that wages were not keeping pace with rising prices, and that land was in greater demand, which led to considerable anger about enclosures. These profound changes did not pass without serious comment. Many moralists identified greed as the chief cause, and by mid-century a number of 'commonwealthsmen' – the foremost being Hugh Latimer – lectured the nation about its moral corruption. Keith Wrightson suggests that they approached economic behaviour as 'a branch of personal and social morality' and 'espoused the ideal of a Christian commonwealth, governed by distributive justice, in which the members of each estate should enjoy an appropriate share in return for performing their duties according to their degree'.[42] Southey was familiar with the views of Latimer, and more generally was influenced by sixteenth-century moralists such as Thomas More and William Harrison.[43] He supplied a number of reasons for the worsening condition of serfs at this time. Because of the need to finance war, and to support courtly lifestyles, landlords increasingly preferred rent to villeinage, and, following More and Latimer, he also believed that they were more eager to extend enclosure and pastoral farming at the expense of their tenants.[44] 'Four-legged animals therefore were wanted for slaughter more than two-legged ones', or, in More's memorable phrase, the sheep became 'so greedy and fierce that they devour men themselves'.[45] Finally, Southey also suggested that the main cause of

in the West Indies: cf. Southey to Wynn, 28 June 1831, and Southey to White, 24 Apr. 1832, *SL* iv. 227, 274.

[40] *BOTC* i. 287.

[41] [Southey], 'Emigration', 552.

[42] K. Wrightson, *Earthly necessities: economic lives in early modern Britain*, New Haven 2000, 149, 150.

[43] See [Southey], 'Inquiry', 330, 332–5; 'The poor', 194–5; *STM* i. 79, 85, 88–92, 96; and *CPB* ii. 296–300.

[44] *STM* i. 76–81.

[45] Ibid. i. 79; More, *Utopia*, 18–19.

inflation was the influx of specie from the new world. In Portugal and Spain this had encouraged a desire for lavish expenditure among the nobility:

> rents were raised; all the necessaries of life advanced in price; the burden fell upon the poor; and of the wealth which poured into the country in full streams, all that reached them was in the shape of more abundant alms, which made them more dependent than they were before, without preventing them from being more miserable.[46]

The same fashion for luxury was also prevalent in England, and produced the same consequence of 'fleecing the tenantry'.[47] The result of all these changes was that the number of free labourers grew dramatically. The lucky few rose to become tradesmen and merchants, but many more were squeezed to the margins of society to swell the number of vagabonds.[48]

The dissolution of the monasteries also remained a central factor in Southey's thinking, and his criticisms again drew liberally on More and Latimer. Monasteries had provided employment for the poor, charity for the aged and helpless, and even a home for needy people. More important, perhaps, was that they generally preferred to receive rents in kind than in cash, and whatever their other failings, the abbots generally did not indulge in the 'prodigal expenditure' of lay landlords, and so did not need to raise rents.[49] With the dissolution, this 'parental tenure' was lost and tenants found themselves paying rents three or four times higher to support the lifestyles of their new landlord-courtiers.[50] 'Nothing of the considerate superintendence which the Monks had exerted, – nothing of their liberal hospitality, was experienced from the Step-Lords.' 'The tenantry were deprived of their best landlords, artificers of their best employers, the poor and miserable of their best and surest friends.'[51] On top of this, the dissolution also worsened the vagabond problem by making members of religious houses effectively homeless. In the Book of the Church, Southey was clear that the proceeds of the dissolution should have been used to establish more bishoprics, to found colleges of divinity, to provide support for single women and to create 'seats of literature and of religious retirement'.[52] This would have helped to reinvigorate the Church, promote education and learning and perhaps also counteract the desire for gain. As it was, the sixteenth century as a whole witnessed a revolution by which the trading spirit had come to supersede the 'rude but kindlier principle of the feudal system'.[53]

From the early seventeenth century the condition of the middling and

---

46 [Southey], 'The poor', 193. See Wrightson, Earthly necessities, 119–20.
47 STM i. 79.
48 [Southey], 'Inquiry', 328–31; STM i. 73, 96–8.
49 STM i. 86.
50 [Southey], 'The poor', 194.
51 BOTC ii. 122; STM i. 88–9.
52 BOTC ii. 54. See also [Southey], 'Hallam', 207–8, and Connell, Romanticism, 241–7.
53 STM i. 79.

upper ranks improved, while that of the lower orders – whatever Frederick Eden and Thomas Bernard claimed – had remained stationary.[54] In making this argument Southey expanded on themes first expressed in *Letters from England*. The commercialisation of agriculture had created large farms which had squeezed out the yeoman class and thereby destroyed a valuable 'link in the social chain'.[55] As Coleridge put it, 'the most important rounds in the social ladder are broken' which meant that 'Hope', which 'distinguishes the free man from the slave', was extinguished'.[56] Those that remained on the land, Southey argued, endured low wages because farmers feared to raise them. The shame of poor relief was lessened as labourers recognised that they had little chance of avoiding it. Hence 'the moral evil results from the physical one: fellowship in degradation takes away the sense of shame, and the more claimants there are upon the eleemosynary funds which the law has provided, the more there will be'.[57] Meanwhile, other labourers flocked to the cities to exacerbate the problems of periodic overproduction and unemployment in manufacturing. There they were degraded mentally and morally, while their children were denied parental affection and useful education. They worked 'to the sacrifice of enjoyment, health, morals, – all of which distinguishes immortal man from brute animals, and all which renders life – mere animal life – desirable'.[58] Yet for all this, Southey accepted that the revolution in farming had brought gains in the yield and quality of crops, while that in manufacturing had produced the armaments and fuelled the trade necessary for victory against France.[59] Even machinery had the potential to liberate humanity: it was 'a great prospective good, and a great present evil; the good permanent, the evil only for a season'.[60]

The worship of wealth, Southey believed, had been growing steadily since the sixteenth century to the point where Britons were encouraged to prize everything that promoted prosperity and to despise everything that did not.[61] As Owen put it, 'the governing principle of trade, manufactures, and commerce, is immediate pecuniary gain, to which on the great scale every other is made to give way'.[62] The functions of government were seen almost solely in terms of increasing revenue and encouraging trade, and it was either forgotten or never known that the aim of government was not just wealth but welfare. In other words, Southey believed that in becoming a major reason

---

[54] [Southey], 'The poor', 191, 195–6.

[55] Ibid. 197.

[56] *LS*, 227; cf. [Southey], 'The poor', 199.

[57] [Southey], 'The poor', 192. See also 'Emigration', 555–6.

[58] [Idem], 'Works on England', 569. This point was restated many times, but see especially *STM* i. 81–2, 166–70.

[59] [Southey], 'Emigration', 555; *Peninsular war*, i. 59; *STM* i. 158–9; ii. 242–3.

[60] [Southey], 'Works on England', 569. He could even commend the steam train to May, 23 Oct. 1837, *SL* iv. 526.

[61] *STM* i. 337–8.

[62] R. Owen, *Observations on the effect of the manufacturing system*, London 1815, in R. Owen, *A new view of society and other writings*, ed. G. Claeys, London 1991, 95.

of state, commerce had largely benefited the rich and powerful, while the poor and weak were ignored and exploited. While a state could never be too rich, its people certainly could.[63] During the war years, landlords and farmers had raised rents and prices, while speculators flooded every sector to increase their wealth. These were 'men who were actually rich, and who in other times would have believed themselves so' but they were not content with the 'safe and regular' returns on their investments, preferring to risk everything to 'chance and circumstances which they could neither foresee nor controul'.[64] The result of all this 'greediness of gain' was production of cheap and flimsy goods, loss of reputation abroad, falsification of weights and measures, adulteration of foodstuffs and so on. While honest farmers and traders went to the wall, the unscrupulous few became very rich.[65] Southey believed that the country would always be liable to the distress produced by overstocking as long as 'men in trade are actuated by selfishness, which is the spirit of trade' and all the while 'competition, which is the life of trade, continues unrestrained'.[66]

Southey and Coleridge did not believe that the modern economy was a self-regulating mechanism that produced harmony as a result of the unintended consequences of economic interest. The effect of untrammelled greed was crisis, and the 'spirit' of trade was dangerous without a counterweight. 'The habits attached to this character', Coleridge argued, 'must, if there be no adequate counterpoise, inevitably lead us, under the specious name of utility, practical knowledge, and so forth, to look at all things thro' the medium of the market, and to estimate the Worth of all pursuits and attainments by their marketable value. In this does the Spirit of Trade consist.' Southey agreed.[67] In the Colloquies he considered how in past times the 'spirit' had been 'confined to a narrow scale and within a narrow sphere' where it had not adversely affected the national interest or the national character because it was widely accepted that covetousness was the root of all evil.[68] What was required was moral reformation, or, as Coleridge put it, a 'change in the mind of the nation'.[69] Southey argued that a man should prepare himself for a future state by 'controlling the unworthy propensities of his nature, and improving all its better aspirations'. It should be his aim 'to promote the welfare and happiness of those who are dependent upon him, or whom he has the means of assisting' and to encourage as far as possible 'whatever is useful and ornamental in society' and 'whatever tends to refine and elevate humanity'.[70] In

63 STM i. 100–1, 193–4.
64 [Southey], 'Works on England', 568.
65 See [idem], 'The poor', 205–6; 'Popular disaffection', 543; STM i. 194; ii. 250–3; and [R. Southey], 'On the corn laws', QR li (Mar. 1834), 246–7, 254–6.
66 [Idem], 'Emigration', 573.
67 LS, 189; Southey to Senhouse, 22 Mar. 1817, LC iv. 258.
68 STM ii. 248. See also [Southey], 'Emigration', 546; The doctor, 233; and CPB iv. 669.
69 LS, 192.
70 STM i. 165.

particular, men of business should take care to exercise 'self-watchfulness' and use the restraint of a 'higher principle' to ensure that the spirit of enterprise did not pass the bounds of 'of prudence and of principle'.[71]

Counteracting Mammon

Southey and Coleridge were, of course, not the only people who feared that Mammon was stalking the land. The tradition of evangelical political economy shared these concerns. Men such as J. B. Sumner, Edward Copleston and Thomas Chalmers opposed the optimistic natural theology of Paley in favour of that of Malthus. The world was a state of trial in which divinely instituted natural laws dealt out rewards and punishments which promoted virtue and discouraged vice. It was therefore undesirable that there should be 'artificial' measures, such as generous poor law provision, which prevented individuals from experiencing the consequences of their actions. Once educated to know the importance of industry and thrift, a man who refused to work would have no recourse to relief: his poverty was his punishment, and acted as an incentive to virtuous behaviour. The rich might also learn lessons from natural laws. In following Malthus by rejecting Say's Law, Chalmers argued that there was retributive justice in the trade cycle. An avaricious man might overproduce or speculate to the point of causing a collapse in his fortunes, and so bankruptcy was a just consequence of vice. By contrast, extreme evangelicals rejected this mechanistic interpretation of the natural order, and argued that special providential intervention was common. It was folly to think that there were 'laws' one could understand and obey so as to avoid punishment in the future. This kind of thinking, it has been argued, was central to evangelicals such as Sadler, Lord Ashley and Henry Drummond, and it helped to shape their belief in the necessity of interventionist government.[72] In other words attitudes to nature and providence were central in explaining whether paternalism or *laissez-faire* should be the order of the day.

Southey was not comfortable with the moderate evangelical position and he was sceptical about the idea that rewards and punishments were the way to motivate people. Sumner had suggested in his *Records of creation* that a schooling in adversity developed the virtues, but Southey believed that while true in a limited sense 'there is a degree of misery which is fatal to them'.[73] Excessive suffering hardened the heart, and extreme poverty reduced man to the level of a beast. It was better to motivate individuals by hope of improvement than by fear of suffering.[74] More generally, because the world as it existed was radically different from how it ought to be, he could not believe that

---

71 Ibid. i. 195, 197.
72 Hilton, *Age of atonement*, 14–19, 91–8, 211–15.
73 [Southey], 'The poor', 209.
74 Ibid. 209–10, 215; cf. *LS*, 224.

its operations mechanistically revealed divine justice. Many people might indeed be poor because they were idle, but there were also many cases where industrious labourers were reduced to poverty

> not by any misconduct of their own, not by any affliction befalling them in the course of nature, not by any natural visitations of pestilence, or famine, – not by the ravages of war, but by those changes in trade, which, though improvements in themselves, and at length greatly beneficial upon the great scale, are injurious and even ruinous to many in their immediate effects.[75]

Similarly, it was self-evident that many avaricious men passed their lives without punishment for their ill-gotten gain. Hence Southey explicitly denied the moderate evangelical argument, stating that for individuals 'the day of reckoning may not always be in this world'.[76] Did he have more sympathy with the extreme evangelicals? Certainly Sadler and Ashley were good friends, though he had no interest in the excessive millenarianism of Edward Irving, who was 'beyond all doubt, insane'.[77] We have also seen his strong belief that nations were subject to providential punishment, although it does not necessarily follow that government should therefore take a large role in social and economic life. Unlike the moderate evangelicals, however, there was little in his thinking which created principled opposition to its intervention.

What was to be done about the post-war social and economic problems? With regards to the manufacturing system, Southey was in agreement with both Owen and Malthus that it had become too large. Like a cancer, it had 'acquired so great a bulk, its nerves have branched so widely, and the vessels of the tumour are so inosculated into some of the principal veins and arteries of the natural system' that simply cutting it out would be fatal.[78] He hoped that sooner rather than later it would lose its competitive edge: as rivals in Europe and America acquired machinery it was natural they would wish to protect their burgeoning industries rather than allow them to be ruined by cheap imports. Indeed, while some were nervous about this prospect, Southey positively looked forward to the gradual and sensible 'euthanasy' of the manufacturing system.[79] In the meantime, however, it had to be controlled or else the 'steam-engine will blow up this whole fabric of society'.[80] Because manufacturers disclaimed all responsibility for their 'calculated system of inhumanity' they must be subjected to legal regulation, and to that end both Southey and Coleridge supported efforts to reform factories in the 1810s and

---

75 [Southey], 'Emigration', 543.
76 [Idem], 'On the means', 91.
77 Southey to C. Bowles, 19 Jan. 1832, in *The correspondence of Robert Southey with Caroline Bowles*, ed. E. Dowden, London 1881, 239.
78 *STM* i. 171.
79 Ibid. ii. 245. See also [Southey], 'Popular disaffection', 542–3, and 'Corn laws', 231, 256–7.
80 Southey to Rickman, 26 Apr. 1826, *LC* v. 250.

1830s.[81] In 1832 Sadler chaired a select committee investigation, and when he lost his Commons seat later that year, Ashley became the leader of the ten hours movement at Westminster. Southey esteemed both men, followed the committee evidence closely, and even sent a petition in support of 'our little white slaves'. He fully endorsed the Factory Bill of 1833, and bemoaned the successful efforts of Lord Morpeth and the 'Cotton Kings' to dilute its contents.[82] In thanking Ashley for his efforts, Southey continued to hope that 'this system of insatiable avarice, or, rather, greediness of gain' would eventually be restrained.[83]

One way to contain manufacturing was by supporting agriculture. As Anna Gambles has shown, protectionists believed not just in encouraging self-sufficiency in food, but also in developing the implications of the under-consumptionist agenda. The corn laws helped to prevent overproduction in manufacture and by preserving the agricultural sector ensured a healthy market for its goods.[84] In the 1810s Southey expressed scepticism or indifference towards the corn laws, but by the 1830s he was increasingly impressed by arguments in their defence.[85] In response to Ebenezer Elliott's *Corn law rhymes* he prepared an article which drew heavily on John Barton's important *In defence of the corn laws*.[86] He argued that protectionism was not about supporting one economic sector against another, but about the whole nation: 'the prosperity of the landed proprietor, the merchant, the manufacturer, and the labourer, are so intimately connected, that a system of policy which seeks to enrich any one of these classes at the expense of the rest, is likely to terminate in the impoverishment of all'.[87] Besides, he doubted many of the claims mounted by opponents. Scrapping the corn laws would dramatically increase unemployment in southern England, causing an escalation in poor rates. These labourers would be unlikely to find employment in the north, and even if they did the abundance of labour would drive down manufacturing wages thereby offsetting any benefits created by cheaper bread. It was also a mistake to deprive the country of a vibrant home market in agriculture in

---

[81] Southey to White, 24 Apr. 1832, SL iv. 273. See S. T. Coleridge, *Shorter works and fragments*, ed. H. J. Jackson and J. R. de Jackson, London–Princeton 1995, i. 714–51; EOT ii. 483–9; iii. 155–8; and Edwards, *Statesman's science*, 165–74.

[82] Southey to Wynn, [3, 4 June 1833], NL ii. 400. See P. Mandler, 'Cain and Abel: two aristocrats and the early Victorian factory acts', HJ xxvii (1984), 83–109, and Lawes, *Paternalism*, 91–6, 150–83.

[83] Southey to Lord Ashley, 24 July 1833, in E. Hodder, *The life and work of the seventh earl of Shaftesbury*, London 1886, i. 169.

[84] A. Gambles, *Protection and politics: conservative economic discourse, 1815–1852*, Woodbridge 1999, 27–36, 50–5.

[85] [Southey], 'Works on England', 567; Southey to May, 30 Dec. 1833, in *Letters to May*, 263.

[86] [Southey], 'Corn laws', 279–82, was by J. W. Croker. See S. Brown 'Ebenezer Elliott and Robert Southey: Southey's break with the *Quarterly Review*', *Review of English Studies* xxii (1971), 307–11.

[87] [Southey], 'Corn laws', 268.

favour of uncertain, and potentially protected, foreign markets for manufac-tured goods.[88] Similarly, the likelihood of cheap corn imports was overstated. 'No sooner shall we have made ourselves dependent upon the foreign grower', Southey argued, 'than he will tax us for his own benefit; and his government, through him, will tax us also.'[89] The security of the nation required a domestic supply of food, and, what was more, it should also aspire to self-sufficiency in goods that by 'nature or habit' had become virtual necessities.[90] Southey opposed free trade because he saw it in terms of dependence:

> International commerce is beneficial when commodities are interchanged to the *mutual* benefit of two countries, and to the promotion of industry *in both*; it is injurious when it renders one country dependent upon another for the conveniences of life – and in the last degree ruinous if it induce a dependence for the necessaries.[91]

This was the free trade argument on its head: rather than creating peace and concord, the possibility of war and discord meant that free trade was a dangerous proposition.

The issue of poverty remained Southey's central concern. He reiterated his fundamental belief that the poor received few of the benefits of civilisation, but his broad acceptance of the existing social and political order, and his belief that 'artificial distinctions' were necessary and desirable, meant that he did not wish to attack the structure of property, only to remedy the fact that 'the poor are too poor'.[92] The post-war depression and the continued acceleration of the poor rates – £7.9m in 1818 – ensured that this was a fundamental area of debate. At one pole were those who drew on Blackstone and Paley to argue that the poor had a right to relief, while on the other were those – including supporters of Sturges Bourne's 1817 select committee – who followed Malthus' view that the poor laws encouraged population growth and prevented self-improvement.[93] If a point of convergence was possible, it centred on whether the able-bodied labourer was responsible for his unemployment, and this helps to explain the growing use of the distinction between 'deserving' and 'undeserving' poor. Coleridge and Southey were also concerned about the cost of the poor rates, and the numbers of 'undeserving' poor. Coleridge denounced the Speenhamland system for paying three-quar-ters of the rates to 'healthy, robust, and ... *industrious, hard-working* Paupers in lieu of Wages'.[94] Southey at one time suggested that because the poor laws

---

[88] Ibid. 231, 249, 256–8, 263–4, 266–7, 276–7.
[89] Ibid. 274.
[90] Ibid. 256.
[91] Ibid.
[92] [Idem], 'Dymond, 86; [idem], 'Saint-Simon, 450.
[93] See Poynter, *Society*, chs vi–vii; P. Mandler, 'Tories and paupers: Christian political economy and the making of the New Poor Law', *HJ* xxxiii (1990), 81–103; Horne, *Prop-erty*, chs iv–vi; and Lawes, *Paternalism*, 45–63.
[94] *LS*, 222.

bred paupers, their 'gradual extinction' was desirable, but at another invoked Blackstone in support of them, and blamed the problem on their 'mal-administration or perversion'.[95] Donald Winch has recently argued that Southey was closer to the anti-poor law argument than has hitherto been recognised because Rickman 'was increasingly influential in changing (even writing) the position' he adopted in his *Quarterly Review* articles.[96] There is some truth in this, but confusion has arisen over the authorship of two essays written in 1818: 'On the means of improving the people' was Southey's, while 'On the poor laws' was Rickman's. These gestated in tandem, but their authorship was largely separate.[97] While the two men freely exchanged ideas about the poor laws, and perhaps influenced each other, they did not, in fact, see eye-to-eye on social and economic matters.

Rickman's article made a vigorous assault on the existing poor laws. He was influenced by the Oriel Noetic, John Davison, whose *Considerations on the poor laws* supported Bourne's findings and recommended abolition of support for the able-bodied within ten years.[98] Rickman presented the poor rates as a great incursion on property, and not just as a tax, because the wages of the industrious poor were also depressed by provision for the idle.[99] He followed Davison in arguing that the laws cancelled out the penalties of vice:

> Proclaim that, for the future, the poor, no more than the rich, are to be exempted from the consequences of their own imprudence and misconduct; that they must suffer misery when they have brought it upon themselves, or have not exerted themselves to avoid it; in fine, that they shall not escape the common lot of human nature, whereby it has been wisely and benevolently ordained that industry shall be rewarded with temporal blessings, and idleness draw after it its proper punishment.[100]

It was important to draw a firm line between 'misfortune and misconduct' and between 'the industrious and the dissolute poor'.[101] There would be measures of provision for children, the infirm and the elderly, and if the pauper could prove his industry and character to a magistrate, he too would be relieved. As for the idle poor, if they had dependent families then they would be supported at subsistence level, while those without families would have to rely on charity to prevent the 'last extremity of human suffering'.[102] Because the manufacturing districts were prone to fluctuations in employment over which the worker had no control, Rickman proposed that employers should

---

95 Southey to Landor, 17 Sept. 1817, *NL* ii. 174; [Southey], 'Emigration', 540.
96 Winch, *Riches*, 311–12.
97 See N. L. Kaderly, 'Southey and the *Quarterly Review*', *Modern Language Notes* lxx (1955), 261–3.
98 [J. Rickman], 'On the poor laws', *QR* xviii (Jan. 1818), 267–9, 281–5, 293–5, 300.
99 Ibid. 259, 261–2, 270.
100 Ibid. 287.
101 Ibid.
102 Ibid. 288. See also pp. 293–6.

contribute a shilling in the pound towards a fund which could be drawn on in times of sickness and distress, assuming the applicant was not profligate or idle.[103] Taken together, he was convinced that these proposals would reduce the poor rates, enable wages to rise and stimulate the growth of charitable foundations. In short, they would enable the labouring classes to become 'moral, respectable, and happy'.[104]

In preparing his article, Southey read the first report of Bourne's committee, Davison's *Considerations* as well as the anti-abolitionist *Treatise on the poor laws* by T. P. Courtenay. He thought Davison's pamphlet 'exceedingly able' but preferred a gradual reduction of the rates rather than outright abolition in ten years.[105] In the main, he accepted the distinction between the idle and the industrious poor, and, adopting Rickman's terminology, wrote of how pauperism was exacerbated by individual failings: 'misfortune in one instance, misconduct in fifty; want of frugality, want of forethought, want of prudence, want of principle' but also 'want of hope', for which the individual could not entirely be blamed.[106] Here, however, he was primarily thinking of reasonably well paid manufacturing workers rather than the impoverished agricultural labourer. Southey asserted the centrality of a reformation of manners, and expressed interest in encouraging financial independence for the poor. Unlike Rickman, he supported friendly societies, noting only that more needed to be done to prevent them being defrauded.[107] Both men agreed, however, on the usefulness of savings banks because they provided not merely insurance but a repository for earned wealth. Such banks had the backing of men as diverse as Colquhoun, Malthus, Ricardo and Wilberforce, and in 1817 George Rose's bill to promote them was passed.[108] Southey and Rickman had high hopes for them, believing that they would help the poor to start a family, and would offer support in hardship. They would also have positive effects on personal character by encouraging industry and frugality and by providing an incentive to save further. As it happened these hopes were to prove largely fanciful, and friendly societies remained the more popular way for the lower orders to protect themselves against distress.[109]

On other issues, however, the two men disagreed about how best to improve the poor. Southey was inspired by the efforts of the Society for Bettering the Condition of the Poor, which since 1796 had been proposing schemes to help the lower orders without making them dependent. In particular, he supported a plan to give cottagers a garden and enough grassland to support a cow or two, and argued – as Coleridge did in his *Lay sermon* – that its success had

103 Ibid. 285.
104 Ibid. 286. See also pp. 290, 298.
105 Southey to Wynn, 20 Nov. 1817, SL iii. 79.
106 [Southey], 'On the means', 85; cf. [Rickman], 'Poor laws', 287.
107 [Southey], 'The poor', 218; [Rickman], 'Poor laws', 278.
108 Poynter, Society, 290.
109 [Southey], 'The poor', 219; 'On the means', 96–7, 104–5; [Rickman], 'Poor laws', 278, 285, 299–300.

already been demonstrated by the earl of Winchilsea. The earl suspected that farmers had slowly but deliberately been depriving labourers of small plots of land in order to make them more dependent. To counteract this, he had on his Rutland estate given nearly eighty labourers enough land to keep a cow, believing that it helped them to improve their condition and so made them more contented with their situation:

> [H]aving acquired a sort of independence, which makes them set a higher value upon their character, they are generally considered in the neighbour-hood as men the most to be depended upon and trusted; that feeling the advantage of possessing a little, their industry is excited by hope; and that when a labourer has obtained a cow, and land sufficient to maintain her, his next thought is to save money enough for buying another.[110]

The 'Wisdom' and 'Goodness' of Winchilsea was self-evident to Coleridge and Southey, and indeed they could not have found a better summary of their own thinking on this subject.[111] Southey was also impressed by a similar experiment in Wiltshire in 1801, where labourers were allowed to occupy and cultivate land at a 'fair rent'.[112] 'Let us multiply farms instead of throwing many into one', he concluded, 'Let the labourer, wherever it is possible, have his grass plot and his garden.'[113] Rickman, however, had little time for such thinking. Wealth – 'all the comforts and conveniences of life' – arose from the surpluses generated by agriculture, and so large and efficient farms made economic sense. 'If the face of the country', he argued, 'were divided into small occupancies' the current population would be reduced to a level 'far inferior to that of the lowest labourer at present.'[114] These sorts of schemes were deceptively attractive, but feeding a cow in winter usually compelled a cottager to steal, while plots and gardens merely took labourers away from waged employment, required other men to fill their places and so helped to increase the poor rates.[115] None of this washed off on Southey. He saw in these schemes not just a chance to recreate the economic independence destroyed by the agricultural revolution, but also sources of psychological independ-ence: pride and hope.

Southey retained his youthful interest in experiments with communal living and communal ownership. In private he occasionally expressed a hope that communities of goods would emerge in a future state of society, and even in public he could be found encouraging the Spenceans as long as their methods were peaceful and voluntary.[116] In 1817 Owen began to publicise his

110 [Southey], 'The poor', 207.
111 LS, 219. See also pp. 226–7, 263–4.
112 [Southey], 'The poor', 207–8.
113 Ibid. 234.
114 [Rickman], 'Poor laws', 278, 279.
115 Ibid. 279–80. See Rickman to Southey, 6 Jan. 1818, in Williams, Lamb's friend, 199.
116 Southey to Rickman, 14 Sept. 1816, SL iii. 45; Southey, Journal, 264–5; Southey to Bowles, 17 Aug. 1829, in Correspondence with Bowles, 171. The positive account of the

plan to alleviate unemployment by building 'villages of union' which could become economically self-sufficient. A mere £60,000 would be sufficient to set up a single community, and he hoped that government would supply the capital. In the *Letter to William Smith*, Southey praised these plans for home colonies, and proposed that the government purchase waste lands on which the poor could be settled in villages.[117] Once this national property had been brought into cultivation it could be leased 'like Church or College lands' and so contribute to the public revenue.[118] Rickman, however, thought such schemes encouraged idleness and dismissed their supporters as 'feeble-minded idiots'.[119] Southey was not convinced, and in 1821 he was impressed by a *Report of the committee of journeymen*, which was based on a plan suggested by the early socialist writer, George Mudie.[120] This pamphlet formed the basis for the discussion of Owenism in the *Colloquies* – indeed much of the account was plagiarised from it.[121] By making co-operation rather than competition the basis of social organisation, genuine progress in civilisation could be achieved. The proposed community would purchase goods wholesale and in bulk, thereby saving 25 per cent of the cost, and it would distribute labour equally so that time was created for 'intellectual enjoyments and rational amusements'.[122] In countering the view that it was hard to ensure amity in such communities, the *Report* suggested (rather unconvincingly Southey thought) that all members take an oath to help each other, and that the community reserved the right to expel members.[123] The objections about communities of goods did not arise because this form of ownership was rejected, although the *Report* recommended that contributions to the community should be regulated according to means. Southey approved, adding that the desire 'to have and to hold' was the 'main spring of all improvements in society'.[124] Overall, however, he believed that the community would have improved character and been an economic success and that its failure was a result not of theoretical deficiencies but of insufficient capital invested at the outset.

In 1829 Southey heard from his friend Robert Gooch about the Brighton Co-operative Benevolent Fund Association which had been founded two years earlier. Members of the association had pooled together a common fund by subscription and invested it in business. Already they possessed a shop, a boat and a large garden, and as their means increased they hoped to employ more people, eventually intending to purchase land in order to create a commu-

---

Spenceans was struck from 'Parliamentary reform' by Gifford, and reappeared in Southey, *Essays*, i. 411–12.

[117] Southey, *William Smith*, 33–4.
[118] Southey to Murray, 14 Jan. 1817, *NL* ii. 148.
[119] Rickman to Southey, 7 Sept. 1816, in Williams, *Lamb's friend*, 182.
[120] See Southey to G. Bedford, 15 Apr. 1821, *LC* v. 64–5, and *Report of the committee appointed at a meeting of journeymen*, London [1821].
[121] Cf. *STM* i. 135–6, and *Report*, 6–9.
[122] *STM* i. 135.
[123] Ibid. i. 137.
[124] Ibid. i. 139.

nity. Gooch was impressed, and wrote a paper for the *Quarterly Review* to publicise these ideas. The plan, Southey commented, was a 'slip of Owenism grafted upon sound common sense stock', although he worried about 'where the limits of private property are to be fixed'.[125] Rickman expressed his usual concerns about how '*Labour in common* produces idleness in all, or injustice to the industrious', yet he was willing to examine the association to see if it encouraged 'thrift and accumulation'.[126] Pleasantly surprised to find that it did, he reported to Southey that such societies increased good behaviour, reduced crime and insolvency, and would be of enormous benefit as they spread.[127] Meanwhile Southey enthused about how co-operation might form the foundation of a new type of political economy, 'existing systems being built either upon sand or bottomless mud'.[128] He too was impressed with the efficiency of these communities and the way in which they brought about a reformation of character, but he also worried that equality would be embraced as a formal aim. These fears proved well founded. Many co-operators – for instance those in Birmingham – refused to recognise the Brighton Association because it did not go far enough towards a community in land and goods. Southey commented that this would create idleness and that it would frighten off middle- and upper-class support. When he read a report of a meeting of co-operators in London in November he confirmed that it displayed the 'rankest levelling language'.[129] For Southey, co-operation was about enabling the lower orders to support themselves throughout the life cycle: it was about creating independence and not about revolutionising the structure of property.

The reformation of morals and manners was central to all these schemes. The immediate necessity was for a gradual removal of what Coleridge called 'encouragements and temptations to Vice and Folly'.[130] Southey criticised existing laws against vice for either not being strong enough, or more often, not being effectively enforced. He attacked excessive gambling, cruel sports, game laws and Sabbath-breaking, but the issue to which he returned repeatedly was the need for stricter regulation of alehouses. Their growth was a sign of 'increased and increasing depravity of manners', for they were places of 'idleness, misery and pauperism' where the labourer squandered wages that should be saved for marriage or spent on the family.[131] In future, he suggested, new alehouses should only be licensed in areas with expanding populations,

---

125 Southey to Rickman, 9 July 1829, and Southey to R. Gooch, 8 Aug. 1829, *LC* vi. 50, 57. See [R. Gooch], 'The co-operatives', *QR* xli (Nov. 1829), 359–75.
126 Rickman to Southey, 14 July 1829, in Williams, *Lamb's friend*, 246.
127 Rickman to Southey, 25 Sept. 1829, ibid. 247–8.
128 Southey to H. Taylor, n.d., *LC* vi. 81.
129 Southey to Rickman, 5 Jan. 1830, ibid. vi. 82. See also Southey to Bowles, 17 Aug., 14 Sept. 1829, in *Correspondence with Bowles*, 171, 176; Southey to Landor, 22 Aug. 1829, *SL* iv. 146–7; [R. Southey], 'French revolution: conspiration de Babeuf', *QR* xlv (Apr. 1831), 167–209; and 'Saint-Simon', 407–50.
130 *LS*, 229.
131 [Southey], 'On the means', 82, 84.

and there should be more willingness to shut down places of habitual disorder and drunkenness. Magistrates should enforce existing laws, and if they were not enough, new laws should be passed. The immediate result would be an improved moral tone in the parish and the reduction of the poor rates.[132] In more general terms, Southey advocated a better system of policing and a reform of the criminal justice system. It is not known what he thought of Peel's reforms while at the home office in the 1820s, but his preference was for simplification and consolidation, for punishment – including execution – which matched the offence, and for more effort to reform the offender.[133] Overall, he summarised his recommendations as 'wholesome chastisement for the dissolute, wholesome encouragement for the well-disposed, and the watchful execution of those minor laws, upon the proper observance of which the general weal is not less dependent than domestic comfort and happiness are upon the minor morals'.[134] This was not, he thought, excessive meddling in the lives of individuals, only the better enforcement of necessary laws.

An improved system of national education was, as we have seen, absolutely essential not just for instilling loyalty but for enabling progress, and Southey continued to press this issue. The existing system of voluntary subscription was useful, but was unable to raise enough money to be extensive or effective, and besides government ought not to rely on charity to provide 'one of the most imperative and important of all public duties'.[135] He was aware that critics would accuse the government of a 'passion for interference' but 'we shall err wickedly and perilously' if nothing was done.[136] Ideally, he wanted to see a system of parochial schools spread across the country. Attached to the establishment, they would provide education for the children of all poor parents, and attendance would be a necessary condition of receiving poor relief. They would be regularly inspected by a salaried overseer and, if the clergy and the wealthy took a benevolent interest in their operation, they would flourish. They need not be expensive: if £200 a year could fund a school, then a mere £26,000 would educate all the poor children of London. This was such good value, Southey mused, that even a hard-hearted economist could not object.[137] Within a few years the young would be provided with the basics of necessary knowledge and a rule of conduct for life, and moreover their manners would be reformed, creating a 'sense of independence, a habit of industry, a sense of prudence, and a feeling of principle'.[138] The eventual result would be that pauperism and crime would decline, and the poor rates and the costs of implementing justice would diminish. This optimism was only possible, however, if education had a solid religious basis, and for this

---

132 Ibid. 83–4, 101–2, 117–18
133 Ibid. 115–16; STM i. 109.
134 [Southey], 'On the means', 87.
135 [Idem], 'The poor', 225.
136 [Idem], 'On the means', 93.
137 Ibid. 96–101, 107–111.
138 Ibid. 96.

reason Southey was strongly opposed to the secular trends evident in educa-tion from the 1820s.[139]

Despite their close friendship, the similarities between Southey and Rickman can be overstated. Rickman was a staunch defender of the 'sacred-ness of private property' and hated poor relief as an unjust 'agrarian law' which in effect legalised plundering the rich. He advised Southey to 'praise *selfishness*' in his writings, 'the only mover of large beneficial action, because general'. The real motor of commercial society was such self-interest, and attempts to limit it invariably caused more harm than good. 'The down-hill path of alms-giving and patronage is pleasant to the individuals who give and who receive', he insisted, but 'cruelly mischievous to the community in an enlarged view of consequences.' His own '*Canons of Benevolence*', he suspected, would seem 'repulsive and severe' to others.[140] Although Southey rarely challenged Rickman on such points, it should by now by evident that it was not to selfishness that he looked, but the transformation of human moti-vation through education. This was why he praised the practical benevolence of Owen, and claimed that he was one of three men who had given a 'moral impulse' to the nation.[141] The points of disagreement between Owen and Southey were important but not fatal, and they were essentially restatements of Southey's objections to Godwin: atheism and necessitarianism. Owen's *Address* was 'much more injudicious than his conversation' and contained ideas that were 'misplaced, injudicious, and reprehensible' and which would lose him the support of the establishment.[142] While Owen despised Christi-anity because it instilled false notions of character, such as original sin, into the mind, Southey thought that founding a system on an irreligious basis was 'building upon sand', and, worse, was to propound views contrary to 'indi-vidual happiness and to the general good'.[143] He also opposed Owen's neces-sitarianism. 'I never regarded man as a machine', he confided to his journal after touring New Lanark, 'I never believed him to be merely a material being; I never for a moment could listen to the nonsense of Helvetius, nor suppose, as Owen does, that men may be cast in a mould (like other parts of his mill) and take impression with perfect certainty.'[144] Owen's mechanistic philosophy seemed to undermine individuality and domesticity and ultimately appeared to oppose the freedom of the will. Yet this should not disguise the weight that Southey attached to education, for he did believe that 'man is as clay in the potter's hands' and that 'the mass of mankind ... are what our institu-

---

[139] See [idem], 'Elementary teaching', *QR* xxxix (Jan. 1829), 126–43, and *The doctor*, 227–9.
[140] Rickman to Southey, 8 May, 29 Oct. 1817, 14 July 1829, in Williams, *Lamb's friend*, 193, 195, 246.
[141] *STM* i. 132. The other two were Thomas Clarkson and Andrew Bell.
[142] Southey to Rickman, 25 Aug. 1816, *LC* iv. 196, 197.
[143] Southey, *William Smith*, 33; *STM* i. 133.
[144] Southey, *Journal*, 264.

tions make us'.[145] Owen and Southey shared an intellectual inheritance from the 1790s but diverged on the role of religion in spreading benevolence and advancing progress.

It should by now be evident that Southey did not attach a huge role to the state in alleviating social distress. Most of what he advocated – cow-cottagers, savings banks, co-operative villages, reformed manners – was designed to create conditions so that individuals could secure themselves independence. He did not think that the implementation of such schemes required excessive intrusion from the state. He was proud of Britain's reputation as a philanthropic nation, and was inclined to agree with Bernard that 'more may be done by well disposed and active individuals, than could be effected by legislative interference'.[146] Benevolence on the part of individuals, such as that exercised by a good landlord like Winchilsea or a good manufacturer like Owen, could perform wonders. The work of 'real radical reform' had to begin in 'the root of the state' which meant 'individuals exerting themselves in their own sphere, for the immediate good of others, and for their own almost equally immediate advantage!'[147] Ideally, if individual behaviour was revolutionised by the principles of the Gospels then many social problems would quickly be alleviated, but in the meantime government was necessary to do what individuals could not or would not do. It had to concern itself with education because private provision was ineffective, and it had to regulate factories because the masters were too selfish to do it themselves. If individuals would not rein in their greed then a degree of 'wholesome restraint' over trade – including tariffs – might be necessary. Although the 'evil of vexatious interference' remained great, it was possible that a revival of the older system of guilds might help to prevent overstocking: 'when trade is conducted by corporate bodies, the check upon fraud may more than compensate for any inconvenience arising from want of competition'.[148] If individuals were what they ought to be, then there would be little need for the state, but that not being the case, its duty was to help prevent the harmful consequences of individual self-interest.

'The benefits of commerce', Montesinos told the ghost of Sir Thomas More, 'cannot be too widely diffused, their general extension being for the general good.'[149] These sorts of economic sentiments are not usually associated with Southey, but it is clear that he believed that commerce had been central to the power and liberty of eighteenth-century Britain. Yet his endorsement of the tradition of *doux commerce* only extended to the pursuit of independence, not to the mania for enrichment. He agreed with Coleridge that there was an 'over-balance' of the commercial spirit which meant that wealth was

---

145 [Idem], 'The poor', 224; Southey to R. H. Inglis, 22 Feb. 1829, *LC* vi. 28–9.
146 [Southey], 'The poor', 205.
147 [Idem], 'On the means', 105. See also *The doctor*, 85.
148 *STM* ii. 250. See also Southey to Rickman, 16 Feb. 1830, *LC* vi. 87.
149 *STM* i. 190.

esteemed beyond happiness and welfare, and that political economy was the intellectual prop of this selfishness. The revolutions in agriculture and manufacture had indeed created wealth, but at the cost of the health, morality and independence of the lower orders. Formerly, Coleridge argued, the commercial spirit had been counterbalanced by feelings of 'rank and ancestry', by the influence of a learned and philosophic class and by religion. None of these were now effective in dampening 'commercial avidity', and so the need for a clerisy was more pressing than ever.[150] Similarly, Southey persisted with his argument that religion and education would reform manners across all classes. The lower orders would become more independent, while the middle and upper classes might be persuaded that there was more to life than the 'love of lucre'. Following the 'commonwealthsmen' agenda laid out by Edward VI, all that was needed was 'good education, good example, good laws, and the just execution of those laws'.[151] Eventually the nation would realise that the 'system which produces the happiest moral effects' was the most beneficial to 'the interest of the individual and to the general weal: upon this basis the science of political economy will rest at last'.[152]

[150] See LS, 170–4, 185–7, 190–1.
[151] STM i. 102–3. See W. K. Jordan, *The chronicle and political papers of King Edward VI*, London 1966, pp. xxiv–xxv, 165.
[152] Southey, 'The poor', 199.

9

In Defence of Church and State

On his way through Brussels in June 1826, Southey was surprised and amused to learn that he had been returned as MP for Downton in Wiltshire. Arriving in London at the end of the month, he found a letter from a 'zealous admirer of the British Constitution' who had been impressed with the *Book of the Church*.[1] Thinking Southey might prove a valuable MP in the upcoming session, Lord Radnor, who controlled the seat, had him installed during the general election. The offer was refused: Southey was ineligible as a government pensioner and besides he lacked the necessary property qualifications. Meanwhile, celebratory preparations were under way in Keswick, and although the organisers decided not to chair the member for Downton, there was a band to salute him, and music on the lake in the evening. Southey soon wrote a letter to the speaker of the House of Commons explaining why he could not take up his seat, and this was read to the House on 22 November. That was the end of the matter, but for an abortive plan formed by Robert Inglis to acquire an estate of £300 a year for his friend.[2] Although Southey conceded that the land might be desirable, it was not really the issue. Rather, he felt that 'my habits, nor talents, nor disposition' were suited to parliament, and he agreed with his friend Henry Taylor that he would make a 'bad statesman'.[3] This otherwise trivial episode provides a glimpse into the importance with which defenders of the unreformed Church and State viewed Southey's voice by the 1820s.

The national Church?

By this time Southey seemed eminently orthodox. He told correspondents whose faith was troubling them that his own was now secure, and he happily toyed with putting together a 'view of the moral & historical, – that is the internal & external evidencies of Xtianity'.[4] He often stated his conviction that the marks of design in creation indicated the existence of God, and the

---

1   [Lord Radnor] to Southey, 10 July 1826, *LC* v. 261.
2   See ibid. v. 262–5, 273–9; *SL* iv. 6–8; and *NL* ii. 306.
3   Southey to H. Taylor, 13 Nov. 1826, and Southey to G. Bedford, 8 Dec. 1826, *LC* v. 269, 274.
4   Southey to J. T. Coleridge, 20 Dec. 1820, in Braekman, 'Letters', 117. See Southey to [E. Hamond], 2 Mar. 1819, *LC* v. 11–13, and G. Carnall, 'A note on Southey's later religious opinions', *PQ* xxxi (1952), 399–406.

constitution of human nature showed religion to be essential to happiness. Biblical history was mainly accurate: 'our first parents' knew their creator, and evidence of the deluge could be found in the modern world. Mosaic law was divine in origin, and the promise of a new revelation had been given to the Jews. As for the New Testament, its authenticity had been proven by detailed scholarship and only a fool could think it fraudulent. Of course, Southey conceded, there were some matters which remained difficult to explain, but he fell back on the argument most clearly stated by Samuel Johnson, that questioning all mysteries merely exposed the arrogance of human intellect.[5] On tests of doctrine, he also now appeared orthodox. The existence of sin, 'an original taint in human nature, – a radical infirmity, – an innate and congenital disease' was self-evident, and the Trinity was no longer a sufficient stumbling block to his 'conscientiously' subscribing to the Thirty-Nine Articles.[6] He also supported episcopacy, arguing that it had 'prevailed among the Britons', and apostolicity, although he did think it could not be proved because the documents were unreliable.[7] It was easy, then, for it to be assumed that he was an orthodox Churchman.

In fact, however, he remained at odds with both Clapham and Hackney.[8] He did not manifest a severe religiosity in his private or public life, remained wary of excessive displays of enthusiasm and was persistently critical of overly ascetic trends, such as strict sabbatarianism. Moreover, for all his commitment to Anglicanism, he could not conceal his dissent from some of its doctrines and perhaps for this reason he avoided theology in favour of religious history. As he explained to Taylor, the purpose of his work, 'whether controversial or historical, is not to disturb established delusions, but to defend established truths'.[9] Occasionally, however, he could not conceal some 'delusions'. In the *Life of Wesley*, for instance, the Methodists were praised for welcoming the 'orthodox of all descriptions, Churchmen or Dissenters, Baptists or Paedobaptists, Presbyterians or Independents, Calvinists or Arminians; no profession, no sacrifice of any kind was exacted'. The *British Critic* was not amused by this latitudinarianism and pointed out that these groups differed on many essential points.[10] The Catholic author Milner made the same point: Southey's criticisms of the 1662 Act of Uniformity, and especially its stipulation that all clergy subscribe to the Articles, undermined his 'professed' support for the episcopal Church.[11] Critics – whether friendly or hostile – could sometimes see the chinks in Southey's armour.

The central problem was his ambivalent view about original sin. Indeed, referring to it as a 'taint' or a 'germ' in human nature conveyed something

---

5 [Southey], 'Infidelity', 528, 531, 532–3.
6 BOTC i. 310; Southey to Wynn, 3 Feb. 1835, NL ii. 420.
7 BOTC i. 82. See LW ii. 441; Butler, Book, 20–1; and Southey, Vindiciae, 57.
8 See Sack, Jacobite, 188–98, 204–16.
9 Southey to Taylor, 22 Oct. 1825, LC v. 236.
10 LW ii. 2; British Critic xiv (1820), 168.
11 [Milner], Strictures, 90. See also pp. 82–3.

less than the depravity of the fallen flesh. He blamed Augustine's works for casting a long shadow over Catholicism and Protestantism in this regard, and could not help believing that Pelagius remained the most reasonable of heretics. He at least had vindicated the goodness of God and the free will of humanity.[12] Similarly, when in the *Life of Wesley* Southey considered the idea that until grace brought about the new birth, a man was damned irrespective of his good works, he asked where Wesley had learned 'this exaggerated and monstrous notion of the innate depravity of man? and who taught him that man, who was created in the image of his Maker, was depraved into an image of the devil at birth?' The Methodist critic Richard Watson responded that one needed to look no further than the Bible and the Articles.[13] Again, Southey commented that when Wesley argued that '*no good works can be done before justification, none which have not in them the nature of sin*', at least he had not preached this doctrine 'in all the naked absurdity of its consequences'. In a pencilled annotation, Coleridge wondered whether his old friend had forgotten that this was in fact one of the Articles of the Church.[14]

Ironically, Southey's views seemed to have much in common with the eighteenth-century latitudinarians that Coleridge and the Methodists attacked. Archbishop Potter had told Wesley to focus on promoting 'real, essential holiness' and Southey thought this good advice. To Coleridge, such thinking was only 'calculated to soothe and justify a Socinian in his Pelagian self-redemption', and, moreover, this focus on good works was why the Church had lost the affections of the people.[15] Watson was perceptive enough to see that ultimately the poet laureate defended the Church not because of its doctrines but because it supported social order. He argued that Southey possessed 'lingering traces of former erring sentiments' and either he had to modify his views or 'renounce his profession of Christianity, and return to Socinianism or infidelity'.[16] This was an overstatement, but Southey's views existed at some point between Arminianism and Pelagianism rather than with the High Church to which he professed allegiance. The path to salvation was broad not narrow. 'I am no bigot', he wrote in 1819, 'I believe that men will be judged by their actions and intentions, not their creed. I am a Christian; and so will Turk, Jew and Gentile be in Heaven, if they have lived according to the light which was vouchsafed them.'[17]

Taken together, the *Book of the Church*, the *Life of Wesley* and various articles in the *Quarterly Review* form a loosely connected religious history of England since the time of the Britons. The purpose of these writings was to defend the Church against the 'unholy alliance' of dissent and Catholicism. Southey did this not just by showing how the Church had created order, but

---

12 BOTC i. 310–11. See also STM i. 28, 127.
13 *LW* i. 297; R. Watson, *Observations on Southey's Life of Wesley*, London 1820, 16–17.
14 *LW* i. 288; Coleridge, *Marginalia*, v. 138.
15 *LW* i. 222; Coleridge, *Marginalia*, v. 135.
16 Watson, *Observations*, 6, 92.
17 Southey to [Hamond], 2 Mar. 1819, *LC* v. 12.

by showing, in the words of Sheridan Gilley, that liberty and civilisation were the 'twin children of English protestant Christianity' and that the Church had improved the 'temporal condition of all ranks'.[18] Unlike earlier Church historians, he was not especially interested in drawing out continuities between Anglicanism and the religious institutions of the Britons, and, though he suggested that they possessed 'glimmerings of the patriarchal faith', he felt that the evidence was too patchy to draw stronger conclusions.[19] Instead, he was more interested in explaining why the heathen Anglo-Saxons so quickly succumbed to the new faith after the arrival of Augustine. He offered naturalistic arguments. The invaders were a long way from their original homes, their paganism lacked foundational texts, its ceremonies were unimpressive, and, finally, it provided nothing 'useful or consolatory' in its tenets. This religion was 'not rooted in their history, nor intimately connected with their institutions and manners; it had no hold upon the reason, the imagination, or the feelings of the people'.[20] The Christian missionaries, however, were respected because the name of Rome carried weight and because they brought sacred texts which proved their beliefs. Their religion offered comfort against the 'frailties, and infirmities, and wants' of life, and, Southey conceded, even its 'errors and fables' were useful to an ignorant people in need of 'rites and ceremonies'.[21]

Christianity helped to establish a paternal and progressive order in early medieval England. The rulers liked a religion which inculcated 'obedience and fidelity' while the lower orders expected 'humanity and beneficence' from their superiors. It was also increasingly appreciated that Christianity was an aid in 'refining the manners' and 'softening the barbarity' of the age.[22] Monasteries became hubs of activity – marshes were drained, woods were cleared and agriculture was improved – and the clergy encouraged the arts and aided the instruction of the people. The tithes released them from temporal concerns, but, Southey stressed, at this stage they were not a 'distinct tribe' but a body which was chosen from all parts of the community for 'moral and intellectual qualifications'.[23] By supporting religion 'the improvement of the country, the civilization of the people, and the security of the states' was increased, and so the Church saved Europe from barbarism.[24] This remained a theme even after the Norman conquest, when the narrative dwelled on the growing power of the papacy and the consequent clash between secular and religious authority. Southey acknowledged that papal power had advantages at a time when regal power lacked defined limits, and suggested that a truly Christian pope, like a patriot king, might be preferable to a secular autocrat. The people, after

18 Gilley, 'Nationality', 419.
19 BOTC i. 3. See Kidd, *British identities* ch. v.
20 BOTC i. 53, 54.
21 Ibid. i. 55.
22 Ibid. i. 27–8, 57.
23 Ibid. i. 85.
24 Ibid. i. 80.

all, looked to the Church rather than to the king when they craved protection. 'With all its errors, its corruptions, and its crimes', it appeared that the Church was 'morally and intellectually, the conservative power of Christendom'.[25] However, before and after 1066, if the priesthood were completely unrestrained it would have become as powerful as it had been in Egypt or Tibet. While this would have prevented the return of barbarism, the lack of innovation in such a society would make it 'as unprogressive as the Chinese, and at a lower stage in civilization'.[26]

As the narrative approached the high Middle Ages, Southey began to elaborate the complaints familiar to Protestant anti-Catholic polemic: an untranslated Gospel made it easy to dupe the people, idolatry was rife in the form of saint-worship and Mary-devotion and the peddling of relics was conveniently profitable. He also detected the growing popularity of dualism, which, he claimed, led some people to think that the worship of God required denying the world and mortifying the flesh to the point where a masochistic pride in suffering was detectable.[27] More important, however, were the 'corruptions' that facilitated the growing temporal power of the papacy. The introduction of indulgences (a 'toll ticket' for the soul) increased the wealth and power of the Church, while the growth of private confession, absolution and the 'astonishing doctrine' of transubstantiation appeared to give the priest enormous influence.[28] The power of the pope over the temporal world appeared vast because the rule of the world belonged to him 'by natural, moral, and divine right'. He even seemed to hold sway over the meanings of right and wrong: 'if the Pope, through error, should enjoin vices to be committed', Southey claimed, 'the Church would be bound to believe that vices were good, and virtues evil, and would sin in conscience were it to believe otherwise. He could change the nature of things, and make injustice justice'. This claim to absolute infallibility and to unlimited jurisdiction was the 'key-stone' of this structure of 'imposture and wickedness', the universal despotism of the papacy over mind and body.[29]

Charles Butler lambasted many of these anti-Catholic arguments in his *Book of the Roman Catholic Church*, and they were in turn dealt with by *Vindiciae Ecclesiae Anglicanae*. Southey thought that there was little good evidence for Butler's claim that the British Isles were originally converted by Pope Eleutherius, opposed the idea that the Anglo-Saxon Church prospered because it had enjoyed God's favour and attacked Butler's defence of miracles.[30] The most fundamental differences, however, were over papal 'corruptions', with Butler insisting that key doctrines – transubstantiation, purgatory, veneration of saints – as well as the celibacy of the clergy were not late innovations,

25 Ibid. i. 293.
26 Ibid. i. 118.
27 Ibid. i. 298–318.
28 Ibid. i. 320, 324.
29 Ibid. i. 327, 329, 330.
30 Butler, *Book*, 20–1, 30–48, 70–1; Southey, *Vindiciae*, 57–63, 95–212.

while Southey saw them as part of a system to increase papal power. Celibacy, he argued, cut the clergy off from 'natural obligations' and encouraged the renunciation of 'national character', while the emergence of clerical immunity from secular jurisdiction was an attempt to make the clergy independent of the state.[31] The aim was to 'exalt the mitre above the crown, and form the clergy throughout all Christendom into a compact body, acting upon one system, animated by one spirit, and directed by one head, and every where independent of all civil power'.[32]

Butler spent considerable energy in arguing that whatever pretensions to temporal power the papacy might once have had, they no longer existed. Catholics believed that the pope held supreme jurisdiction in spiritual but not temporal matters. Southey, Butler argued, was confusing the old Transalpine with the current Cisalpine position. The former, which had stated that in pursuit of spiritual good the pope might depose rulers, absolve subjects from obedience and enforce civil penalties, had been disavowed by the Gallican declaration of 1682.[33] Southey was not convinced by this. Butler argued that Catholicism should be judged only by its articles of faith, but Southey insisted that the Tridentine Creed affirmed all previous canons and councils, including the fourth Lateran Council which defined the power to absolve subjects of their allegiance to a heretical sovereign, and the Council of Constance, which declared that faith was not to be kept with heretics. The creed also spoke of the Church as the 'mother' and 'mistress' of all Churches, and demanded that Catholics 'condemn, reject, and anathematize' all heretical Churches.[34] Southey added that in quoting the creed, Butler had silently omitted the passage affirming that Catholics should endeavour to convert others.[35] To the poet laureate, the very articles of faith that Butler lauded contained 'all those obnoxious opinions' which ensured that modern Catholicism remained a threat to Protestant security and sovereignty.[36]

Unsurprisingly, Southey's treatment of the Reformation was also controversial. Butler accused him of relying too heavily on John Foxe's *Actes and monuments*, of painting the sufferings of Protestants but not of Catholics with feeling, and in general of refusing to recognise that this period damaged wisdom, morality and happiness.[37] Southey did not respond to these points because he never completed the second volume of *Vindiciae*, but his views were already well established. The Henrician Reformation was limited and flawed. There was little effective doctrinal change and it was of course responsible for the extensive and unjustified spoliation of the Church.[38] Only

[31] Butler, *Book*, 28–9, 64–6, 99–118; Southey, *Vindiciae*, 299–304, 346–54.
[32] Southey, *Vindiciae*, 355–6.
[33] Butler, *Book*, 93–8, 121–3.
[34] Southey, *Vindiciae*, 25.
[35] Ibid. 28.
[36] Ibid. 29.
[37] Butler, *Book*, 169–224. See also [Milner], *Strictures*, 49–54.
[38] BOTC ii. 52–70, 78–83, 115–21.

under Edward was there an attempt to define the new religious order against Catholicism, and under Elizabeth the Church was finally anchored and stabilised. Southey praised moderates and pragmatists like Thomas Cranmer who ensured that Catholics could be reconciled to the transition by not departing 'unnecessarily from what had been long established'.[39] The founders wanted a 'comprehensive Church' which would leave 'as much latitude of opinion as possible upon points not clearly defined in scripture'.[40] In dealing with Elizabeth's relations with Catholics, Southey claimed that she was more tolerant than her father, believing that in time most would eventually have drifted into Anglicanism. However, she could not allow the Catholic clergy to form their own churches, which she rightly saw as a threat to her security. Southey argued that it was only with her excommunication, coupled with the threat of Mary of Scotland and Catholic insurgency in the north, that she adopted stricter measures. The pope, by ruling against occasional conformity and encouraging the assassination of the queen, had in effect made treason a duty for Catholics. Plotters were therefore caught and executed not because of their religion, but because they taught that the queen must be deposed. Southey felt it important to stress that, first, the government was moderate until 'it was compelled, by the duty of self-preservation, to regard its Papistical subjects with suspicion, and treat them with severity'. Second, he wanted to underline his belief that Catholics were not persecuted because of their beliefs. They 'suffered for points of State, and not of Faith … not for religion, but for treason'.[41]

At the other extreme was Calvinism. The Puritans, Southey insisted, were imbued with a spirit of 'insubordination' which was rooted in their insistence that Scripture was the sole rule of action. They lacked any ties of obligation to the state Church and wrongly believed that the system of church government pioneered in Geneva – a 'turbulent democracy' – was applicable to England.[42] James I did his best to improve the Church, but this failed to appease the Puritans: their books became popular, their preachers were active and their leaders entered parliament. By the 1630s they were allying themselves with critics of the monarchy, and by the 1640s their demands included the abolition of episcopacy, the Prayer Book and the House of Lords. Once in power, Southey thought that their contempt of law and intolerance of opponents was worse than anything Charles I would have done. They supported illegal arrests, punishments and taxation, demanded the execution of Catholics and the prosecution of the clergy, destroyed churches and suppressed theatres.[43] In reconstructing the Church, Charles II's hopes of conciliating a wide range of opinion were to be frustrated. The Act of Uniformity required, first, epis-

---

39 Ibid. ii. 288.
40 Southey to J. T. Coleridge, 14 Nov. 1825, in Braekman, 'Letters', 165.
41 BOTC ii. 267–8, 278. See also [Southey], 'Hallam', 219–27, and Coleridge, *Marginalia*, v. 143.
42 BOTC ii. 293.
43 Ibid. ii, chs xvi–xvii passim. See also Coleridge, *Marginalia*, v. 124, 144–5.

copal ordination for all ministers, and second, assent to the Book of Common Prayer. The result was that some 2,000 men left their livings, and were then expected to take an oath supporting the structure of Church and State or else be subject to the Five Mile Act. As we have seen, Southey was critical of the Act of Uniformity because he believed it effectively created a sect hostile to the state. A more moderate approach embracing 'comprehension' would have ensured that the Church of England retained a better claim to be the national Church.[44]

The *Book of the Church* concluded with a fairly conventional account of the Glorious Revolution. There were, however, two points that stood out. The first was that because James II had initially courted the dissenters they turned a blind eye to his ultimate ambitions. Only with the indictment of the seven bishops in 1688 for refusing to support the Declaration of Indulgence – which exempted Catholics and dissenters from penal statutes – did they realise their error. 'The better part', Southey suggested, 'felt now how much more important were the points on which they agreed with the Church, than those on which they differed; and the scheme of comprehension was revived with less improbability of success than on any former occasion.'[45] The other notable point was his sympathetic treatment of the nonjurors for their 'conservatism'. The 400 men who left the Church may have 'judged errone-ously' in opposing William III, but, it was claimed, they were respectable men untainted by Jacobitism. Their offence was that they remained loyal to inher-ited institutional forms, that is to say, they adhered 'to the principle without which no Government can be secure'.[46] At this point Southey concluded the *Book of the Church*, but more because of 'want of room' than because there was nothing else to say.[47]

Even during the eighteenth century, the work of reformation had barely begun, and Southey continued to believe that ordinary people 'had been Papists formerly, and now they were Protestants, but they had never been Christians'.[48] The demographic explosion and the growth of towns had only worsened matters, and the Church was ill-equipped to deal with these prob-lems. In the *Life of Wesley* he suggested a number of reforms that had been necessary: the condition of the lower clergy needed improving, the number of religious instructors had to be increased, a system of parochial education was essential and, finally, the clergy must be awakened to their duty.[49] The first three measures required legislative intervention, but at the beginning of the eighteenth century even the 'most convincing arguments' would have fallen on deaf ears.[50] Money raised from the lease of church lands was not spent on

44 *BOTC* ii. 463–72.
45 Ibid. ii. 496.
46 Ibid. ii. 509, 510.
47 Southey to J. T. Coleridge, 21 Oct. 1823, in Braekman, 'Letters', 133.
48 *LW* i. 330. See also [Southey], 'New churches', 549–91.
49 *LW* i. 333–4.
50 Ibid. i. 334.

the Church, and Queen Anne's Bounty was simply insufficient.[51] As for the lack of zeal in the Church, this was largely inevitable all the while it offered an undemanding life (especially for younger sons of the gentry) rather than requiring 'all the heart, and all the soul, and all strength' of man. Its effects, however, were devastating because it was at the parochial level that clergymen had the potential to do the most good, and by neglecting their duty they damaged the religious feelings of the whole nation.[52]

By the time the *Life of Wesley* was published in 1820, Southey had altered his earlier stance on Methodism. Now he was prepared to add ecstatic praise to strong criticisms. This puzzled some readers: Milner thought him an enthusiast for Wesley and Coleridge worried that he was too favourable, while Watson claimed that the biography was a very partial account and the *British Critic* concluded that Methodism had 'never received so deadly a wound'.[53] On the negative side, Southey presented Wesley as being overly ambitious, too domineering and gripped by intense spiritual pride. Methodists were excessively ascetic – they praised plainness, disliked jewellery, opposed card-playing, dancing, theatre and even too much laughter was frowned upon.[54] More significantly, Southey continued to stress the dangerous effects of fervent preaching on 'weak minds, ardent feelings, and disordered fancies'.[55] He lamented that Methodists approached religion as 'a thing of sensation and passion, craving perpetually for sympathy and stimulants' rather than as something that brought 'peace and contentment'.[56] While enthusiasm inspired and drove people to spread the word, it was also accompanied by 'much that was erroneous, much that was mischievous, much that was dangerous'.[57] Yet for all this there were countervailing positives, which included the awakening of Anglican zeal. While Wesley knew that field preaching was an irregular practice, it was also crucial in bringing about a thorough reformation of character among the lower orders, as well as inculcating due loyalty to the state.[58] In time, Southey hoped that the impulse set off by Wesley would bring about a 'national reformation' which in turn would lead eventually to the 'fulfilment of those prophecies which promise us that that kingdom of our Father shall come, and His will be done in earth, as it is in heaven'.[59]

In the meantime, the central problem was that the sectarian spirit of Methodism undermined attachment to the established Church, even though this had not been Wesley's intention.[60] At the end of the *Life of Wesley* (and

51 Ibid. i. 324; [Southey], 'New churches', 563–4.
52 *LW* i. 326, 327.
53 *British Critic* xiv (1820), 16; [Milner], *Strictures*, 82–3; Coleridge, *Marginalia*, v. 153–4; Watson, *Observations*, passim.
54 See *LW* i. 96–7, 389–90; ii. 159–60, 197ff., 498–504, 519–23.
55 Ibid. i. 246.
56 Ibid. ii. 217.
57 Ibid. i. 336. See also *STM* ii. 70, 80; Coleridge, *Marginalia*, v. 135.
58 *LW* i. 399–402; ii. 528–30.
59 Ibid. i. 335–6.
60 Ibid. ii. 440–2.

again in the *Colloquies*) Southey suggested that because the principles of Methodism were close to those of the Church, it could in time be reconciled to the establishment.[61] Watson doubted that this would ever happen, while the *British Critic* loftily insisted that Methodism would wither away.[62] Others, however, were more sympathetic. In 1824 Mark Robinson, a Methodist leader from Beverley, wrote of how he and Sadler had been promoting the idea of Church Methodism, and that they had the support of the archbishop of York. The bishop of London, however, foresaw great difficulties.[63] Southey, nevertheless, thought it would encourage Methodists to abandon the extremes of enthusiasm and to become an active wing of the Church as catechists, itinerants and carers. It would also have the advantage, if linked with co-operative societies, of bringing various groups and associations back within the parochial framework.[64] These ideas came to nothing, but they once again reveal Southey's interest in extending the appeal of the national Church in response to the growth of religious pluralism.

This was a pressing concern in the 1820s because he had now come to believe that the spread of infidelity was a major issue. He believed its origins were not in England so much as in France, because disillusion with Catholicism commonly led to atheism. The courts of François I and Henri IV had an irreligious reputation which quickly spread profanity and obscenity to the realm of literature, and eventually affected philosophy, especially in its adoption of the view that selfishness was the source of virtue. England had its freethinkers at this time, such as Hobbes, but it was only in the eighteenth century that infidelity was actively promoted. Hume, Rousseau and especially Voltaire helped to popularise scepticism towards (and even hatred of) Christianity, while philosophical materialism undermined the basis of faith.[65] Added to this was the trend – formerly denied, now accepted – whereby Arianism was supplanted by Socinianism which in turn led to 'blind necessity and gross materialism' and nothing else.[66] By the early nineteenth century, while there was evidence that religiosity was reviving among the upper classes, Southey believed that 'an absolute fanaticism of unbelief' was spreading fast to the middle and even the lower orders. Aided by the popularity of Paine, Volney and Mirabeau, as well as the scurrilous journals of Hone and Carlile, preachers freely travelled the land stirring the people with tales of how religion was a fabrication designed to keep them in subjection.[67] The effects of

---

61 Ibid. ii. 563–5; *STM* ii. 82–3.

62 Watson, *Observations*, 156–7; *British Critic* xiv (1820), 185.

63 M. Robinson to Southey, 13 Jan. 1824, and the bishop of London to Southey, 25 Feb. 1824, *LC* v. 161–4, 165–6. See *The early correspondence of Jabez Bunting, 1820–1829*, ed. W. R. Ward, London 1972, 98–114, 149–50.

64 *STM* ii. 82–7; Southey to J. J. Hornby, 27 Aug. 1829, *LC* vi. 60–5; Southey to Bowles, 14 Sept. 1829, in *Correspondence with Bowles*, 175–6.

65 See [Southey], 'Popular disaffection', 525–8; 'Infidelity', 493–4, 510–20; and *STM* ii. 44–53, 105–6.

66 [Southey], 'Popular disaffection', 536; cf. *LS*, 181–4, 249–60.

67 [Southey], 'Infidelity', 520–2 at p. 522.

this, he thought, were to destroy morality and religion and to undermine patriotism and loyalty. The solution was more vigorous zeal on the part of the Church: already young clerics were more committed and better trained than ever before, and new churches were finally being built.[68] All this effort, however, would amount to nothing, he believed, if the state caved in to the demands of the 'unholy alliance', for this would ultimately sink Anglicanism in a sea of pluralism.[69]

The conclusion of the *Book of the Church* reminded readers that the Church had not only saved the country from 'temporal as well as spiritual despotism', but that it was also responsible for 'our moral and intellectual character as a nation'.[70] By this time Southey claimed to be a devotee of Richard Hooker, and quoted Burke's argument against Warburton that in a Christian country Church and State were 'one and the same thing, being different integral parts of the same whole'.[71] When Hooker had defended the idea that subjects of the state were also members of the Church, it had largely been true, but by the 1820s this had long ceased to be the case. Given that Southey believed salvation was possible outside the Church, why was he so strong on the establishment? His interest in 'comprehension' provides a clue: he wanted a Church of Protestants which could truly claim to be a national Church. That way its functions of securing order, encouraging learning and promoting morality could best be served. In the *Constitution of Church and State*, Coleridge trod similar ground. The purpose of a national Church – which need not necessarily be Christian – was 'to secure and improve that civilization, without which the nation cannot be either permanent nor progressive'. The clerisy was charged with disseminating culture and making possible the moral development of the nation. The Church of Christ, by contrast, was concerned purely with religious matters: it was not subject to the laws of any state and the magistrate had no right to interfere in it. While it was a 'blessed accident' that in England these two Churches existed together, their functions were quite distinct from one another.[72] Similarly, if with less subtlety, Southey wanted the Church to have an intellectual and educative role for the whole nation, but this was rarely recognised by opponents who saw in him little more than a High Church 'bigot'.

---

68 [Idem], 'New churches', passim; *STM* ii, ch. xi passim.

69 *STM* i. 248–55.

70 *BOTC* ii. 511.

71 [R. Southey], 'The Roman Catholic question: Ireland', *QR* xxxviii (Oct. 1828), 556, quoting Burke, 11 May 1792, in *Parliamentary history*, xxix. 1393. Positive references to Hooker are in *BOTC* ii. 292, and [Southey], 'Dymond', 114. For Hooker's legacy see J. Gascoigne, 'The unity of Church and State challenged: responses to Hooker from the Restoration to the nineteenth-century age of reform', *JRH* xxi (1997), 60–79, and D. MacCulloch, 'Richard Hooker's reputation', *EHR* cxvii (2002), 773–812.

72 S. T. Coleridge, *On the constitution of Church and State*, ed. J. Colmer, London–Princeton 1976, 44. See Smith, *Gothic bequest*, 146–56; Morrow, *Coleridge's political thought*, ch. v; and Edwards, *Statesman's science*, chs viii–ix.

The constitution of the state

In the years after Waterloo, Southey amplified the political thoughts he had first articulated in 1812. As Jonathan Parry and Dror Wahrman have shown, these years saw increasing calls for 'corrupt' government to be opened up to public opinion. In the hands of its defenders, this concept referred to the results of deliberation by informed persons. In time all sound minds would adopt its conclusions for it was 'a tribunal which cannot err … its decision being the only standard of right and wrong'.[73] Typically, it was rhetorically paired with the 'middle class', thereby creating the impression that by the 1820s there was a respectable voice outside parliament that MPs ought to heed. Southey, along with other opponents of reform, adopted the older perspective that while 'public opinion' did have a role to play in government, it was capricious and subject to twists and turns that would lead the statesman astray. He was contemptuous of the idea that *vox populi* was *vox dei*, pointing to the Gordon riots and the French Revolution as ample proof otherwise.[74] 'By *the people*', he suggested, 'the discontented faction is meant – the deceivers and the deceived – according to that figure of speech by which a part is put for the whole.'[75] He repeatedly argued in the *Quarterly Review* that publications like Cobbett's *Political Register* and Hone's *Reformer's Register* used satirical and abusive language to undermine trust in established institutions. This vocal minority persistently impugned the motives and misrepresented the actions of government. The real danger, as we have seen, was that the radical press was designed for the comparatively new class of reader among the working classes who were as yet 'the credulous, the ignorant and the half-informed'.[76] Southey often likened these writings to dangerous 'poisons'. In *A vision of judgement* he endorsed the Machiavellian view that the corruption of the manners of the people invariably produced the destruction of governments, and that there was 'no means better whereby that corruption can be so surely and rapidly diffused, as by poisoning the waters of literature'.[77]

Southey believed that the advocates of reform rested their arguments on a number of errors. He criticised their defences of contract theory and insisted that discussions of 'abstract right and imaginary compacts' were redundant.[78] In a review of Jonathan Dymond's *Essays on the principles of morality*, he also opposed the view that political power was rightly held only with the consent of the community. He interpreted this assertion as a demand for extension

---

73 Cited in D. Wahrman, 'Public opinion, violence and the limits of constitutional politics', in J. Vernon (ed.), *Re-reading the constitution: new narratives in the political history of England's long nineteenth century*, Cambridge 1996, 91. See also Parry, *Rise and fall*, 27–34.
74 [Southey], 'Parliamentary reform', 276.
75 Ibid. 262.
76 [Idem], 'Works on England', 564. See also 'Popular disaffection', 545–52, and *LS*, 145–55.
77 R. Southey, *A vision of judgement*, London 1821, pp. xxi, xix–xx generally.
78 *STM* i. 254.

of the franchise, and insisted that the right to govern must be founded on 'principles and laws' rather than the 'weather-cock of public opinion'.[79] As we have seen, Coleridge dealt with the issue of consent more subtly. In the *Constitution of Church and State* he repeated his belief that it was 'pure fiction' to suppose that a historical contract had ever existed, but that the '*idea* of an ever-originating contract' was much more plausible. He explained that no constitution deserved reverence unless it supported the 'general good' and once it lost that, it rightly lost respect. The forces of permanence and progression were balanced because on the one hand laws and institutions were fixed on the basis of their utility, but on the other hand they evolved when they were no longer thought useful: consent was expressed as the trust of a people in its developing institutions.[80] Southey did not state his views in these terms, though it is unlikely he would have dissented from them.

One probable influence on Southey's thinking was Hume, whom he had described as a 'sagacious' writer 'upon all points in which a sense of religion is not required'.[81] He knew the *History of England* well, and probably the *Essays* also.[82] In 'Of the original contract', originally written in 1748, Hume spent some time unpicking the Whig idea that government was founded on the consent of the people. He was prepared to accept that in the very earliest times, when all humans were equal, a form of consent must have enabled some people to acquire power over others. But this was of marginal relevance, because he went on to show that all governments had been founded on 'usurpation or conquest', and that the idea that the entire people either actually or tacitly consented to them was absurd.[83] Far from being an instance of consent, the Glorious Revolution merely altered the succession of the regal part of the government, and even that was enacted by less than 700 out of a population of ten million who had no say at all. But the absence of a contract did not take away the obligation to obey government, for without that no society could be maintained. 'The general bond or obligation, which binds us to government', Hume insisted, 'is the interest and necessities of society; and this obligation is very strong.' The specific forms of government were less important: what mattered most was what the people felt strongly attached to, and this usually meant rulers who had the claim of longevity. 'Present possession has considerable authority in these cases', Hume continued, 'because of the disorders which attend all revolutions and changes of government.'[84]

Southey argued that in the earliest ages of mankind government was 'patriarchal'. By this he did not mean to lend support to Filmer – who had drawn 'unwarrantable and injurious deductions' about absolute monarchy

[79] [Southey], 'Dymond', 106.
[80] Coleridge, *Constitution*, 15.
[81] Southey, *Essays*, i. 300.
[82] See Southey to Taylor, 31 Dec. 1825, *LC* v. 242.
[83] D. Hume, 'Of the original contract', in *Political essays*, 189.
[84] Ibid. 200. See D. Forbes, *Hume's philosophical politics*, Cambridge 1975, and Pocock, *Narratives*, chs xi–xv.

from the idea – but merely to indicate that authority was organised and experienced through the family. In some parts of Asia and Africa there were still the remnants of this early form of 'patriarchy', but it had not survived in the rest of the world:

> This natural order was overthrown as soon as violence began to prevail; government was then established by force; and forms, more or less favourable to the general good, were introduced, as strength or wisdom prevailed. Custom and convenience sometimes, and sometimes craft and superstition, perpetuated what chance and circumstance had induced, and colonies carried with them the forms and institutions of the parent stock.[85]

The origin of government, then, was in the fact that some people were able to use force to subjugate others. The forms that it took were unplanned, and whether the wider welfare of the people was attended to was largely a matter of chance. Many societies had never experienced anything other than government by force, and even free societies could be reduced to that level.[86] Even despotism was better than anarchy, because it at least provided one of the functions of government: security. But while safety was the 'first object of civil society', 'welfare and happiness' also had to be considered.[87] Southey agreed with Dymond that political power was rightly exercised when it served the welfare of the community, and so it would appear that although governments originated in conquest rather than with consent, they derived their legitimacy from what they did for the people.[88]

Unlike Hume, Southey adopted a religious approach to natural law.[89] The legitimacy of government was not wholly secular and the obligation of obedience was not entirely self-interested. In the *Colloquies* he insisted, to Macaulay's annoyance, that 'nothing is more certain than that religion is the basis upon which civil government rests, – that from religion power derives its authority, laws their efficacy, and both their seal and sanction'.[90] This is an ambiguous statement, but one interpretation might be that governments should act in accordance with the laws of God, thus turning mere 'power' into genuine 'authority'. In addition, religion was helpful in fostering obedience. The ghost of Thomas More explained that governments were held together 'either by force' or by 'the attachment of the people' and that while the former could ensure submission, 'the willing obedience of a free people' was far better.[91] This willingness emerged either from a sense of interest or from a sense of duty. In the former case, as in the United States, the people obeyed because they felt content or prosperous, but Southey believed that this was a

---

85 [Southey], 'Dwight', 25. See also 'Hallam', 206, and *Admirals*, i. 18.
86 *STM* ii. 198.
87 [Southey], 'Works on England', 565', and 'Parliamentary reform', 252.
88 [Idem], 'Dymond', 106.
89 See Forbes, *Hume's philosophical politics*, chs i–ii.
90 *STM* ii. 47. See [Macaulay], 'Southey's colloquies', 547–8.
91 *STM* ii. 198.

precarious basis for submission. Religion was better because it created a sense of duty by insisting that observance of the law was the will of God. The duty to obey the magistrate was not, however, unbounded, and Southey argued that if the 'requisitions of government' were opposed to the 'higher law', the subject could legitimately resist government, though by non-compliance rather than by active opposition.[92] Hume had argued that ideas of resistance were best kept obscure because they undermined the security of governments, and Southey agreed. In the *Book of the Church* he stated that resistance was a doctrine 'subjects ought never to remember, and rulers never to forget'.[93]

He also agreed with Hume about the longevity of institutions: 'political power', he claimed, 'is rightly possessed by that individual, or that body, to whom it had devolved according to the laws and institutions of their ancestors'.[94] This was primarily because people were attached to what was familiar. The chief lesson of the English and French revolutions was the danger of undermining the 'principle and habit of obedience'. Cromwell, for instance, had only belatedly understood 'the beauty, the utility, and the necessity' of the structures he had helped tear down.[95] It remained to be seen if any of the 'liberal' governments which were springing up across the globe would prove enduring.[96] At the same time, however, Southey believed that liberty was a modern invention: he continued to dismiss the supporters of the Anglo-Saxon constitution, and believed that the real aim of the baronial revolt under John was to establish aristocratic despotism, 'the worst and most incurable of all governments'.[97] Like Hume, he viewed the Tudors more critically than did many Whigs (who wished to play up the contrasts with Stuart absolutism), claiming that to all intents and purposes Henry VIII and Elizabeth had been absolute monarchs, with parliaments virtually powerless to resist them.[98] Similarly, he was far less harsh than Whigs in his treatment of the Stuarts, arguing that if moderation had prevailed it might have been possible to have 'defined and balanced' the constitution without bloodshed, but unfortunately opinion polarised between republicans and Puritans on one side and the king's men on the other.[99] He defended Charles, Strafford and Laud as far as he was able, and doubted that they were pursuing policies of absolutism.[100]

---

92 [Southey], 'Dymond', 85.
93 BOTC ii. 471. See D. Hume, *The history of England*, Indianapolis 1983, v. 544; vi. 293–4.
94 [Southey], 'Dymond', 106.
95 BOTC ii. 450, 451.
96 STM ii. 175.
97 BOTC i. 287.
98 Ibid. ii. 48, 337; [Southey], 'Parliamentary reform', 253.
99 BOTC ii. 338–9.
100 See ibid. ii, ch. xvii; [Southey], 'Hallam', 229–48; S. Lang, *The Victorians and the Stuart heritage: interpretations of a discordant past*, Cambridge 1995; and Pocock, *Narratives*, ch. xiii.

Of James II, however, he was in no doubt: if he had remained king he would have destroyed England's civil and religious liberty.[101]

Only with the Glorious Revolution was the constitution 'well balanced and defined'.[102] This was not the restoration of an earlier constitution but an almost accidental stumbling (by the 'blessing of Providence') on a near perfect form of government, something which by the middle of the eighteenth century was recognised by most other nations.[103] In his eulogies to the constitution, Southey sounds very much like the 'vulgar Whigs' made infamous by Duncan Forbes.[104] First, he explicitly adhered to the lessons inculcated by Cicero and Tacitus that the best way to prevent abuses in each of the forms of government was to mix them. Britain had blended monarchy, aristocracy and democracy 'in one harmonious system' to create 'political freedom and legitimate authority'. Second, in phrasing that recalls Burke, he stressed that the constitution was not a 'creature of theory'. It 'has arisen out of our habits and necessities; it has thus grown with our growth, and been gradually modified by the changes which society is always passing in its progress'. (This was exactly the point that moderate reformers denied: the constitution, they believed, was not evolving at the same pace as society.) Finally, he was mainly interested in the supposed wider effects of the constitution. Under it 'we are as free as our own thoughts' and, moreover, it contributed to the wealth of the nation and ensured that the people abounded 'in charity, in knowledge, in piety and in virtue. The constitution is our Ark of the Covenant'.[105] Even accepting that this polemical hyperbole was designed to resist reformers, it is clear that Southey attached great significance to the broad shape of the constitution. Yet it is also important to note that while he viewed it as the product of ages, it had only been perfected in the eighteenth century.

By the 1810s and 1820s he did not think that politics was in a healthy shape. While moderate and extreme reformers agreed that some measures were needed to create more independence for legislators, he thought that such demands threatened to upset the balance of the constitution. He was opposed to the Whig conviction that, in the words of Dunning, 'The power of the Crown has increased, is increasing, and ought to be diminished.' He doubted whether this had been true in the 1770s, agreed with Burke that it was not true of the 1790s and certainly thought it wrong for the 1810s. Indeed, he claimed there was 'no proof – no indication – no suspicion' of any attempt by the monarchy since the late seventeenth century to increase its powers.[106] He was inclined to agree with Rickman, by contrast, that the power of the

---

101 BOTC ii. 473.
102 STM i. 99.
103 [Southey], 'British empire', 267.
104 See Forbes, Hume's philosophical politics, 142ff.
105 [Southey], 'Parliamentary reform', 253. Cicero and Tacitus are discussed in 'British empire', 267–8.
106 [Idem], 'British empire', 268. See J. Fulcher, 'The English people and their constitution after Waterloo: parliamentary reform, 1815–1817', in Vernon, Re-reading, 52–82.

democracy 'has increased, is increasing and ought to be diminished'.[107] This was evident in the way that the opposition seemed to be overstepping the legitimate bounds of its role. Wordsworth followed Burke in arguing that a vigorous opposition was formed of men bound together by conscience, honour and friendship which ought to hold the executive to account by expressing contrary opinions and slowing its business when necessary.[108] It should also act as a parliamentary focal point if the nation had grievances against the government, and so should be primed to 'assume command of the ship' if called upon.[109] While this was the ideal, Southey and Wordsworth felt that in opposing the war and flirting with reform the Whigs were not basing their prac-tice on 'political views or moral principles' but on the debased desire for party gain.[110] Until they regained a proper sense of the 'kind and degree of hostility to the executive government, which is fairly warrantable' they deserved no respect.[111] Behind these thoughts lay more traditional eighteenth-century concerns about the dangers of extreme factionalism. Southey's real worry was about the ability of the king's ministers to carry on the king's government, and for this reason he was strongly opposed to 'economical reformers' who wished to rein in the influence of the crown.[112] He agreed with Hume that every magistrate 'must either possess a large revenue and a military force, or enjoy some discretionary power, in order to execute the laws and support his own authority'.[113] By the 1810s it was already becoming hard for the govern-ment to rely on a large body of support among MPs, and by the 1820s Southey was firmly agreeing with Stuart Wortley, who had warned that if many more offices were abolished the influence of the crown would be at an end, and the system of government impossible to continue.[114]

In any event, Southey rejected the idea of 'old corruption'. He had insisted for some time that increased expenditure was caused by the war, rather than by state profligacy, and that the abolition of all useless pensions, places and sinecures would barely reduce the annual tax burden by 2½d. per person.[115] If anything, the machinery of state needed more not less money. With the exception of a few excessively remunerated posts, the rewards for high office were so inadequate that even Pitt had died in debt.[116] Since MPs were not paid, some incentive was essential, for 'in no other way could men of talents

107 [Southey], 'Parliamentary reform', 252. See Rickman to Southey, 25 Nov. 1816, in Williams, *Lamb's friend*, 186–7.
108 [W. Wordsworth], *Two addresses to the freeholders of Westmorland*, Kendal 1818, in *Prose works*, iii. 157.
109 [Southey], 'Popular disaffection', 545.
110 Ibid. 522. See idem, *Peninsular war*, i. 55–6, and *CPB* iv. 663.
111 [Wordsworth], *Two addresses*, 160.
112 A. S. Foord, 'The waning of "the influence of the crown"', *EHR* lxii (1947), 484–507, and *His Majesty's opposition, 1714–1830*, Oxford 1964.
113 Cited in [Southey], 'British empire', 267, from Hume, *History*, v. 129.
114 [Southey], 'British empire', 269, 271.
115 [Idem], 'Parliamentary reform', 259; cf. *LS*, 167.
116 [Southey], 'Europe, 1810', 212, 214.

be tempted so frugally into the service of the state'.[117] If fully implemented, economical reform would turn government into an 'oligarchy of the rich'. Lower down the bureaucracy its effects would be 'unequivocally mischievous'. Men in these offices, Southey claimed, were grievously underpaid, their salaries having decreased in value for twenty years. Young clerks of 'activity and merit find better situations in life', he argued, 'leaving behind them the stupid and idle to succeed in due seniority to the higher stations of every office'.[118] If one wanted the best public servants, rather than the cheapest, the rewards of office had to be increased. Nor did he see why certain classes of public servant were disbarred from holding a seat or from voting, as if 'the very act of serving the public ... rendered an Englishman unworthy of exercising an English freeman's rights!'[119]

If economical reform was unsafe, then parliamentary reform, even of a moderate kind, was positively hazardous.[120] Southey's views had hardened since the 1800s. He accepted that the electoral system was not perfect, but thought that the violence, bribery and corruption of many constituencies were caused not by the government but by the people themselves. He also thought that in due course larger towns should be allowed their own representatives, and that the poll should take place in every parish. More important, while he suggested that the freehold franchise should be raised to £20, he thought that it could be extended to persons leasing land of a certain value, or assessed in direct taxation for a given sum. In other words he was happy that a wider number of propertied men be allowed within the pale of the constitution so long as the social reach of the franchise was not expanded.[121] Aside from this, he offered an exceptionally rosy view of the representative system, stating that it would be hard to find a body of men 'among whom more individual worth and integrity can be found, and more collective wisdom; or who have more truly represented the complicated and various interests of the community'. The county representatives were generally above 'sinister motives' and were 'perfectly independent'. They belonged to families which had 'hereditary claims to the confidence of their constituents'.[122] Wordsworth developed this idea in his pamphlets opposing Brougham's candidacy for Westmorland in 1818. True patriotism, he argued, was based on enduring local attachments and it contrasted favourably with that of outsiders like Brougham who attacked 'habit' and 'old ties'.[123] The electoral influence of the Lowthers was the 'natural and reasonable' result of the 'long-continued possession of large

117 [Idem], 'Parliamentary reform', 260.
118 [Idem], 'Europe, 1810', 213, 214, 215.
119 [Idem], 'British empire', 269.
120 See Sack, *Jacobite*, 146–55, and Parry, *Rise and fall*, 45–9.
121 [Southey], 'Parliamentary reform', 255–7; Southey to Rickman, 20 Nov. 1816, *LC* iv. 220. See also Southey, *Essays*, i. 385, 388, for passages removed by Gifford which deal with representation for new towns and the purchase of seats.
122 [Southey], 'Parliamentary reform', 255, 256.
123 [Wordsworth], *Two addresses*, 170.

property'.[124] This promised, if not ensured, that the candidate had a reasonable education, a firm stake in the constituency and that his integrity was intimately known to voters. This was the 'the wisdom that lurks in circumstances', and it contributed to what Coleridge called the forces of permanence.[125] By contrast, the cities, ports and boroughs returned 'members of the manufacturing, mercantile, distributive, and professional classes', and so contributed to the forces of progression.[126] Southey accepted that some large boroughs should return 'ultra-liberty' men such as Wilkes and Burdett, but he also believed it important that patrons could provide seats for talented men 'more richly endowed with the gifts of nature than of fortune'.[127] The key point, as in the 1800s, was that the existing system be able to return a range of talented men who collectively could 'represent' the nation.

After the 'liberal' economic and religious reforms of the 1820s, however, Southey began to be more apprehensive about the quality of parliament. He feared that the Commons was becoming less a deliberative legislative body and more a clamorous popular assembly. In the *Colloquies* he even mooted the idea that its size could be reduced by a half or even two-thirds and still ensure that 'all who, by character, ability, station and stake in the country, are entitled to a place' would have a place.[128] He speculated that the quality of MPs had declined because too many peerages had been offered to propertied men, thereby creating a vacuum in the Commons which all too often was filled by men 'of a lower class and of a dangerous disposition'.[129] On the other hand, there were also too many younger sons of the aristocracy who, despite lacking 'qualities or merits', crowded the benches.[130] As for the House of Lords, Southey remained a vigorous supporter of the need for a second chamber to slow down legislative change, and was convinced of the 'utility and necessity' of a titular aristocracy acting as hereditary legislators.[131] These families ought to have performed great service to the nation and ought also to possess great landed estates. In general he thought that the nobility was not a 'degenerate race', and that its members, unlike their continental counterparts, had not experienced excessive political power or legal privileges, both of which created an 'unchristian pride of caste'. The true nobleman felt attached 'to his posterity and to his country' and so the feeling of nobility 'became a virtuous principle of action, and justifies the name of *noble*'.[132] Southey, however, worried that the character of the House of Lords was being

---

124 Ibid. 172.
125 Ibid. 175.
126 Coleridge, *Constitution*, 27. See [Southey], 'Parliamentary reform', 256–7.
127 [Southey], 'Parliamentary reform', 257, 258.
128 STM ii. 210.
129 Ibid. ii. 231.
130 Ibid. ii. 237; cf. Coleridge, *Constitution*, 88–91.
131 Southey to Hodson, 24 Oct. 1832, *NL* ii. 385. See Landor to Southey, Nov. 1820, and Southey to Landor, 19 Dec. 1821, in Forster, *Landor*, i. 467–8, 494.
132 STM ii. 214–15, 216, 217, 218.

radically altered by the influx of new men since the late eighteenth century. Still, in spite of all this, his most important concerns were clearly stated in a letter to Wynn in 1831. 'If you continue to represent the property of the nation and not its mere numbers', he argued, 'I should not care what alterations were made; for as soon as the machine was in use it would work in the same way. But base it upon numbers, make all elections popular, and nothing can avert a revolution in its fullest extent of the word.'[133]

Finally, it is important to consider Southey's thinking about the state. In his review of the *Colloquies*, Macaulay ridiculed 'the intermeddling of Mr Southey's idol – the omniscient and omnipotent State'.[134] In fact, the state was not quite such an idol, because Southey's preference was for what have been called 'organic' local communities. In the sixteenth and seventeenth centuries, relations of paternalism and deference were preached and practised in many communities, but Southey's wistful tone indicates that they were largely dissipated.[135] 'The representative of an old family', he wrote, 'who resides on the land of his ancestors, and sees around him their portraits in his mansion, and their tombs in his parish church, is surrounded by hereditary attachments; he succeeds to their principles and feelings and duties as part of his inheritance.'[136] The landowner exercised his responsibilities to the local people, and they felt devotion to him. Similarly, they were impressed by the 'dignity and importance' of the Church because of its buildings and its ceremonies, and because of the memory of ancestors in the churchyard.[137] Southey firmly agreed with Wordsworth's view in the preface to *Lyrical ballads* that in the 'condition of low and rustic life the essential passions of the heart find a better soil in which they can attain their maturity'.[138] He often stated the central link between 'topography and patriotism' and insisted that whatever strengthened local attachment was favourable to 'individual and national character'.[139] The ideal of locality was that the squire and the parson presided over good order and good morals, but the reality was that in all but the most rural areas the influence of the clergyman had declined, while the consolidation of landed estates had deprived many communities of their gentleman. As More's ghost lamented, 'old mansions fall to decay, old hearts grow cold, and hereditary attachments wither; the beneficent presence which should invigorate them being withdrawn'.[140] The 'little commonwealths' – or 'parish

---

133 Southey to Wynn, 3 Mar. 1831, *SL* iv. 210.
134 [Macaulay], 'Southey's colloquies', 565.
135 K. Wrightson, *English society, 1580–1680*, London 1982, 57–65. For nineteenth-century paternalism see H. Perkin, *The origins of modern English society, 1780–1880*, London 1969, 182–92, 237–52; D. Roberts, *Paternalism in early Victorian England*, London 1979; and Lawes, *Paternalism*.
136 *STM* ii. 221. See also [Southey], 'Popular disaffection', 542.
137 [Southey], 'New churches', 556–8.
138 Cited in [idem], 'The poor', 201, from Wordsworth, 'Preface', 124.
139 Southey, *The doctor*, 81.
140 *STM* ii. 224.

states' as John Clare called them – still kept up the 'machinery' of their function, but 'it no longer works according to its original design'.[141]

The decline of the parish at a time when individuals were not yet ideal
Christians meant that government had an important role. At a future point
when 'all our institutions were as perfect as they could be' its business could
be reduced to necessary matters such as emigration, 'for the other parts of the
machine would regulate themselves'.[142] Even in the present Southey accepted
that giving too much power to government – as in utopian schemes – robbed
individuals of their freedom, and the French Revolution was only the most
recent instance of this. In the *Colloquies*, he had recognised how the 'just
medium between too much superintendence and too little, – the mystery
whereby the free will of the subject is preserved, while it is directed by the
fore purpose of the state, (which is the secret of true polity) – is yet to be found
out'.[143] As Pamela Edwards has recently shown, there were similar ambiva-
lences in Coleridge's thought. He did not attach overweening importance
to government intervention because it undermined the moral autonomy of
the individual, but he did attempt to define its functions. In his *Lay sermon*
he argued that the negative ends of the state – security – had already been
achieved, but that its positive ends remained incomplete: '1. To make the
means of subsistence more easy to each individual. 2. To secure to each of
its members THE HOPE of bettering his own condition or that of his children.
3. The development of those faculties which are essential to his Humanity,
i.e. to his rational and moral Being.'[144] Southey held the same opinions, as
a discussion of 'utility' made clear. This he defined as 'consulting the interests, the welfare, and the happiness of mankind', and he distinguished it from
secular utilitarianism because it took account of eternal as well as the temporal
factors in defining what counted as 'welfare'. Hence 'universal benevolence'
and improvement of the nation ought to guide the behaviour not just of individuals, but of the state as well.[145] While Southey did not provide an elaborate theory of the state, he and Coleridge agreed that its main functions were
to enable moral autonomy and economic independence and so to promote
real happiness.

The positive functions of the state had 'never seriously been attempted'.[146]
Since the early modern period, statesmen had been so occupied with commercial reasons of state – raising revenue and waging war – that their wider duties
to promote civilisation had barely been understood. 'The ancient legisla-

---

[141] Ibid. i. 142; [Southey], 'New churches', 564. See *CPB* iv. 402, and D. Eastwood,
Government and community in the English provinces, 1700–1870, Basingstoke 1997, 13–14,
26–49.

[142] Southey to White, 4 Sept. 1826, *SL* iv. 28; cf. B. Hilton, *A mad, bad and dangerous
people? England, 1783–1846*, Oxford 2006, 312–15.

[143] *STM* i. 105.

[144] *LS*, 216–17. See Edwards, *Statesman's science*, 125–32, 165–74.

[145] [Southey], 'Dymond', 86, 87.

[146] *STM* i. 100.

tors', Southey argued, 'understood the power of legislation', but 'no modern government' – with the possible exception of Napoleon's – 'seems to have perceived that men are as clay in the potter's hands'. There would always be innate differences in individual character but 'national character is formed by national institutions and circumstances, and is whatever those circumstances may make it. ... Till governments avail themselves of this principle in its full extent, and give it its best direction, the science of polity will be incomplete'.[147] If men were what institutions made them, then those institutions could be used to encourage progress. In this respect the duties of government were 'patriarchal' or 'parental'.[148] Macaulay had dismissed this idea by suggesting that it could only be true if governments were vastly superior in wisdom to the people. Southey, conversely, argued that 'He who maintains that men are best dictated by a sense of their own interest, should be prepared to show that they always know what their own interests really are.'[149] A nation led by wise rulers would better understand the real interests of humanity and could devote its attention to promoting them. With 'good laws, good institutions, and good governments' it would be possible for 'the sum of both moral and physical evil' vastly to be diminished.[150]

In an article for the *Edinburgh Review* in 1824, Francis Jeffrey distinguished between two types of Toryism. There was '*practical* Toryism' which arose in individuals from little more than 'personal servility to the Government' and the desire for 'unearned emoluments and undeserved distinctions'. To its opponents, this was all that there was to Toryism, but Jeffrey was 'liberal enough' to accept the existence of '*sincere* Tory opinions'.[151] This has sometimes been neglected by historians who have chosen to stress the pragmatics rather than the principles of Toryism. It should be evident that Southey was utterly sincere in his profession of Toryism, or, as he preferred, conservatism. By the early 1830s he was wishing that other 'conservatives' had been as committed. He believed that from around the early 1820s, Lord Liverpool had let the 'liberal' elements of his government gain the upper hand. Thinking that concession to 'public opinion' was the best way to appease it, they had not realised that they were unleashing a constitutional revolution.[152] This Southey opposed because he believed he was defending an order which provided liberty and security, and which was little more than a hundred years old. The supporters of the Protestant constitution, he believed, were fighting to save the principles established during the Glorious Revolution. This was not about holding back the forces of progress but about preserving the institutions by which it was

---

147 *LW* i. 333. See also *STM* i. 104, 192; Southey, *Admirals*, i. 17, 47; and *CPB* iv. 690.
148 *STM* i. 105.
149 Ibid. ii. 195. See [Macaulay], 'Southey's colloquies', 550.
150 *STM* i. 29.
151 [F. Jeffrey], 'Brodie's constitutional history: corrections of Mr Hume', *ER* xl (Mar. 1824), 93.
152 See [Southey], 'British empire', 270–6.

made possible. 'The most turbulent democracy of the ancients', he claimed, 'was not more under rule of popular opinion, than the English Government is now, and must continue to be, till the inevitable inconveniences which result and the serious sufferings which may be expected to bring the nation to a sense of its folly or of its sins.'[153]

[153] Southey to J. W. Warter, 23 Jan. 1833, NL ii. 391.

Conclusion

One of the few things that Robert Peel was able to do during his short-lived first ministry was to honour the name and ease the burdens of Robert Southey. In February 1835 he wrote formally to offer the poet laureate a baronetcy, and also informally to ask if there was anything else he could do for a man who had served 'not only literature but the higher interests of virtue and religion'.[1] Southey refused the title and explained that his financial situation remained precarious, so Peel increased his pension by £300 a year on the grounds of 'public principle – the recognition of literary and scientific eminence as a public claim'.[2] This released Southey from further financial pressures. He remained prolific throughout the 1830s, but in the aftermath of the constitutional revolution he no longer wrote to persuade the public and his contributions to the *Quarterly Review* gradually dried up. In private, however, he remained as apprehensive as ever, and frequently worried about the consequences of political and religious reform. In early 1835 Thomas Carlyle was introduced to him, and later perceptively recollected that 'in the eyes especially was visible a mixture of sorrow and of anger, or of angry contempt, as if his indignant fight with the world had not yet ended in victory, but also never should in defeat. A man you were willing to hear speak'.[3]

Too often historians have been reluctant to listen. They have been inclined to judge Hazlitt's characterisation of apostasy as appropriate, and Southey's own explanation that his opinions did not alter drastically as dissimulation. It is only possible to hold such views if one ignores religion: this was the pivot upon which everything else turned. Southey's theological beliefs remained remarkably consistent throughout his life and would have been recognised easily by a Unitarian. He believed in the superintendence of God, the moral teachings of Christ and the promise of an afterlife. It was not necessary to have knowledge of revelation or faith in atonement in order to be 'saved', because people were not in any real sense 'damned'. Pelagius was a better guide than Augustine because he argued for a soteriology that stressed humanity's capacity to reform and redeem itself. Southey believed that all humans – whatever their professed religion – had the capacity to reach into their souls to hear the voice of God. By listening to their conscience, men and women would grow to be real Christians: they would be animated by the spirit of the Gospel (even if they had never read it), and demonstrate love in their

---

1 R. Peel to Southey, 1 Feb. 1835, *LC* vi. 255.
2 Peel to Southey, 4 Apr. 1835, ibid. vi. 263.
3 T. Carlyle, *Reminiscences*, ed. J. A. Froude, London 1881, ii. 313. Carlyle incorrectly remembered the year as 1836 or 1837.

thoughts and deeds. This was a vision of Christian sociability and benevolence. The *telos* of humankind was the achievement of such a state on earth,
and even though it was to be created by free will it was assured by the guiding
hand of providence. In later life Southey grew less sceptical about scriptural
history, and accommodated the idea that sin was 'a mortal taint – in heart and
will', but this did not substantially alter his fundamental convictions.[4] He was
at his most candid in the *Colloquies*, when he looked towards a time when the
world would become 'perfect according to its capacity for perfection', a time
'when men become Christians in reality, as well as in name, something like
that Utopian state of which philosophers have loved to dream, – like that
millennium in which Saints as well as enthusiasts have trusted'.[5]

In the 1790s Southey's radicalism arose from his belief that political and
religious institutions prevented the emergence of a natural and benevolent
sociability, and so impeded progress towards a superior state of society. Over
many centuries hereditary elites had arisen and structured legal and economic
systems in their favour, and pursued their politics of reason of state against the
interests of the people. These institutions of force drew support from institutions of fraud. The various priesthoods of Europe – whether Catholic or Protestant – promulgated corrupt versions of true Christianity in order to prop
up Church and State, and to keep the people in ignorance. Southey drew
both sustenance from Thomas Paine, who strengthened his taste for republicanism, and convinced him that stripping away force and fraud would enable
just social relations to emerge; and from William Godwin, who insisted on
the centrality of unimpeded free inquiry as the mechanism of social progress.
He thought that politics would eventually become practically unnecessary
as natural human equality and sociability was established. The key problem,
however, was one of transition. Sometimes he hoped that benevolence would
emerge once corrupt institutions were stripped away and at other times he
thought that republican institutions should be used to establish it. By the turn
of the century he was coming to accept, first, that reforming manners was a
difficult process, and second, that without such reform dismantling political
institutions was dangerous. French republicanism had failed because it was
unable to transform a corrupt and unsuitable 'national character', and so had
led to anarchy and eventually despotism.

These thoughts were to form the basis of Southey's later conservatism. If
it was accepted that institutions shaped manners, and also that the populace became deeply attached to those which were familiar, it followed that
any radical alteration of those institutions was hazardous. It also meant that
Southey became increasingly interested in historical continuity and 'national
character', though he did not eulogise antiquity for its own sake. He now agreed
with Hume that the origins of government in conquest did not automatically
make it illegitimate, and that one must focus instead on the utility of existing

---

4 Southey, *Paraguay*, 52.
5 *STM* i. 152, 27.

institutions. How far did they promote liberty and security, morality and wisdom? In Spain, for instance, the despotism of Church and State impeded progress, but the country retained the elements of a freer constitution which was acceptable to its national character. England, by contrast, had acquired desirable political and religious forms in the seventeenth century, and while they were useful they ought to be defended until the time was right for further reform. While people 'are what they are' there needed to be a strong executive, but once knowledge and morality were improved then the liberalisation of politics could proceed safely.[6] For the same reasons, although Southey reluctantly accepted that property was the basis of political participation, he preferred education as a yardstick of ability. Indeed, wise 'statesmen' were better suited to the prime task of government which was to promote social progress. While he opposed Owen on many points, he agreed that because people were like 'clay' in the hands of institutions it was possible to reform them substantially. He was convinced that national education under the auspices of the national Church would encourage the growth of knowledge and morality without impairing the cohesion of the nation. In other words, his institutional conservatism had become the best means of enabling the social reformism that he had desired since the 1790s.

In those days, Southey had contended that the greed of an idle minority condemned the majority of the populace to incessant labour at the cost of their physical and mental well being. He and Coleridge shared a vision of a future state of society which had abolished property and in which equality was maintained by the reign of benevolence. This 'utopia' would have eliminated the vast majority of physical and moral evils which afflicted the world, and which currently ensured that the world was very different from the 'perfection' intended by God. The strength of these convictions explains why Southey reacted so ferociously to Malthus. The *Essay on population* seemed to argue that evil was part of the natural order, and so provided the basis for the emerging tradition of political economy to legitimise individual selfishness and deny social improvement. Although Southey retained a hope that communities of goods would be possible at some distant state in the future, and continued to believe that inequality was too extreme, he had by the 1800s come to accept the basic defence of commercial society. The desire to acquire riches and to transmit property was now viewed as a means of advancing civilisation, so long as it was kept within due bounds. He wanted a *via media* between ambition and benevolence so that while the desire for independence was acceptable, the lust for wealth was not. Indeed, it was the greed of landowners, commercialists and manufacturers which caused overproduction, overspeculation and overwork. This was, then, primarily a moral rather than an economic critique, and the solution was a reformation of the morals of all classes. Ultimately much could be done by voluntary methods

---

6 [Southey], 'British empire', 267.

– hence the interest in co-operation – but if these failed it was the duty of government to promote the welfare of the nation.

More so than many figures in the 'romantic' period, Southey has been subject to the enormous condescension of posterity. In part this was because of the perceived inferiority of his poetry, but mainly because of his supposedly reactionary politics. The aim of this book has not been to argue that he was the unrecognised equal of Wordsworth or Coleridge, but simply to restore some coherence to his social and political world view and to place him more accurately within the intellectual firmament of the late eighteenth and early nineteenth centuries. By paying attention to the particular religious frame-work that underlies his thought it is possible to see the strong continuities running through it, and to appreciate how the 'radical' sympathies of the 1790s were extruded through the 'conservatism' of the 1820s. More broadly, it also becomes possible to place him within a longer historical framework. A. V. Dicey suggested that Southey was the 'prophetic precursor of modern collectivism', but as with the wider arguments of *Law and public opinion* this is an oversimplification. It would be better to say that he was a prophet of the 'age of incarnationalism'.[7] To invite comparisons between Southey's views and, for example, the new liberalism of T. H. Green might seem an odd undertaking; nevertheless there are strong family resemblances in their views about theology, perfection and the state.[8] Indeed, by stepping back from the complex intellectual genealogies running through discussions of idealism and romanticism in Britain and Germany in the nineteenth century, one can appreciate that similarities between diverse thinkers arose because of a grounding in broader traditions of ethical activism, Protestant millennialism and, ultimately, the long Reformation.[9]

Carlyle met Southey again in 1838 and noted a melancholy air about him, observing that his eyes seemed filled with 'gloomy bewilderment and incur-able sorrows' as if he were looking back on his own life 'with a kind of ghastly astonishment rather than with triumph or joy!'[10] The poet laureate's literary labours were nearly at an end. For the first time in his adult life he found concentrating on writing difficult, and was to be seen in his study, hand pressed to forehead, muttering 'memory, memory, where art thou gone'.[11] Between 1839 and 1843 his condition slowly but inexorably deteriorated into senility and debility, but still, his son recalled, his books 'were a pleasure to him almost to the end, and he would walk slowly round his library looking at

---

7   Hilton, *Age of atonement*, 255-339.
8   See D. P. Leighton, *The Greenian moment: T. H. Green, religion and political argument in Victorian Britain*, Exeter 2004. Coleridge's importance to Green has long been recognised.
9   See especially L. Dickey, *Hegel: religion, economics, and the politics of spirit, 1770–1807*, Cambridge 1987, 1–137.
10   Carlyle, *Reminiscences*, ii. 323.
11   C. C. Southey, *LC* vi. 390.

them, and taking them down mechanically'.[12] Wordsworth, visiting Keswick in July 1840, made a similar observation. Southey was 'past taking pleasure in the presence of any of his friends. He did not recognise me till he was told. Then his eyes flashed for a moment with their former brightness, but he sank into the state in which I had found him, patting with both hands his books affectionately, like a child'.[13] It is perhaps an appropriate and fitting end to his career that, as the tides of dementia washed over him, Robert Southey's love of books – which represented so much to him – was among the last cares to be held above the rising swell.

[12] Ibid. vi. 389.
[13] Wordsworth to Lady F. Bentinck, [30 July 1840], in *Letters*, vi. 97.

Bibliography

[This book draws extensively on contributions to early nineteenth-century periodicals, in particular the *Annual Review*, the *Edinburgh Annual Register* and the *Quarterly Review*. Owing to limited space individual journal articles are not listed. The reader is referred to the first footnote to each article for full bibliographical information.]

Unpublished primary sources

London, British Library
MS Add. 30927 Southey letters
Microfilm MS RP 719 Southey letters
Microfilm MS RP 1222 Southey, 'Joan of Arc' (1793)

Manchester, Chetham's Library
MS Mun. A.4.2 Southey, 'Letters of D. Manuel Alvarez Espriella on England'

Oxford, Bodleian Library
MS Eng. Lett. c. 22 Southey letters

Published primary sources

Newspapers and periodicals
Analytical Review
Annual Review
Blackwood's Magazine
British Critic
Cobbett's Political Register
The Courier
Critical Review
Edinburgh Annual Register
Edinburgh Review
The Examiner
The Flagellant
Foreign Quarterly Review
Foreign Review
Fraser's Magazine
London Magazine
Monthly Magazine
Quarterly Review

The Times
Westminster Review

Contemporary books and articles
Allen, J., *Suggestions on the cortes*, London 1809
Barton, B., *Selections from the poems and letters of Bernard Barton*, London 1849
Braekman, W., 'Letters by Robert Southey to Sir John Taylor Coleridge', *Studia Germania Gandensia* vi (1964), 103–230
Brissot, J. P., *New travels in the United States of America*, London 1792
Bunting, J., *The early correspondence of Jabez Bunting, 1820–1829*, ed. W. R. Ward, London 1972
Butler, C., *The book of the Roman Catholic Church*, London 1825
Canning, G. and others, *The poetry of the anti-Jacobin*, London 1799
Carlyle, T., *Reminiscences*, ed. J. A. Froude, London 1881
Cartwright, J., *The life and correspondence of Major Cartwright*, ed. F. D. Cartwright, London 1826
Coleridge, S. T., *Collected letters of Samuel Taylor Coleridge*, ed. E. L. Griggs, Oxford 1956–71
—— *The Friend*, ed. B. E. Rooke, London–Princeton 1969
—— *Lectures, 1795: on politics and religion*, ed. L. Patton and P. Mann, London–Princeton 1971
—— *Lay sermons*, ed. R. J. White, London–Princeton 1972
—— *On the constitution of Church and State*, ed. J. Colmer, London–Princeton 1976
—— *Essays on his times in the* Morning Post *and the* Courier, ed. D. V. Erdman, London–Princeton 1978
—— *Marginalia*, ed. H. J. Jackson and G. Whalley, London–Princeton 1980–2001
—— *Biographia literaria*, ed. J. Engell and W. J. Bate, London–Princeton 1983
—— *Lectures, 1808–1819: on literature*, ed. R. A. Foakes, London–Princeton 1987
—— *Table talk*, ed. C. Woodring, London–Princeton 1990
—— *Shorter works and fragments*, ed. H. J. Jackson and J. R. de Jackson, London–Princeton 1995
—— [and R. Southey], *The fall of Robespierre*, Cambridge 1794
De Quincey, T., *Recollections of the lakes and the lake poets*, ed. D. Wright, Harmondsworth 1970
—— *The works of Thomas De Quincey*, ed. B. Symonds and others, London 2000–3
Forster, J., *Walter Savage Landor: a biography*, London 1869
Gibbon, E., *The history of the decline and fall of the Roman empire*, ed. D. Womersley, London 1994
Godwin, W., *An enquiry concerning political justice*, London 1793, in Godwin, *Political and philosophical writings*, iii
—— *The enquirer: reflections on education, manners, and literature*, London 1797, in Godwin, *Political and philosophical writings*, v
—— *Thoughts occasioned by the perusal of Dr. Parr's Spital sermon*, London 1801, in Godwin, *Political and philosophical writings*, ii

────── *The political and philosophical writings of William Godwin*, ed. M. Philp, London 1993

Harford, J. S., *The life of Thomas Burgess, bishop of Salisbury*, London 1840

Harrington, J., *The political works of James Harrington*, ed. J. G. A. Pocock, Cambridge 1977

Hazlitt, W., *Political essays, with sketches of public characters*, London 1819, in Hazlitt, *Selected writings*, iv

────── *The spirit of the age*, London 1825, in Hazlitt, *Selected writings*, vi

────── *The selected writings of William Hazlitt*, ed. D. Wu, London 1998

Hodder, E., *The life and work of the seventh earl of Shaftesbury*, London 1886

Holland, J. and J. Everett, *Memoirs of the life and writings of James Montgomery*, London 1854

A house of letters, ed. E. Betham, London 1905

Hume, D., *The history of England*, Indianapolis 1983

────── 'Of national characters' and 'Of the original contract', in Hume, *Political essays*, ed. K. Haakonssen, Cambridge 1994

John Dryden, ed. K. Walker, Oxford 1987

Jordan, W. K., *The chronicle and political papers of King Edward VI*, London 1966

Jovellanos, G. de, *Obras completas*, ed. J. M. Caso Gonzalez, Oviedo 1984–99

Lang, A., *The life and letters of John Gibson Lockhart*, London 1897

Malthus, T. R., *An essay on the principle of population*, 1st edn, London 1798, ed. A. Flew, London 1970

────── *An essay on the principle of population*, 2nd edn, London 1803, ed. D. Winch, Cambridge 1992

The manuscripts of Lord Kenyon, London 1894

Marsh, H., *The national religion the foundation of national education: a sermon*, London 1811

Mill, J. S., *The earlier letters of John Stuart Mill, 1812–1848*, ed. F. E. Mineka, Toronto–London 1963

[Milner, J.], *Strictures on the poet laureate's* Book of the Church, London 1824

Montesquieu, C. L., *The spirit of the laws*, ed. A. M. Cohler and others, Cambridge 1989

More, T., *Utopia*, ed. G. M. Logan and R. M. Adams, Cambridge 1988

Owen, R., *Observations on the effect of the manufacturing system*, London 1815, in R. Owen, *A new view of society and other writings*, ed. G. Claeys, London 1991

Paley, W., *Reasons for contentment*, London 1793

────── *Natural theology*, London 1802

The parliamentary history of England, London 1806–20

Pasley, C. W., *An essay on the military policy and institutions of the British empire*, London 1810

Poole, T., *Thomas Poole and his friends*, ed. M. E. Sandford, London 1888

Price, R., *Observations on the importance of the American Revolution*, London 1784, in R. Price, *Political writings*, ed. D. O. Thomas, Cambridge 1991

────── *The correspondence of Richard Price*, ed. W. B. Peach and D. O. Thomas, Durham, NC–Cardiff 1983–94

Report of the committee appointed at a meeting of journeymen, London [1821]

Ricardo, D., *The works and correspondence of David Ricardo*, ed. P. Sraffa, Cambridge 1951–73

Rousseau, J. J., *Confessions*, ed. J. M. Cohen, London 1953

———— *Emile: or, on education*, ed. A. Bloom, Harmondsworth 1991

———— *Letter to Voltaire*, in J. J. Rousseau, *The Discourses and other early political writings*, ed. V. Gourevitch, Cambridge 1997

———— 'Considerations on the government of Poland and its projected reformation', in J. J. Rousseau, *The Social contract and other later political writings*, ed. V. Gourevitch, Cambridge 1997

Saint-Pierre, J. H. B. de, *Studies of nature*, trans. H. Hunter, London 1796

Scott, W., *The letters of Sir Walter Scott*, ed. H. J. C. Grierson, London, 1932–7

Shelley, P. B., *The letters of Percy Bysshe Shelley*, ed. F. L. Jones, Oxford 1964

Smiles, S., *A publisher and his friends: a memoir and correspondence of the late John Murray*, London 1891

Smith, A., *An enquiry into the nature and causes of the wealth of nations*, ed. R. H. Campbell and A. S. Skinner, Oxford 1976

Smith, S., *The letters of Sydney Smith*, ed. N. C. Smith, Oxford 1953

Southey, R., *Joan of Arc*, Bristol 1796, in *Poetical works*, i

———— *Letters written during a short residence in Spain and Portugal*, Bristol 1797

———— *Madoc*, London 1805, in *Poetical works*, ii

[————] *Letters from England: by Don Manuel Alvarez Espriella*, London 1807

———— *The curse of Kehama*, London 1810, in *Poetical works*, iv

———— *The history of Brazil*, London 1810–19

———— *The origin, nature, and object of the new system of education*, London 1812

———— *The life of Nelson*, London 1813

———— *The poet's pilgrimage to Waterloo*, London 1816

———— *A letter to William Smith, Esq. MP*, London 1817

———— *Wat Tyler*, London 1817

———— *The life of Wesley and the rise and progress of Methodism*, London 1820

———— *A vision of judgement*, London 1821

———— *History of the peninsular war*, London 1823–32

———— *The book of the Church*, London 1824

———— *A tale of Paraguay*, London 1825

———— *Vindiciae Ecclesiae Anglicanae*, London 1826

———— *Sir Thomas More: colloquies on the progress and prospects of society*, London 1829

———— 'Introduction', to J. Jones, *Attempts in verse*, London 1831

———— *Essays moral and political*, London 1832

———— *Lives of the British admirals*, London 1833–40

———— *The life of the Rev. Andrew Bell*, London 1844

———— *The doctor*, ed. J. W. Warter, London 1848

———— *Common-place book*, ed. J. W. Warter, London 1849–51

———— *The life and correspondence of Robert Southey*, ed. C. C. Southey, London 1849–50

———— *Selections from the letters of Robert Southey*, ed. J. W. Warter, London 1856

———— *The correspondence of Robert Southey with Caroline Bowles*, ed. E. Dowden, London 1881

———— *Journal of a tour in Scotland in 1819*, ed. C. H. Herford, London 1929

———— *Journals of a residence in Portugal, 1800–1801 and a visit to France, 1838*, ed. A. Cabral, Oxford 1960

———— *New letters of Robert Southey*, ed. K. Curry, New York 1965

———— *The letters of Robert Southey to John May, 1797 to 1838*, ed. C. Ramos, Austin 1976

———— *Poetical works: 1793–1810*, ed. L. Pratt, London 2004

———— (ed.), *The chronicle of the Cid*, London 1808

———— (ed.), *Horae lyricae by Isaac Watts, with a memoir of the author by Robert Southey*, London 1834

Taylor, W., *A memoir of the life and writings of the late William Taylor of Norwich*, ed. J. W. Robberds, London 1843

Wakefield, G., *A reply to some parts of the bishop of Llandaff's address to the people of Great Britain*, London 1798

Warburton, W., *The alliance between Church and State*, London 1736, in *The reception of Locke's politics*, ed. M. Goldie, London 1999, v

Watson, R., *An address to the people of Great Britain*, London 1798

Watson, R., *Observations on Southey's Life of Wesley*, London 1820

Williams, O., *Lamb's friend the census taker: life and letters of John Rickman*, London 1912

The Windham papers, ed. [A. P. Primrose], earl of Roseberry, London 1913

Wordsworth, W., 'Preface' to *Lyrical ballads*, London 1800, in Wordsworth, *Prose works*, i

———— *The Convention of Cintra*, London 1809, in Wordsworth, *Prose works*, i

[————], *Two addresses to the freeholders of Westmorland*, Kendal 1818, in Wordsworth, *Prose works*, iii

———— *Poetical works*, ed. T. Hutchinson and E. de Selincourt, Oxford 1936

———— *The letters of William and Dorothy Wordsworth*, ed. E. de Selincourt and others, Oxford 1967–93

———— *The prose works of William Wordsworth*, ed. W. J. B. Owen and J. W. Smyser, Oxford 1974

Yonge, C. D., *The life and administration of Robert Banks Jenkinson, second earl of Liverpool*, London 1868

Young, E., *Night thoughts*, ed. S. Cornford, Cambridge 1989

Secondary sources

Armitage, D., *The ideological origins of the British empire*, Cambridge 2000

Bainbridge, S., *Napoleon and English romanticism*, Cambridge 1995

Baker, K. M., *Inventing the French Revolution: essays on French political culture in the eighteenth century*, Cambridge 1990

Baugh, D. A., 'Maritime strength and Atlantic commerce: the uses of "a grand marine empire"', in L. Stone (ed.), *An imperial state at war: Britain from 1689 to 1815*, London 1994, 185–223

———— 'Withdrawing from Europe: Anglo-French maritime geopolitics, 1750–1800', *International History Review* xx (1998), 1–32

Baughman, R., 'Southey the schoolboy', *Huntington Library Quarterly* vii (1944), 247–80

Beer, M., *A history of British socialism*, London 1919

Bellenger, D., 'The émigré clergy and the English Church, 1789–1815', *JEH* xxxiv (1983), 392–410

Bennett, S., 'Catholic emancipation, the *Quarterly Review* and Britain's constitutional revolution', *Victorian Studies* xii (1969), 283–304

Berg, M., *The machinery question and the making of political economy, 1815–1848*, Cambridge 1980

Berlin, I., 'The counter-Enlightenment', in P. P. Wiener (ed.), *The dictionary of the history of ideas: studies of selected pivotal ideas*, New York 1973, ii. 100–12

Best, G., 'The Protestant constitution and its supporters, 1800–29', *Transactions of the Royal Historical Society* 5th ser. viii (1958), 105–27

Boulger, J. D., *Coleridge as religious thinker*, New Haven 1961

Brinton, C., *The political ideas of the English romanticists*, Oxford 1926

Broers, M., *Europe under Napoleon, 1799–1815*, London 1996

Brown, S., 'Ebenezer Elliott and Robert Southey: Southey's break with the *Quarterly Review*', *Review of English Studies* xxii (1971), 307–11

Buchan, B., 'The empire of political thought: civilisation, savagery and perceptions of indigenous government', *HHS* xviii (2005), 1–22

Butler, M., *Jane Austen and the war of ideas*, Oxford 1975

—— *Romantics, rebels and reactionaries: English literature and its background, 1760–1830*, Oxford 1981

—— *Literature as heritage: or reading other ways*, Cambridge 1988

Cannon, J., *Parliamentary reform, 1660–1832*, Cambridge 1973

Carnall, G., 'A note on Southey's later religious opinions', *PQ* xxxi (1952), 399–406

—— *Robert Southey and his age: the development of a conservative mind*, Oxford 1960

Chandler, J. K., *Wordsworth's second nature: a study of the poetry and the politics*, Chicago 1984

Claeys, G., 'The French Revolution debate and British political thought', *History of Political Thought* xi (1990), 59–80

—— 'The origins of the rights of labor: republicanism, commerce and the construction of modern social theory in Britain, 1796–1805', *Journal of Modern History* lxvi (1994), 249–90

Clark, J. C. D., *English society, 1660–1832: religion, ideology and politics during the ancien régime*, Cambridge 2000

Clive, J., *Scotch reviewers: the* Edinburgh Review, *1802–15*, London 1957

Cobban, A., *Edmund Burke and the revolt against the eighteenth century: a study of the political and social thinking of Burke, Wordsworth, Coleridge and Southey*, 2nd edn, London 1960

Coleman, D., *Coleridge and* The Friend *(1809–1810)*, Oxford 1988

Coleman, D. C., 'Mercantilism revisited', *HJ* xxiii (1980), 773–91

—— *Myth, history and the industrial revolution*, London 1992

Collini, S., D. Winch and J. Burrow, *That noble science of politics: a study of nineteenth century intellectual history*, Cambridge 1983

Colmer, J., *Coleridge: critic of society*, Oxford 1959

Connell, P., *Romanticism, economics and the question of 'culture'*, Oxford 2001

Cookson, J. E., *The friends of peace: anti-war liberalism in England, 1793–1815*, Cambridge 1982

—— *The British armed nation, 1793–1815*, Oxford 1997

Curry, K., 'Southey's contributions to the *Annual Review*', *Bulletin of Bibliography* xvi (1939), 195–7

———— *Southey*, London 1975

———— 'The text of Robert Southey's published correspondence: misdated letters and missing names', *Papers of the Bibliographical Society of America* lxxv (1981), 127–46

———— and R. Dedmon, 'Southey's contributions to the *Quarterly Review*', *WC* vi (1975), 261–72

Dart, G., *Rousseau, Robespierre, and English romanticism*, Cambridge 1999

Dicey, A. V., *Lectures on the relation between law and public opinion during the nineteenth century*, 2nd edn, London 1914

———— *The statesmanship of Wordsworth: an essay*, Oxford 1917

Dickey, L., *Hegel: religion, economics, and the politics of spirit, 1770–1807*, Cambridge 1987

Dolson, G. B., 'Southey and Landor and the *Consolation of philosophy* of Boethius', *American Journal of Philology* xliii (1922), 356–8

Eastwood, D., 'Robert Southey and the intellectual origins of romantic conservatism', *EHR* civ (1989), 308–31

———— 'Patriotism personified: Robert Southey's *Life of Nelson* reconsidered', *Mariner's Mirror* lxxvii (1991), 143–9

———— 'Robert Southey and the meanings of patriotism', *JBS* xxxi (1992), 265–87

———— 'Ruinous prosperity: Robert Southey's critique of the commercial system', *WC* xxv (1994), 72–6

———— *Government and community in the English provinces, 1700–1870*, Basingstoke 1997

Edwards, P., *The statesman's science: history, nature and law in the political thought of Samuel Taylor Coleridge*, New York 2004

Esdaile, C., 'War and politics in Spain, 1808–1814', *HJ* xxxi (1998), 295–317

Foakes, R. A., '"Thriving prisoners": Coleridge, Wordsworth and the child at school', *Studies in Romanticism* xxviii (1989), 187–206

Foord, A. S., 'The waning of "the influence of the crown"', *EHR* lxii (1947), 484–507

———— *His Majesty's opposition, 1714–1830*, Oxford 1964

Forbes, D., *Hume's philosophical politics*, Cambridge 1975

Fortescue, J. W., *The county lieutenancies and the army, 1803–1814*, London 1909

Frappell, L. O., 'The Reformation as negative revolution or obscurantist reaction: the liberal debate on the Reformation in nineteenth-century Britain', *JRH* xi (1980), 289–307

Fulcher, J., 'The English people and their constitution after Waterloo: parliamentary reform, 1815–1817', in Vernon, *Re-reading the constitution*, 52–82

Fulford, T., 'Blessed bane: Christianity and colonial disease in Southey's *Tale of Paraguay*', *RN* xxiv (2001), unpaginated

Gambles, A., *Protection and politics: conservative economic discourse, 1815–1852*, Woodbridge 1999

[Garnett, R.], 'Robert Southey', in *The dictionary of national biography*, ed. L. Stephen and S. Lee, London 1885–1900, liii. 284–90

Gascoigne, J., 'Anglican latitudinarianism and political radicalism in the late eighteenth century', *History* lxxi (1986), 22–38

———— 'The unity of Church and State challenged: responses to Hooker from the Restoration to the nineteenth-century age of reform', *JRH* xxi (1997), 60–79

Gilley, S., 'Nationality and liberty, Protestant and Catholic: Robert Southey's *Book of the Church*', in S. Mews (ed.), *Religion and national identity*, Oxford 1982, 409–32

Gould, E. H., *The persistence of empire: British political culture in the age of the American Revolution*, Chapel Hill 2000

Graham, W., 'Robert Southey as Tory reviewer', *PQ* ii (1923), 97–111

Green, K., 'The passions and the imagination in Wollstonecraft's theory of moral judgement', *Utilitas* ix (1997), 271–90

Gueniffey, P., 'Cordeliers and Girondins: the prehistory of the republic?', in B. Fontana (ed.), *The invention of the modern republic*, Cambridge 1994, 86–106

Gunn, J. A. W., 'Influence, parties and the constitution: changing attitudes, 1783–1832', *HJ* xvii (1974), 301–28

Haller, W., *The early life of Robert Southey, 1774–1803*, New York 1917

——— 'Southey's later radicalism', *PMLA* xxxvii (1922), 281–92

Hammett, B. R., 'Spanish constitutionalism and the impact of the French Revolution, 1808–1814', in H. T. Mason and W. Doyle (eds), *The impact of the French Revolution on European consciousness*, Gloucester 1989, 64–80

Hampsher-Monk, I., 'John Thelwall and the eighteenth-century radical response to political economy', *HJ* xxxiv (1991), 1–20

Harling, P., 'The duke of York affair (1809) and the complexities of war-time patriotism', *HJ* xxxix (1996), 963–84

——— *The waning of 'old corruption': the politics of economical reform in Britain, 1779–1846*, Oxford 1996

——— 'Robert Southey and the language of social discipline', *Albion* xxx (1998), 630–55

Hastings, A., *The construction of nationhood: ethnicity, religion and nationalism*, Cambridge 1997

Hedley, D., *Coleridge, philosophy, and religion: Aids to reflection and the mirror of the spirit*, Cambridge 2000

Herr, R., 'The constitution of 1812 and the Spanish road to parliamentary monarchy', in I. Woloch (ed.), *Revolution and the meanings of freedom in the nineteenth century*, Stanford 1996, 65–102

Hicks, P., *Neoclassical history and English culture: from Clarendon to Hume*, Basingstoke 1996

Hilton, B., *The age of atonement: the influence of evangelicalism on social and economic thought, 1795–1865*, Oxford 1988

——— *A mad, bad, and dangerous people? England, 1783–1846*, Oxford 2006

Himmelfarb, G., *The idea of poverty: England in the early industrial age*, London 1984

Hirschman, A. O., *The passions and the interests: political arguments for capitalism before its triumph*, Princeton 1977

Hoadley, F. T., 'The controversy over Southey's *Wat Tyler*', *SP* xxxviii (1941), 81–96

Holmes, R., *Coleridge: early visions*, London 1989

——— *Coleridge: darker reflections*, London 1998

Hont, I., *Jealousy of trade: international competition and the nation state in historical perspective*, Cambridge, MA 2005

Horne, T. A., *Property rights and poverty: political argument in Britain, 1605–1834*, Chapel Hill 1990

Humphreys, R. A., *Robert Southey and his History of Brazil*, London 1978

Johnston, H. J. M., *British emigration policy, 1815–30: 'shovelling out paupers'*, Oxford 1972

Jones, C., *Radical sensibility: literature and ideas in the 1790s*, London 1993

Jordan, G. and N. Rogers, 'Admirals as heroes: patriotism and liberty in Hanoverian England', *JBS* xxviii (1989), 201–24

Kaderly, N. L., 'Southey and the *Quarterly Review*', *Modern Language Notes* lxx (1955), 261–3

Kaufman, P., 'The reading of Southey and Coleridge: the record of their borrowings from the Bristol library, 1793–1798', *Modern Philology* xxi (1924), 317–20

Kidd, C., *British identities before nationalism: ethnicity and nationhood in the Atlantic world, 1600–1800*, Cambridge 1999

Lang, S., *The Victorians and the Stuart heritage: interpretations of a discordant past*, Cambridge 1995

Lawes, K., *Paternalism and politics: the revival of paternalism in early nineteenth-century Britain*, Basingstoke 2000

Leask, N., 'Pantisocracy and the politics of the "Preface" to *Lyrical ballads*', in A. Yarrington and K. Everest (eds), *Reflections of revolution: images of romanticism*, London 1993, 39–58

Leighton, D. P., *The Greenian moment: T. H. Green, religion and political argument in Victorian Britain*, Exeter 2004

Logan, E., 'Coleridge's scheme of pantisocracy and American travel accounts', *PMLA* xlv (1930), 1069–94

Long, A. A., *Hellenistic philosophy: stoics, epicureans, sceptics*, London 1974

Lovejoy, A. O., 'On the discrimination of romanticisms', *PMLA* xxxix (1924), 229–53

——— 'The meaning of romanticism for the historian of ideas', *Journal of the History of Ideas* ii (1941), 257–78

MacCulloch, D., 'Richard Hooker's reputation', *EHR* cxvii (2002), 773–812

McGann, J., *The romantic ideology: a critical investigation*, Chicago 1983

MacGillivray, J. R. 'The pantisocracy scheme and its immediate background', in M. W. Wallace (ed.), *Studies in English at University College, Toronto*, Toronto 1931, 131–69

McKusick, J. C., '"Wisely forgetful": Coleridge and the politics of pantisocracy', in T. Fulford and P. J. Kitson (eds), *Romanticism and colonialism: writing and empire, 1780–1830*, Cambridge 1998, 107–28

Machin, G. I. T., *The Catholic question in English politics, 1820–1830*, Oxford 1964

Madden, L. (ed.), *Robert Southey: the critical heritage*, London 1972

Magnusson, L., *Mercantilism: the shaping of an economic language*, London 1994

Majeed, J., *Ungoverned imaginings: James Mill's The history of British India and orientalism*, Oxford 1992

Mandler, P., 'Cain and Abel: two aristocrats and the early Victorian factory acts', *HJ* xxvii (1984), 83–109

225

—— 'Tories and paupers: Christian political economy and the making of the New Poor Law', *HJ* xxxiii (1990), 81–103

Manogue, R. A., 'Southey and William Winterbotham: new light on an old quarrel', *The Charles Lamb Bulletin* n.s. xxxviii (1982), 105–14

Marshall, P. J. and G. Williams, *The great map of mankind: British perceptions of the world in the age of Enlightenment*, London 1982

Meachen, E. W., 'From an historical religion to a religion of history: Robert Southey and the heroic in history', *Clio* ix (1980), 229–52

Meek, R. L., *Social science and the ignoble savage*, Cambridge 1976

Miller, J. T., *Ideology and Enlightenment: the political and social thought of Samuel Taylor Coleridge*, New York 1988

Mitchell, L. G., *Holland House*, London 1980

—— *Charles James Fox*, Oxford 1992

Morrow, J., *Coleridge's political thought: property, morality and the limits of traditional discourse*, London 1990

Murphy, M., *Blanco-White: self-banished Spaniard*, New Haven 1989

Muthu, S., *Enlightenment against empire*, Princeton 2003

Pagden, A., 'The defence of "civilisation" in eighteenth-century social theory', *HHS* i (1988), 33–45

—— *European encounters with the new world: from renaissance to romanticism*, New Haven 1993

—— *Lords of all the world: ideologies of empire in Spain, Britain and France c. 1500–c. 1800*, New Haven 1995

Parry, J., *The rise and fall of liberal government in Victorian Britain*, London 1993

Perkin, H., *The origins of modern English society, 1780–1880*, London 1969

Phillips, M. S., *Society and sentiment: genres of historical writing in Britain, 1740–1820*, Princeton 2000

Phillipson, N., 'Providence and progress: an introduction to the historical thought of William Robertson', in S. J. Brown (ed.), *William Robertson and the expansion of empire*, Cambridge 1997, 55–73

Philp, M., *Godwin's political justice*, London 1986

—— 'English republicanism in the 1790s', *Journal of Political Philosophy* vi (1998), 235–62

Pocock, J. G. A., *The Machiavellian moment: Florentine political thought and the Atlantic republican tradition*, Princeton 1975

—— 'Cambridge paradigms and Scotch philosophers: a study of the relations between the civic humanist and the civil jurisprudential interpretation of eighteenth-century social thought', in I. Hont and M. Ignatieff (eds), *Wealth and virtue: the shaping of political economy in the Scottish Enlightenment*, Cambridge 1983, 235–52

—— 'Clergy and commerce: the conservative Enlightenment in England', in R. Ajello and others (eds), *L'età dei Lumi: studi storici sul settecento europeo in onore di Franco Venturi*, Naples 1985, i. 523–62

—— *Virtue, commerce and history: essays on political thought and history, chiefly in the eighteenth century*, Cambridge 1985

—— *Barbarism and religion*, II: *Narratives of civil government*, Cambridge 1999

—— *Barbarism and religion*, IV: *Barbarians, savages and empires*, Cambridge 2005

Porter, A. N., '"Commerce and Christianity": the rise and fall of a nineteenth-century missionary slogan', *HJ* xxviii (1985), 597–621

Poynter, J. R., *Society and pauperism: English ideas on poor relief, 1795–1834*, London 1969

Pratt, L. (ed.), Special issue: 'Robert Southey', *RN* xxxii–xxxiii (2003–4)

—— (ed.), *Robert Southey and the contexts of English romanticism*, Aldershot 2006

Richardson, A., *Literature, education and romanticism: reading as social practice, 1780–1832*, Cambridge 1994

Rivers, I., *Reason, grace and sentiment: a study of the language of religion and ethics in England, 1660–1780*, Cambridge 1991–2000

Roberts, D., *Paternalism in early Victorian England*, London 1979

Roe, N., *Wordsworth and Coleridge: the radical years*, Oxford 1988

—— *The politics of nature: Wordsworth and some contemporaries*, Basingstoke 1992

Romani, R., *National character and public spirit in Britain and France, 1750–1914*, Cambridge 2002

Rosenblatt, H., *Rousseau and Geneva: from the First discourse to the Social contract, 1749–1762*, Cambridge 1997

Sack, J. J., *From Jacobite to conservative: reaction and orthodoxy in Britain c. 1760–1832*, Cambridge 1993

Schneewind, J. B., *The invention of autonomy*, Cambridge 1998

Simmons, J., *Southey*, London 1945

Smith, C., *A quest for home: reading Robert Southey*, Liverpool 1997

Smith, R. J., *The gothic bequest: medieval institutions in British thought, 1688–1863*, Cambridge 1987

Spadafora, D., *The idea of progress in eighteenth-century Britain*, New Haven 1990

Speck, W. A., 'Robert Southey and *The Flagellant*', *Harvard Library Bulletin* xiv (2003), 25–8

—— *Robert Southey: entire man of letters*, New Haven 2006

Spence, P., *The birth of romantic radicalism: war, popular politics and English radical reformism, 1800–1815*, Aldershot 1996

Stack, D., *Nature and artifice: the life and thought of Thomas Hodgskin*, Woodbridge 1998

Stanley, B., 'Christianity and civilisation in English evangelical mission thought, 1792–1857', in B. Stanley (ed.), *Christian missions and the Enlightenment*, Grand Rapids 2001, 169–97

Stedman Jones, G., 'National bankruptcy and social revolution: European observers on Britain, 1813–44', in D. Winch and P. O'Brien (eds), *The political economy of British historical experience, 1688–1914*, Oxford 2002, 61–92

—— *An end to poverty? A historical debate*, London 2004

Storey, M., *Robert Southey: a life*, Oxford 1997

Taylor, C., *Sources of the self: the making of modern identity*, Cambridge 1989

Taylor, S., 'William Warburton and the alliance between Church and State', *JEH* xliii (1992), 271–86

Thomas, G. K., *Wordsworth's dirge and promise: Napoleon, Wellington, and the Convention of Cintra*, Lincoln 1971

Thompson, E. P., 'Disenchantment or default? A lay sermon', in C. C. O'Brien and W. D. Vanech (eds), *Power and consciousness*, London 1969, 149–81

Todd, J., *Sensibility: an introduction*, London 1986

Tuck, R., *The rights of war and peace: political thought and the international order from Grotius to Kant*, Oxford 1999

Turner, F. M., *Contesting cultural authority: essays in Victorian intellectual life*, Cambridge 1993

Tyacke, N. (ed.), *England's long Reformation, 1500–1800*, London 1998

Varouxakis, G., *Mill on nationality*, London 2002

Vernon, J. (ed.), *Re-reading the constitution: new narratives in the political history of England's long nineteenth century*, Cambridge 1996

Viroli, M., *For love of country: an essay on patriotism and nationalism*, Oxford 1995

Wahrman, D., 'Public opinion, violence and the limits of constitutional politics', in Vernon, *Re-reading the constitution*, 83–122

Ward, W. R., *Religion and society in England, 1790–1850*, London 1972

Waterman, A. M. C., *Revolution, economics and religion: Christian political economy, 1798–1833*, Cambridge 1991

——— 'The nexus between theology and political doctrine in Church and dissent', in K. Haakonssen (ed.), *Enlightenment and religion: rational dissent in eighteenth-century Britain*, Cambridge 1996, 193–218

Watts, M. R., *The dissenters: expansion of evangelical nonconformity*, Oxford 1995

Wellek, R., 'The concept of "romanticism" in literary history', *Comparative Literature* i (1949), 1–23, 147–72

Wells, J. E., 'The story of Wordsworth's *Cintra*', *SP* xviii (1921), 15–76

Whatmore, R., '"A gigantic manliness": Paine's republicanism in the 1790s', in S. Collini, R. Whatmore and B. Young (eds), *Economy, polity and society: British intellectual history, 1750–1950*, Cambridge 2000, 135–57

——— *Republicanism and the French Revolution: an intellectual history of Jean-Baptiste Say's political economy*, Oxford 2000

Winch, D., *Riches and poverty: an intellectual history of political economy in Britain, 1750–1834*, Cambridge 1996

Wokler, R., 'Isaiah Berlin's Enlightenment and counter-Enlightenment', in R. Wokler and J. Mali (eds), *Isaiah Berlin's counter-Enlightenment*, Philadelphia 2003, 13–31

Wood, M., *Slavery, empathy and pornography*, Oxford 2002

Wootton, D., 'The republican tradition: from commonwealth to common sense', in D. Wootton (ed.), *Republicanism, liberty and commercial society, 1649–1776*, Stanford 1994, 1–41

Wordsworth, J., 'Introduction', to R. Southey, *Joan of Arc*, Oxford 1993

Wrightson, K., *English society, 1580–1680*, London 1982

——— *Earthly necessities: economic lives in early modern Britain*, New Haven 2000

Young, B. W., *Religion and Enlightenment in eighteenth-century England: theological debate from Locke to Burke*, Oxford 1998

——— '"The lust of empire and religious hate": Christianity, history and India, 1790–1820', in S. Collini, R. Whatmore and B. Young (eds), *History, religion, culture: British intellectual history, 1750–1950*, Cambridge 2000, 91–111

Index

Addington, Henry, *see* Sidmouth, 1st viscount
Africa, 146, 147, 152, 157, 202. *See also* Egypt
agriculture: and depression, 133, 169–70; effects of revolution in, 70, 72–4, 172–4, 181–2, 188; improvement of, 142–3, 146, 159, 192; and protectionism, 178–9; virtues of, 16, 33, 69, 74, 208. *See also* land, distribution of
All the Talents, ministry of, 48, 51–2, 82
Allen, John, 109–11
America, 93, 142–3, 145, 147–8; conquest of, 84, 152–3, 155, 158–9; emigration to, 13, 33–5; republicanism in, 17, 163–5. *See also* America, United States of; Brazil; Canada; Mexico; Venezuela
America, United States of, 16, 34, 72, 163–4, 177, 202. *See also* American Revolution; New England; Pennsylvania
American Revolution, 128, 163
Amiens, peace of (1802), 46–7
Analytical Review, 20
Anglicanism, *see* Church of England
Anglo-Saxons, 6, 52, 192, 193, 203
Annual Review, 45, 61, 84, 97
Anti-Jacobin, 37, 50
Arianism, *see* dissent
aristocracy, 9–10, 55, 204; criticism of, 16–18, 32, 121, 203; defence of, 207–8
Arminianism, 87, 191
army, British, 49, 51–3, 55, 103, 113, 119
Ashley, Anthony Ashley Cooper, Lord, *see* Shaftesbury, 7th earl
Asia, 145–6, 147, 158, 202. *See also* China; India
atheism, 18–19, 112, 151; and dissenters, 85; and infidelity, 22, 86, 191, 198–9; and Godwinism, 25, 37–9, 186; and Owen, 186. *See also* deism
Augustine, of Hippo, 90, 191, 212
Australia, 157
Austria, 55, 88, 102–3, 129

Baker, Keith Michael, 128
Baptist Missionary Society, 160

Barton, John, 178
Beer, Max, 8
Behmen, Jacob, 87, 91
Belgium, 129
Bell, Andrew, 96–9, 186 n. 141
benevolence, 24–5, 27–9, 54, 93, 209, 213, 214; and Malthus, 62–3, 64, 66; and selfishness, 186–7. *See also* self-love
Berlin, Isaiah, 5
Bernard, Thomas, 174, 187
Bible, the, 97, 142, 193, 195; and conversion, 161–2; veracity of, 19, 22, 39, 89–90, 189–90, 213
Blackstone, William, 179–80
Blanco-White, Joseph, 108, 109, 112, 163
Bohemia, 102–3
Bonaparte, Napoleon, 39, 154, 210; abdication of, 129; and peace of Amiens, 46–8; and Spain, 103–4, 107, 111; war against, 49, 50, 55, 102
Book of Common Prayer, 97, 195
Bourne, Sturges, 179–81
Brazil, 157–8
Brighton Co-operative Benevolent Fund Association, 183–4
Brissot, Jacques Pierre, 16–18
British Critic, 37, 54, 190, 197, 198
Brougham, Henry Peter, 1st baron, 49, 206
Burdett, Francis, 113–14, 116, 119, 121, 122, 132, 207
Burke, Edmund, 5, 7, 80, 106, 128, 199, 204–5
Butler, Charles, 138, 140, 193–4

Calvinism, 22, 84–5, 86, 87, 91, 195. *See also* evangelicalism
Cambridge, University of, 18, 62
Canada, 157
cannibalism, 143–5, 156
Carlyle, Thomas, 8, 212, 215
Carnall, Geoffrey, 9
Cartwright, John, 52, 116
caste, 147, 149–50, 161, 207
Castlereagh, Robert Stewart, Viscount, 52
Catholic emancipation, 48, 62, 81–3, 123, 132–3

229